European Security in a Global Context

An up-to-date approach, representative range of authors and deft handling of theoretical aspects make this study of European security both user-friendly and authoritative. It portrays a continent of many institutions, yet one where challenges, responsibilities and outside perceptions are converging above all on the still evolving and (in security terms) ambivalent European Union. A rich and helpful source both for general readers and the educational world.

Ambassador Alyson Bailes, University of Iceland

This collection offers the first comprehensive analysis of European internal and external security dynamics. With contributions from some of the world's leading strategic analysts, the book is a must for all those interested in understanding European security and the EU's emerging profile on the international stage.

Professor Jolyon Howorth, University of Yale

This new edited volume examines contemporary European security from three different standpoints. It explores security dynamics, first, within Europe; second, the interaction patterns between Europe and other parts of the world (the United States, Africa, the Middle East, China and India); and, finally, the external perceptions of European security.

The first part of the book analyses the European security landscape. The roles of EU, NATO and the OSCE are given particular attention, as is the impact of their evolution – or enlargement – on the European security architecture and European security dynamics. In this context, Russia's repositioning as a major power appears as a shaping factor of contemporary European geopolitics. The second part presents European security from an external perspective and considers interactions between Europe and other states or regions. Security trends and actors in Europe are examined from an American, Chinese, and Indian perspective, while Europe–Africa and Europe–Middle East relations are also addressed.

This book will be of great interest to students of European Security, European politics and IR in general.

Thierry Tardy is Director of the European Training Course in Security Policy at the Geneva Centre for Security Policy.

Contemporary security studies
Series Editors: James Gow and Rachel Kerr
King's College London

This series focuses on new research across the spectrum of international peace and security, in an era where each year throws up multiple examples of conflicts that present new security challenges in the world around them.

Security Strategies and American
World Order
Lost power
*Birthe Hansen, Peter Toft and
Anders Wivel*

War, Torture and Terrorism
Rethinking the rules of
international security
*Edited by Anthony F. Lang, Jr. and
Amanda Russell Beattie*

America and Iraq
Policy making, intervention and
regional politics
*Edited by David Ryan and
Patrick Kiely*

European Security in a Global
Context
Internal and external dynamics
Edited by Thierry Tardy

European Security in a Global Context
Internal and external dynamics

Edited by Thierry Tardy

This book is edited by Thierry Tardy, with the support of the Geneva Centre for Security Policy

LONDON AND NEW YORK

First published 2009
by Routledge
2 Park Square, Milton Park, Abingdon, Oxon OX14 4RN

Simultaneously published in the USA and Canada
by Routledge
270 Madison Ave, New York, NY 10016

Routledge is an imprint of the Taylor & Francis Group, an informa business

Typeset in Sabon by Wearset Ltd, Boldon, Tyne and Wear
Printed and bound in Great Britain by TJI Digital, Padstow, Cornwall

British Library Cataloguing in Publication Data
A catalogue record for this book is available from the British Library

Library of Congress Cataloging-in-Publication Data
European security in a global context : internal and external
dynamics / edited by Thierry Tardy.
p. cm. – (Contemporary security studies)
Includes bibliographical references.
1. National security–Europe. 2. Europe–Foreign relations–1989–
3. Europe–Politics and government–1989– I. Tardy, Thierry.
UA646.E923558 2009
355'.03304–dc22

2008025469

ISBN10: 0-415-47682-8 (hbk)
ISBN10: 0-203-88535-X (ebk)

ISBN13: 978-0-415-47682-9 (hbk)
ISBN13: 978-0-203-88535-2 (ebk)

Contents

Contributors

Roland Dannreuther is Senior Lecturer in International Relations in the Politics Department of the School of Social and Political Studies of the University of Edinburgh. During 2000–02, he directed the New Issues in Security Course at the Geneva Centre for Security Policy. His research interests include international security and the post-Cold War security agenda, Middle Eastern and Central Asian politics, Soviet and Russian foreign policy, the international politics of energy, and international relations theory.

Pál Dunay is a Faculty Member at the Geneva Centre for Security Policy and currently Director of the International Training Course in Security Policy. In 2007, he was also Director of the Hungarian Institute of International Affairs. Between 2004–07, he was Senior Researcher at the Stockholm International Peace Research Institute. From 1982–96, he was Assistant Professor and later Associate Professor at the International Law Department of *Eötvös Loránd* University, Budapest. During that period, he was also Legal Adviser to the Hungarian Delegation to the Conventional Forces in Europe and to the Open Skies negotiations.

Victor-Yves Ghebali retired from the Department of Political Science at the Graduate Institute of International Studies, Geneva in 2007. Member of the faculty since 1980, he became full professor in 1990. He is Scientific Director of the collections *Axes* and *Organisation internationale et relations internationales* as well as Director of the OSCE Cluster (Swiss contribution to the Partnership for Peace programme). He is also Associate Fellow at the Geneva Centre for Security Policy. His research interests concentrate on the League of Nations and the United Nations, East–West relations, the OSCE, the Mediterranean and national minorities.

François Heisbourg is Chairman of the Council of the International Institute for Strategic Studies (IISS) in London, and of the Foundation Council of the Geneva Centre for Security Policy. He has also been Director of the *Fondation pour la Recherche Stratégique* in Paris, Professor at *Sciences-Po* in Paris, Senior Vice-President of strategic development at MATRA-Défense-Espace, and Director of the IISS. In the early 1980s, he was the international security adviser to the French Minister of Defence as well as a founding member of the French–German Commission on Security and Defence. He began his career in the French foreign ministry working on issues of nuclear non-proliferation, international security and disarmament.

Graeme P. Herd is a Faculty Member at the Geneva Centre for Security Policy, an Associate Fellow in the International Security Programme at Chatham House, London, and an Honorary Research Fellow in the Department of Politics and International Relations of the University of Aberdeen, Scotland. Between 2002–05 he was variously Professor of Civil–Military Relations, Associate Director of the Senior Executive Seminar and Faculty Director of Research at the George C. Marshall European Center for Security Studies, Garmisch-Partenkirchen Germany, where he was also a guest lecturer at the NATO School in Oberammergau. Prior to this, he was a lecturer in international relations at the University of Aberdeen (1997–2002) and Staffordshire University (1994–97) and a Projects Officer in the Department of War Studies, King's College London (1993–94).

Christophe Jaffrelot is the director of *Centre d'Etudes et de Recherches Internationales* (CERI), Paris, and lectures in South Asian politics at *Sciences Po*, Paris. He holds degrees from the Paris *Institut d'Etudes Politiques (IEP)*, University Paris I – Sorbonne, and the *Institut National des Langues et Civilisations Orientales*, as well as a PhD in political science from the *IEP* Paris. His current research includes theories of nationalism and democracy, the rise of the lower castes and the untouchables in North Indian politics, and ethnic conflicts in Pakistan.

Julian Lindley-French is Professor of Military Operational Science at the Netherlands Defence Academy, and Senior Associate Fellow at United Kingdom Defence Academy. He has worked for the British Government and managed projects for the United Nations in Geneva and New York, as well as for the International Olympic Committee in Lausanne. He was formerly a lecturer at the Department of War Studies, King's College London, Deputy Director of the International Centre for Security Analysis and Senior Research Fellow at the EU Institute for Security Studies in Paris. He has also acted as a consultant to NATO in Brussels. From 2003–05, he directed courses and lectured at the Geneva Centre for Security Policy. His main areas of interest are US foreign and security policy and strategic developments in European security and defence structures.

Catherine McArdle Kelleher lectures at College Park, University of Maryland. She also holds a research appointment as Senior Faculty Associate at the Watson Institute, Brown University, Providence, Rhode Island,

and is an Associate Fellow at the Geneva Centre for Security Policy. She was Professor of Military Strategy at the National War College and was also named an *Honorarprofessor* at the Free University of Berlin. In the Clinton Administration, she held posts as the Personal Representative of the Secretary of Defence in Europe and as Deputy Assistant Secretary of Defence for Russia, Ukraine and Eurasia. Her areas of policy analysis include cooperative European security, American–Russian relations, the evolution of NATO, the acquisition of theatre nuclear forces, and European defence and security policies. In 2004, she was awarded the Manfred Wörner Medal by the German Ministry of Defence for her contributions to peace and security in Europe.

Gorm Rye Olsen is Head of the Department of Society and Globalisation at the University of Roskilde in Denmark. He was formerly Head of the European Studies department at the Danish Institute for International Studies. His research interests are the external relations of the European Union, EU relations with Africa, Danish foreign policy, European security and development issues. Currently, he is working on the changing relationship between the EU and Africa and in particular on the new role of Africa in international security politics.

Waheguru Pal Singh Sidhu is Director of the New Issues in Security Course at the Geneva Centre for Security Policy. He lectures on the United Nations, regional organisations, Southern Asia (particularly China and India), nuclear and missile disarmament, arms control and proliferation, especially in the Middle East and Asia. Before joining GCSP, he was Senior Associate at the International Peace Academy, New York, where he directed a project on the United Nations and regional organisations and a project on *Kashmir: New Voices, New Approaches* and co-directed a project on *Iraq Crisis and World Order*. He was appointed as a Consultant to the first and second United Nations Panel of Governmental Experts on Missiles in 2001–02 and 2004 respectively. He was also appointed as a member of the Resource Group established to assist the United Nations High-Level Panel on Threats, Challenges and Change in 2004.

Thierry Tardy is Director of the European Training Course in Security Policy at the Geneva Centre for Security Policy. Prior to joining the GCSP, he was a researcher at the Foundation for Strategic Research in Paris and Lecturer at the *Institut d'Etudes politiques* of Paris as well as at the War College (*Collège interarmées de Défense*, Paris). His area of expertise covers security studies, peace operations, the United Nations and European security.

Lanxin Xiang lectures in international history and politics at the Graduate Institute of International and Development Studies, Geneva. He also serves as a Zijiang Chair and Chairman of the Council at the School of Advanced International and Area Studies (SAIAS), East China Normal University, Shanghai. He held the Henry A. Kissinger Chair of Foreign Policy and International Affairs at the Library of Congress in Washington (2003–04). A graduate of Fudan University in Shanghai, he earned a PhD from the Paul Nitze School of Advanced International Studies (SAIS), Johns Hopkins University. He has published widely in numerous journals on China–US, China–EU and China–Japan relations. He is a policy consultant on China–EU relations. He is also Director of the newly established Centre for China Policy Analysis (CCPA) at HEID in Geneva.

Foreword

Conceived as a training centre of excellence in the framework of the Partnership for Peace programme in 1995, the Geneva Centre for Security Policy (GCSP) defined its programmes in the area of Euro-Atlantic security. At that time, European security was marked by the violent aftershocks of the Cold War: the implosion of the former Yugoslavia, separatism and civil strife in the Caucasus and civil war in Algeria. The European Union had no capabilities to deal with such conflicts effectively. The best it could do was contain spillover into the EU area. It required the interventions of the United States through NATO to finally terminate armed hostilities in the Balkans. In view of the unsettling nature of the 1990s security landscape, the curricula of the GCSP training courses focused on ethnic conflicts, conflict management, and human and humanitarian consequences of war.

Today, European security has evolved and must be understood in a global context. In both a post-Cold War and post-9/11 world, security policies respond to different assumptions about threats and vulnerabilities. Also, the capabilities to respond to threats and risks in and outside Europe have changed significantly. The security of Europe is threatened by terrorist movements with global reach and the EU is preoccupied with weak states and post-conflict reconstruction in its closer and wider neighbourhood. Europe can rely today on a relatively well-functioning security architecture that is built on the enlarged EU and NATO on the one hand, and on 'soft security' cooperation with neighbouring regions on the other. The EU and its member states have developed capabilities for wide-ranging engagements outside the EU, combining military means and socio-economic instruments of cooperation.

Despite this remarkable evolution in the domain of peace and security over the last 15 years, European security remains ill-defined. Globalisation has increased the complexity of security and its impact on advanced industrialised societies. The European public is today vulnerable to multitudes of disruptions in sectors as diverse as critical infrastructure, energy, cyberspace, group identity and public health. These 'new' threats and risks to European security require a different set of policy instruments than those dealing with 'classic' security threats. European security institutions such as the EU, NATO or the OSCE have started to adapt to the new environment, while still being very much involved in traditional threat management. In this context, the transformation of Europe into a zone of peace will depend very much on the future conduct of larger powers outside the European Union that are closely tied to the destiny of European peace and security: the United States and Russia. Equally, globalisation has made the Middle East and Africa, but also powers such as China and India much more relevant to Europe and its security.

As the thorough understanding of European security in its global confines is essential to the work at the GCSP, both in terms of training and research, there is a clear need to tackle contemporary European security issues in a comprehensive fashion. This publication draws on the expertise of the GCSP faculty, its network of accomplished scholars, as well as on interactions with the diversity of professionals trained at the Centre. This project benefits from and contributes to the teaching and research done in the context of GCSP courses. I am confident that this publication will make an important contribution to the debate and understanding of current and future predicaments and opportunities of European security.

Ambassador Dr Fred Tanner
Director of the Geneva Centre for Security Policy

Acknowledgements

This book is the result of a collective effort of the Geneva Centre for Security Policy (GCSP). It would not have come about without the intellectual and logistical support from the GCSP faculty and staff. My warm thanks go to Fred Tanner, GCSP Director, and Peter Foot, Academic Dean, who have supported this project from the beginning and made its realisation possible.

All contributors to this volume are either faculty members of the GCSP or closely associated with its work. This has given a genuine intellectual cohesion and collegiality to this endeavour. Above all, I am most thankful to Miriam Fugfugosh, for her contributions to editing and research, and for her dedicated and professional involvement at all stages of this project.

Thierry Tardy
Geneva Centre for Security Policy

Abbreviations

ACP	African, Caribbean, and Pacific countries
ALTBMD	NATO Active Layered Theatre Ballistic Missile Defence system
APC	Asian Partner for Cooperation
APF	African Peace Facility
ARF	ASEAN Regional Forum
ASEAN	Association of Southeast Asian Nations
AU	African Union
BMD	Ballistic Missile Defence
CAR	Central African Republic
CATs	NATO-EU Crisis Action Teams
CFE	Conventional Armed Forces in Europe
CFSP	EU Common Foreign and Security Policy
CIS	Commonwealth of Independent States
CIVCOM	EU Committee for the Civilian Aspects of Crisis Management
CNCI	US-India Civil Nuclear Cooperation Initiative
CoE	Council of Europe
CPG	Comprehensive Political Guidance, NATO
CSBMs	Confidence and Security-Building Measures
CSCE	Conference on Security and Cooperation in Europe
CSDP	Common Security and Defence Policy (Lisbon Treaty name for ESDP)
CSTO	Collective Security Treaty Organization
CTBT	Comprehensive Test Ban Treaty
DCI	Defence Capabilities Initiative, NATO
DDR	Disarmament, Demobilization, and Reintegration
DPC	Defence Planning Committee, NATO
DRC	Democratic Republic of the Congo
EADS	European Aeronautic Defence and Space Company
ECAP	European Capabilities Action Plan
ECDPM	European Centre for Development Policy Management
ECFR	European Council on Foreign Relations

ECHO	European Community Humanitarian Aid
EDA	European Defence Agency
EDF	European Development Fund
EEC	European Economic Community
EED	Economic and Environmental Dimension, OSCE
EMP	Europe–Mediterranean Partnership
ENP	European Neighbourhood Policy
ESDI	European Security and Defence Identity
ESDP	European Security and Defence Policy
ESS	European Security Strategy
EU	European Union
EU3	France, the United Kingdom and Germany (Iran talks)
EUFOR	European Force
EULEX	EU Rule of Law Mission
FMCT	Fissile Material Cut-off Treaty
FRONTEX	EU Border Force
FSC	Forum for Security Cooperation, OSCE
G8	Group of 8 industrialised countries: Canada, France, Germany, Italy, Japan, Russia, the United Kingdom and the United States
GCC	Gulf Cooperation Council
HCNM	High Commissioner on National Minorities, OSCE
ICC	International Criminal Court
ICI	Istanbul Cooperation Initiative, NATO
IEA	International Energy Agency
ISAF	International Security Assistance Force in Afghanistan, NATO
ITER	International Thermonuclear Reactor Project
JAP	EU–India Joint Action Plan
KFOR	NATO Force in Kosovo
LTM	Long-Term Missions, OSCE
MAP	Membership Action Plan, NATO
MD	Missile Defence
MDGs	Millennium Development Goals
MEPP	Middle East Peace Process
NACC	North Atlantic Cooperation Council
NATO	North Atlantic Treaty Organisation
NPT	Non-Proliferation Treaty
NRC	NATO–Russia Council
NSF	British-led NATO Security Force
ODIHR	Office for Democratic Institutions and Human Rights, OSCE
OECD	Organisation for Economic Cooperation and Development
OEF	Operation Enduring Freedom in Afghanistan
OPEC	Organization of the Petroleum Exporting Countries
OSCE	Organization for Security and Cooperation in Europe

PCC	Prague Capabilities Commitment, NATO
PfP	Partnership for Peace
PHARE	Poland and Hungary Assistance with Reconstructing the Economy, European Commission
PJC	Permanent Joint Council, NATO
PRT	NATO's Provincial Reconstruction Teams in Afghanistan
PSC	Political and Security Committee of the EU
PSI	US Proliferation Security Initiative
SALW	Small Arms and Light Weapons
SCO	Shanghai Cooperation Organization
SHAPE	NATO's Supreme Headquarters Allied Powers Europe
SSR	Security Sector Reform
UNMIK	United Nations Interim Administration Mission in Kosovo
UNSC	United Nations Security Council
WMD	Weapons of Mass Destruction
WTO	World Trade Organization

Introduction

Thierry Tardy

European security and Europe

The notion of 'European security' is well accepted in the academic and policy communities. In Europe in particular, states, international institutions, non-governmental organisations, university departments and think tanks refer to the idea of European security as a generic concept that has found its place in the broader framework of international policy thinking and policy-making.

In the meantime, what 'European security' actually means remains ill-defined and varies from one actor and definition to the other. Not surprisingly, the debates on the concept of European security have revolved around what is to be secured (states, regions, institutions, individuals), by whom (European states, United States, NATO, the EU), from what kind of threats (traditional or non-traditional), and through what kind of instruments (military, civilian, diplomacy, economics, etc.). A related question is whether European security is about security *in* Europe, understood as a geographic space, or about security *of* Europe, understood as an entity. Jahn Egbert (1987, quoted in Wæver 1995) made the distinction between two conceptions of European security: one refers to 'regional international security', that is, international security dynamics as replicated at the regional level. In other words, European security is a reflection, at the level of a region, of security patterns that are mainly defined at the international level. The second conception refers to 'Euronational security', that is, the security of Europe understood as a political, geographical and cultural entity. As much as national security refers to the security of a nation-state, European security would apply to Europe as a referent object of security. The latter approach evolved in the 1990s with the European Union's aspiration to become a security actor, and consequently a referent object of security, that is, a political unit that needs to be secured from threats. European security has then become the security of the European Union (and its member states) rather than that of Europe as a geographic space. Indeed, the December 2003 European Security Strategy, or the European Security and Defence Policy (ESDP) refer to the security of the European Union.

Although this approach focusing on the EU has acquired some salience, especially with the evolution of the Union in the security field, 'European security' understood as 'regional international security' remains nonetheless relevant to the conceptualisation of European security. In parallel with the development of the EU, European security is also about security developments in a region. It is about actors (governmental or non-governmental), threats (inherent or constructed), sources of threat (the 'other'), and policy responses at the level of a region that is Europe. Beyond the security of the EU and its member states, issues such as Russian foreign policy, Balkan stability, the evolution of threats or the role of security institutions such as NATO or the OSCE belong to the European security spectrum. Therefore, a need exists to conceptualise European security by taking Europe as a geographical or political framework in which security-related events take place. However, in so doing, it is not the intention of this book to see regional security as a direct replication of international security at an inferior level. Regions do produce their specificities that shape regional security patterns and that make them distinct from other regions and also from the international level (Buzan and Wæver 2003). European security is distinct from Asian security, African security, or that of any other region.

While European security can simultaneously be understood as being about regional security and about the security of the EU, it is rather the former approach that is favoured in this book. Contributors have been asked to look at a particular aspect of European security or at interactions between Europe and other parts of the world with a broad understanding of Europe, that is not confined to the European Union. In some cases though, chapters looking at patterns of interactions between Europe and other parts of the world tend to focus on the EU rather than Europe per se, or even to amalgamate both entities. In particular, when perceptions of Europe are being addressed, from a Chinese, Indian or Middle Eastern point of view, it is often the EU that is considered rather than Europe as a region. As a matter of fact, it is a tendency both in academic and policy literature, including in official EU documents, to associate Europe with the EU.

This association is interesting in two respects in the context of this book. First, it tends to blur the distinction between the two above-mentioned conceptions of European security. If Europe is often and increasingly associated with the EU, then the security of the EU can easily be equated to that of Europe. Second, the amalgam reflects a self-appropriation of Europe by the European Union, which in a way pretends that it is Europe. Viewed from Russia or Switzerland, the assumption appears presumptuous, yet it is a characteristic of the EU and its member states to equate the EU with Europe, and in so doing to marginalise a large portion of non-EU Europe.

These issues lead to the question of what Europe is. What is it we are talking about when talking about security in Europe? Again, two levels of debate need to be distinguished. One is a broad debate on what Europe is in historical, geographical and political terms (Van Der Dussen and Wilson 1995; Heffernan 1998), as one would ask what Asia is or what America is. This debate relates to discussions about the existence of the West and the values it is supposed to carry, and about the relationship between Europe and the West (Ifversen 2008).

The other debate is directly related to the nature of the EU and to its theoretical membership. As being a 'European state' is a pre-condition to apply for EU membership, knowing what exactly this means is essential to the understanding of the EU and of its future shape (Bourlanges 2004). The first debate informs the second but the two are not identical. One is meant to have no policy relevance while the other is grounded in the policy debate.

In general terms, Europe remains difficult to define and none of the actors that operate in Europe, be they states, international organisations or non-state actors, have come up with clear definitions.

One problem with defining Europe stems from the variety of theoretical approaches to the very concept of 'regions'. The literature on regionalism reveals the difficulty in defining regions (Russet 1967; Fawcett and Hurrell 1995; Katzenstein 2005), and Europe is no exception. The most common dichotomy opposes a materialist approach – Europe as a material entity based on territory – to a sociological approach – Europe as social construct. In the first case, Europe is identifiable by looking at territory and frontiers. In the second case, Europe is a more subjective entity, the definition of which may change over time, depending on the identity of whoever defines it. This dichotomy is particularly interesting in the case of Europe because the very project of European integration was initially – and still is to a large extent – aimed at overcoming geopolitics in Europe. The European Community in the wake of the Second World War and the European Union after the end of the Cold War were largely built on the idea that the Westphalian system based on states, territories and frontiers had to be transcended. As Robert Cooper put it (2003: 26), the Treaty of Rome is 'a conscious and successful attempt to go beyond the nation state', while 'modern Europe was born with the peace of Westphalia'.

It follows that the EU is better defined in terms of values than in terms of frontiers, even if the geographical reality cannot be ignored. As a matter of fact, all European institutions combine an ill-defined geographical and a value-based approach to Europe. The EU Lisbon Treaty poses that 'any European state which respects' the values of the EU 'may apply to become a member' (EU Member States 2007: art.49), but neither the consolidated treaty nor any other EU document defines what a 'European state' is. At the same time, in 1987, Morocco was denied the status of applicant to the European Community on the grounds that it was not a European state, while Turkey was granted that status (European Council 1997).

The same confusion exists in other European international institutions. The NATO Washington Treaty does not define the North Atlantic area apart from referring to Europe as one of its components, and states in article 10 that 'any European State in a position to further the principles of this Treaty' can be invited to accede to it. Turkey joined the Alliance in 1952, together with Greece, but the protocol on Turkey's accession (NATO 1951) makes it a particular case (contrary to Greece) by specifying that 'For the purpose of Article 5, an armed attack on one or more of the Parties is deemed to include an armed attack [. . .] on the territory of any of the Parties in Europe or North America' or 'on the territory of Turkey . . .'. Furthermore, the Istanbul Declaration of 2003 wishes that the 'Alliance remains open to all European democracies, regardless of geography, willing and able to meet the responsibilities of membership, and whose inclusion would enhance overall security and stability in Europe.' At the 2008 Bucharest Summit, Georgia and Ukraine were officially recognised as future NATO members.

In the same vein, the Council of Europe, that counts Russia, Turkey, and the Caucasus countries as members, talks in its Statute (CoE 1949: preamble) about 'like-minded countries of Europe', and poses (CoE 1949: art.4) that 'Any European State which is deemed to be able and willing to fulfil the provisions of Article 3 may be invited to become a member of the Council of Europe'.[1] As far as the Organization for Security and Cooperation in Europe (OSCE) is concerned, its inclusive nature makes it the 'world's largest regional security organization whose 56 participating States span the geographical area from Vancouver to Vladivostok' (OSCE website). The reference to Europe here is specious, as membership includes North America and Central Asia.

It is not the purpose of this book to propose a definition of Europe, on which contributors would likely diverge in any case. However, this volume acknowledges that Europe is at once an amalgam of three overlapping but not mutually exclusive notions: a territory, a social construct based on values and, possibly, an institution through the EU. The general approach is therefore inclusive, with Russia being fully part of Europe and of its internal security dynamics. Russia belongs to the European security problematique regardless of the debate led within EU circles on the frontiers of Europe. As Herd notes in his chapter, Russia sees itself as 'alternative Europe', which puts Russia in Europe as well as it distinguishes it from 'Western' Europe, be it the EU or not. By the same token, institutions such as NATO and the OSCE, whose memberships reach outside Europe and whose activities, at least for NATO, are increasingly 'out-of-area', are considered as actors that shape the European security landscape.

When analysing European security trends, it is also our view that a certain degree of ambiguity on terms needs to be accepted. The expression 'European security' is composed of two terms with subjective and evolving meanings which makes any consensus on definition unlikely. Furthermore, as one objective of this volume is to examine perceptions of European security from American, Chinese, Indian, African, Russian and Middle Eastern perspectives, the added-value is precisely in the diversity of conceptions of what Europe and European security invoke.

Internal and external security dynamics

This book intends to study European security by examining internal and external dynamics. The debate surrounding European security includes the question of the degree of autonomy of the regional context from the international. Can a region be taken as a level of analysis? Is it possible to analyse regional security dynamics as such? A realist/systemic approach would contend that regional trends are primarily determined by the international landscape, that the structure of the international system shapes security dynamics at all levels, and that therefore the analysis of the regional level is of little relevance.

Without dismissing the systemic approach, this volume subscribes to the idea that the regional level can also be taken as a level of analysis, between the national and the global level. The analysis of security dynamics at the level of Europe is relevant because the region offers some degree of cohesion and autonomy. Insofar as European security is about the actors and institutions that are Europe-based, the analysis of the roles of the EU, NATO and the OSCE, of their internal evolutions and of the policies of their member states, sheds light on the bigger picture of European security. By the same token, internal security dynamics as epitomised by the changing role of Russia in Europe and by its relationships with other European states or with the EU, are key to understanding European security. The growing issue of energy security for Western Europe and the Russian policy in this respect are at the heart of European security developments.

In the meantime, the interdependence that characterises international relations makes it difficult to confine the analysis of security dynamics to a finite geographical space. If, because of globalisation, the world has become one of 'porous regions' (Katzenstein 2005: 1), then the interactions between regions and between the regional and the global levels must also be considered.

The analysis of such interactions is all the more important as the place of Europe in international security has significantly changed since the end of the Cold War. Throughout the Cold War, Europe was at the political and geographic centre of the confrontation between the United States and the Soviet Union. For the United States, a stable and secure Western Europe was both a means and an objective of the containment policy. For the Soviet Union, a docile Eastern Europe was equally important in the ideological struggle with the West. In this confrontation, the only security institutions that mattered were NATO and the Warsaw Treaty Organization, as classic military alliances. Neither the European community nor any other institution played a significant role in shaping the European security landscape.

With the end of the Cold War, two fundamental evolutions characterise Europe in the security domain. The first is the political reunification of Europe as a direct consequence of the cessation of bloc-to-bloc confrontation. The second is the fact that Europe as a region has lost its centrality in world politics, its strategic importance for the United States and for post-Soviet Russia. As Mead (2004) put it, 'Kurdistan matters more to the United States than Kosovo, and Mesopotamia means more [...] than Macedonia.'

These evolutions significantly shape European security in both positive and negative ways. On the positive side, what these evolutions mean for Europe is that it is at peace; that an EU, having embraced Eastern Europe, has become a security community where the recourse to force among members is now obsolete (Adler and Barnett 1998); and that, through the EU, NATO and the OSCE, Europe has shifted from the status of security-consumer to that of security-provider. Contrary to the Cold War period, when Europe was importing security, it has turned into an exporter of security. One consequence of this shift is the increasing presence of the EU and NATO in 'out-of-area' activities, in the Balkans, but also in Africa, the Middle East and Asia. This change leads back to the question of the meaning of European security when two key European security institutions are increasingly and predominantly operating outside of Europe. The presence of the EU in the Democratic Republic of the Congo or Chad or that of NATO in Afghanistan means that these two institutions shape the local security environments where they operate, but presumably also that the European security landscape is being shaped by security environments outside of Europe. This is what former German Defence Minister Peter Struck meant when making the link between the security of Germany and security in the Hindu Kush (Struck 2004). It is this very link that makes it indispensable to examine European security in a global context.

On the negative side, recent evolutions – as much as future trends – tend to weaken Europe's position in the world. The emergence of China and India, global economic and demographic trends as well as climate change are likely to make Europe more rather than less vulnerable (Gnesotto and Grevi 2006; Grant and Valasek 2007; Howorth 2007; High Representative for CFSP and European Commission 2008). As said before, a more vulnerable Europe is also likely to benefit less from American protection. Whether European states, leaders and institutions have fully understood the scope of the shift and the risks that it carries is questionable. Have Europeans, and the most atlanticist among them, grasped the consequences for Europe of no longer being at the centre of American strategic thinking? Have the EU, NATO and the OSCE taken measure of the changes and their impact on their existence and relevance?

The present and future roles of China and India in global security governance are equally important. Their economic roles are often referred to with both countries being fierce competitors of the EU, but the security implications of this are less clear. Do the Europeans have a clear idea of the challenges raised by China and India as global security actors and of the potential of cooperation with them? Is China the greatest threat to global stability for Europeans, as a 2008 survey indicates (HarrisInteractive 2008: table 10)? Conversely, how do Chinese or Indians see Europe as a region? How do they see the EU as a security actor? Does Europe matter to them?

This questioning is about the interaction between the global and the regional level, as well as about the interaction between different regions or between different 'regional security complexes' (Buzan and Wæver 2003). The globalisation process and the porosity of regions makes it necessary for the regional level to comprehend the global context, the external perceptions and the interaction patterns between different regions. In a way, the end of European strategic centrality only reinforces the need for a better understanding of external dynamics and perceptions of what Europe is. This is necessary to understand potential sources of vulnerabilities, but also to identify how European states or institutions can minimise the effects of relative decline and maximise their assets.

Insofar as the EU is concerned, the extent to which it is perceived by others as a security actor matters a lot (Bertelsmann Stiftung 2007; Lucarelli 2007). Do the United States, India or China see the EU as a security actor? To what extent have they integrated the EU into their security discourses and policies?

At the systemic level, debates about multipolarity and the relative weights of each of the theoretical poles are informed by this analysis. If China, India, Russia and the EU are supposed to be independent poles competing with the United States, then the understanding of the interaction between them is central to the study of the international system. By the same token, the way Europe, and in this case the EU, is perceived by Russia, China and India, impacts on their respective relationship with the United States. What role then for Europe in each of the triangular relationships involving Europe, the US and alternatively China, India and Russia? Are these relationships likely to challenge the transatlantic link and the existence of the political West? Understanding external dynamics and interactions is equally important where cooperation prevails, for example through the establishment of 'strategic partnerships' between the EU and other key actors. Be it in a competitive or cooperative manner, Europe is likely to interact increasingly with other regions, according to rules that have yet to be defined.

Book structure

This book aims at providing a better understanding of contemporary European security by looking at both internal and external security

dynamics. It considers European security with a broad, inclusive conception of the term, with the understanding that it goes beyond the role and
activities of the EU. How have state actors in Europe evolved over the
past 15 years and how does Europe interact with other parts of the
world? How central is Europe to other parts of the world? How are European security institutions evolving and how are they perceived from the
outside? These are some of the questions that this volume addresses, in
two parts.

The first part focuses on the European security landscape and some of
its key recent evolutions. The three main European security institutions –
the EU, NATO and the OSCE – are given particular attention, with chapters studying their roles, the challenges they are facing, and the extent to
which they have managed to adapt to the new security environment. In
this context, the attraction that the EU and NATO have exerted on
Eastern European countries and the impact of this on European security
is of key importance. By the same token, Russia's repositioning as a
major European power appears as one of the shaping factors of European
security.

Insofar as security institutions are concerned, the three chapters on
respectively the EU (Tardy), NATO (Lindley-French) and the OSCE
(Ghebali) all converge in presenting institutions that are traversing a
period of crisis, but that are not equally equipped to address the challenges
they face. In general terms, the crisis is one of multilateral action, that is,
of the virtues and comparative advantages of institutions in tackling security threats.

Tardy's account of the European Union aims at assessing the scope,
meaning, and degree of success of the recent evolutions of the EU in the
security field, and questions the extent to which the EU has become a
security actor. Still a relatively small institution at the end of the Cold
War, the EU has evolved into a political entity, now present in various
activities on a global scale, and part of the international security architecture. However, what the EU has become remains uncertain. The EU is a
civilian power that has taken steps on the way to militarisation, but does
not yet qualify as a full-fledged military power. The EU has developed
some elements of an EU-specific strategic culture, or rather a security
culture, but this is only emerging and needs to be further defined. While
pursuing its goal of becoming an actor able to shape the international
security environment, the EU faces huge difficulties, some being endogenous (national divergences, lack of resources, institutional confusion, crisis
of European integration, etc.), some being exogenous (diversity of threats
in a post-Westphalian system, complexity of security governance, competition with other security actors, etc.). In the end, the chapter concludes,
in concurrence with other chapters, that if the EU has the potential to play
a global role, the influence that it has acquired at a global scale remains
limited.

In the second chapter, on NATO, Lindley-French draws a pessimistic picture of what used to be the most successful collective defence organisation. NATO was founded to deal with high politics and hard security, and therefore always benefited from American involvement. Yet the nature of such a commitment seems to be at stake, as well as is the propensity of European allies to agree with the objectives, method and conduct of the US strategy. Lindley-French focuses on hard security issues and the role NATO can play in global security governance, much beyond crisis management missions. His assessment describes a 'two-tiered alliance', characterised by an institutional crisis as much as by fundamental transatlantic divergences about security governance. There is no doubt for him that the West needs a strong NATO, one that will have to tackle all kinds of threats beyond the Euro-Atlantic area. However, drawing on the Afghan experience, Lindley-French raises serious doubts about the readiness of European allies to take up the challenge posed by the new security environment.

A further account of the crisis of multilateralism is given in Chapter 3 by Ghebali, looking at the Organization for Security and Cooperation in Europe (OSCE). Together with NATO, the EU and the Council of Europe, the OSCE forms the quadripartite element of the institutional constellation operating in European security management. Ghebali puts forward the comparative advantages that the OSCE displays in the field of conflict prevention, standard-setting and institution-building, enabling the organisation to contribute to the consolidation of stability in its vast geopolitical area over the last 15 years. However, its added-value as a security institution is increasingly questioned. Reasons include a decreased relevance in meeting the security concerns of its participating states; inter-institutional competition, particularly with the EU, which encroaches upon the OSCE's turf; and a blatant loss of interest from key states, epitomised by a relative disinterest from the US and Russia's recurrent criticism of OSCE policy.

Amongst European allies, the new EU and NATO member states play an often overlooked role in both institutions. Dunay's analysis (in Chapter 4) of their performance is mixed. Overall, most new EU and NATO members seem to be lagging behind the promises made during the accession processes, ranging from their defence budget committed to NATO to the Maastricht criteria of economic and monetary union, reducing corruption, and tightly controlling their (EU-external) borders. To Dunay, the fact that all new members are small and medium-size countries is of key importance and explains their limited input in policy-shaping. Interestingly, while acknowledging that integration has contributed to the anchoring of East-central Europe in the West, he also questions whether EU and NATO enlargements have indeed meant the re-unification of Europe, or whether they have rather redrawn the borders between 'East' and 'West'.

Finally, Russia's comeback in the power politics game in Europe is a key feature of the European security landscape. Herd (Chapter 5) examines

Russian security policy in relation to Europe, to conclude that a genuine strategic dissonance between the two camps has emerged, as demonstrated in the Summer 2008 Russia–Georgia crisis. In the wake of the Berlin–Moscow–Paris axis in opposition to preventative intervention in Iraq, Russia's strategic partnerships with both the EU and NATO have notably deteriorated. The US ballistic missile defence project, the independence of Kosovo, a moratorium on Russian obligations to the Treaty on Conventional Armed Forces in Europe (CFE), energy security and the nature of Russian governance have all risen in strategic importance, negatively shaping European–Russian relations, and leading to the Russian response to Georgia's move in South Ossetia. Most importantly, Herd argues that the cumulative impact of these tensions is indicative of deep-rooted divergences in identities, ideas, institutions and interests, which makes Russia a clearly distinct European power, and leads to the idea that Russia is an alternative Europe.

The second part of the volume aims at presenting European security from an external perspective as well as looking at interactions between Europe and other states or regions. Security trends and actors in Europe are examined from an American, Chinese, and Indian perspective, while Europe–Africa and Europe–Middle East relations are also addressed. In different ways, all chapters concur on a picture of Europe characterised by a changing environment, a potential, and a relative decline in the broad field of world politics.

In her account of European security viewed from an American perspective, McArdle Kelleher (Chapter 6) confirms that Europe is no longer at the centre of US strategic thinking. In 2008, transatlantic relations are in better shape than in the wake of the Iraq crisis, but there is also a widely shared perception that all is not well in the transatlantic framework. Interestingly enough, as put by Lindley-French, after Iraq in 2003, the litmus test of transatlantic cooperation is Afghanistan, a political and military endeavour far away from Europe. McArdle Kelleher examines two other critical tests of transatlantic relations: the fight against terrorism and WMD proliferation globally; and missile defence. In both cases, European states and the EU do not appear as driving forces and the tests reveal strategic divides between the United States and Europe more than convergences on a few solid principles or policies. As in Lindley-French's chapter, doubts are expressed on the ability of Europe to exist in the security field, which questions the idea that Europe has become a security-provider rather than a security-consumer.

Dannreuther's chapter on Europe and the Middle East (Chapter 7) stresses the gap between Europe's relative material wealth and power, its strategic ambition in the Middle East, and the difficulties to translate a potential into policy. The Middle East is no doubt an area of strategic interest for Europe and the EU, but also a direct challenge to EU solidarity. Dannreuther identifies the many weaknesses of EU policy towards the Middle East, and what he calls missed opportunities. But he also analyses the efforts put forward in defining a more effective set of frameworks and institutions for managing Europe's policy in the region: namely the European Neighbourhood Policy (ENP) and the increasingly important engagement of the EU and European states with the wider Middle East, such as in Lebanon, Iran, Afghanistan and Israel/Palestine.

European commitment in Africa is of a different nature. Olsen (Chapter 8) examines the role of the EU in sub-Saharan Africa. While acknowledging the importance of the continent for Europe in economic and security terms, Olsen's main thesis is that Africa remains a secondary security challenge for the EU. The EU is present in Africa through development and humanitarian aid and has become increasingly involved on the continent through operations falling within the European Security and Defence Policy (ESDP) and the development of the EU Africa Strategy. However, this does not mean that the region has become a high-priority security concern for Europe, as indicated by the limited attention that the fight against terrorism attracts in the actual implementation of the EU's Africa policy, or by the lack of strategic thinking about the development-security nexus.

The last two chapters offer external perspectives on European security, from a Chinese and Indian perspective. Xiang on China (Chapter 9), and Jaffrelot and Sidhu on India (Chapter 10), concur in their analysis that Europe is not central in the strategic thinking of China and India and that the EU is not perceived as being an actor able to shape the world security landscape. However, they diverge significantly when it comes to the potential of Chinese–Europe or India–Europe relations. For Xiang, the EU ambition to become a global power that promotes the rule of law fits well in Beijing's broad geopolitical vision and grand strategy of 'Peaceful Rise'. Xiang stresses the absence of major strategic confrontations between Europe and China, and talks about an ideological convergence that could well be used in the triangular relationship between China, Europe and the United States.

Jaffrelot and Sidhu provide a less optimistic account of India's perception of Europe and the potential carried by the EU. They wonder whether Europe really matters to India, that has yet to re-discover Europe in any significant political, security or social way. The main reason explaining India's relative lack of interest towards Europe is that Europe matters to India much less than other parts of the world, namely the United States, Russia and East Asia. Jaffrelot and Sidhu stress that unless Europe, namely the EU, asserts itself as a genuine power in political, military, cultural, social and even economic terms, there is a risk of being even further marginalised.

In his conclusion, Heisbourg draws on all these contributions and analyses the impact of internal and external dynamics on the place and role of the EU. Heisbourg starts with the paradox by which the EU is not a coherent, centrally governed international actor comparable to the United States, Russia, China or India, yet, in less than two decades, the EU has managed to move from the absence of any permanent and specific foreign and security role to a situation in which it has acquired an existence of its own.

What is striking in the context of this book is that although contributors dealing with the external dynamics and perceptions of European security were not asked to focus on the EU as a point of reference in their analysis, all authors gave the EU an importance that would most probably not have been given just a decade ago. The paradox is therefore that while Europe as a geopolitical space is losing its centrality, the EU as an institution focuses the attention. For the EU, the long-term trends of global security make it indispensable to transform what is still seen as potential security actorness into reality: because, Heisbourg concludes 'the weight of not being' is simply unbearable.

Notes

1 Article 3 of the Statute of the CoE states that, 'Every member of the Council of Europe must accept the principles of the rule of law and of the enjoyment by all persons within its jurisdiction of human rights and fundamental freedoms, and collaborate sincerely and effectively in the realisation of the aim of the Council.'

References

Adler, E. and Barnett, M. (1998) *Security Communities*, Cambridge: Cambridge University Press.

Bertelsmann Stiftung (2007) 'Who Rules the World? The Results of the Second Representative Survey in Brazil, China, France, Germany, India, Japan, Russia, the United Kingdom, and the United States', Berlin, 22 October 2007.

Bourlanges, J.-L. (2004) 'De l'identité de l'Europe aux frontières de l'Union', *Etudes*, 6(400), pp. 729–741.

Buzan, B. and Wæver, O. (2003) *Regions and Powers*, Cambridge: Cambridge University Press.

Cooper, R. (2003) *The Breaking of Nations. Order and Chaos in the Twenty-First Century*, New York: Grove Press.

Council of Europe (1949) *Statute of the Council of Europe*, London, 5 May.

Egbert, J., Lemaitre, P., and Wæver, O. (1987) *European Security: Problems of Research on Non-Military Aspects*, Copenhagen: Copenhagen Papers of the Centre for Peace and Conflict Research.

EU Member States (2007) *Lisbon Treaty*, Lisbon, 17 December.

European Council (1997) *Presidency Conclusions*, Luxembourg, 12–13 December.

Fawcett, L. and Hurrell, A. (eds) (1995) *Regionalism in World Politics: Regional Organization and International Order*, Oxford: Oxford University Press.

Gnesotto, N. and Grevi, G. (eds) (2006) *The New Global Puzzle. What World for the EU in 2025?*, Paris: EU Institute for Security Studies.

Grant, C. with Valasek, T. (2007) *Preparing for the multipolar world: European foreign and security policy in 2020*, London: Centre for European Reform, December.

HarrisInteractive (2008) *Monthly Opinions of Adults from Five European Coun-*

tries and the United States, Financial Times/Harris Poll, April. Online. Available at www.harrisinteractive.com/news/FTHarrisPoll/HI_FinancialTimes_HarrisPoll_ Apr2008.pdf (accessed 25 April 2008).

Heffernan, M. (1998) *The Meaning of Europe: Geography and Geopolitics*, London: Hodder Arnold.

High Representative for CFSP and European Commission (2008) *Climate Change and International Security*, Paper to the European Council, S113/08, 14 March.

Howorth, J. (2007) *Security and Defence Policy in the European Union*, London & New York: Palgrave.

Ifversen, J. (2008) 'Who are the Westerners?', *International Politics*, 45(3), pp. 236–253.

Katzenstein, P. (2005) *A World of Regions. Asia and Europe in the American Imperium*, Ithaca: Cornell University Press.

Lucarelli, S. (ed.) (2007) 'The external image of the European Union', Garnet Working Paper no. 17/07.

Mead, W.R. (2004) *Power, Terror, Peace, and War: America's Grand Strategy in a World at Risk*, New York: Knopf.

NATO (1951) 'Protocol to the North Atlantic Treaty on the Accession of Greece and Turkey', London, 22 October.

Organization for Security and Co-operation in Europe (2008). Online. Available at www.osce.org/ (accessed 28 April 2008)

Russet, B. (1967) *International Regions and the International System*, Chicago: Rand McNally.

Struck, P. (2004) Keynote Address to the 21st International Workshop on Global Security, 'Global Security: A Broader Concept for the 21st Century', Berlin, 7–10 May. Online. Available at www.csdr.org/2004book/PeterStruckKeynote.htm (accessed 28 April 2008).

Van Der Dussen, J. and Wilson, K. (eds) (1995) *The History of the Idea of Europe (What Is Europe?)*, London: Routledge.

Wæver, O. (1995) 'Securitization and Desecuritization', in Lipschutz, R. (ed.), *On Security*, New York: Columbia University Press.

Part I

European security

Internal dynamics

1 The European Union, a regional security actor with global aspirations

Thierry Tardy

Introduction

The European Union (EU) has gone through fundamental changes over the last 20 years. At the end of the Cold War, what was then the European Economic Community (EEC) was a relatively small organisation composed of 12 member states, dealing mainly with economic issues and with little connection with the broad international security environment. Eleven out of the 12 EEC members were also NATO members, at a time when NATO was the exclusive security guarantor, and when the two organisations had no relations whatsoever. Close to 20 years later, the EU counts 27 members, is de facto present through various activities at a global scale, and has transformed itself into a political entity that is part of the international security architecture.

The changes within the EU have been the result of several trends: the end of the Cold War and the subsequent evolving security environment, the globalisation process, and the intrinsic necessity for any institution to constantly adapt to new circumstances are among the main factors driving transformation. Although still modest in terms of resources allocated and scale of activity, one of the most visible evolutions has been the launching of the European Security and Defence Policy (ESDP) in the late 1990s, as one segment of the Common Foreign and Security Policy (CFSP). Through these two parallel processes, the EU is supposed to become an actor in foreign and defence affairs, although not as a substitute for state action.

The rationale, meaning, and degree of success of these evolutions in the security sphere are constantly under scrutiny, and analysts and policy makers diverge on whether the EU is doing the right thing in the right way. For some, the EU has indeed become an actor of security management as it is now involved in crisis management operations that both mirror the identity of the EU and translate its security strategy into policy. For others, the EU is still constrained by a lack of resources, institutional inertia and national resistance to play any significant role in global security governance.

At a higher level, the evolutions of the EU have led to debates on what it is that the EU is becoming, on the extent to which member states share similar policy objectives when acting through the EU, and on the nature of policy instruments that should be developed in the EU framework. Is the EU becoming a fully fledged security actor, with all the attributes which are traditionally associated with security actorness? Is ESDP transforming the EU into a military power, and if yes, how will that impact on the normative/civilian dimension of the EU? Has the EU developed a strategic culture that would reflect a qualitative evolution in nature?

Finally, as an organisation that is regionally based but that aspires to be of global reach, one challenge for the EU has been to square its global aspirations with its non-global capabilities; in other words, to reconcile regional and global parameters, to define a role for itself that combines regional constraints and global aspirations.

This chapter draws on the recent evolutions of the European Union in the security sphere to provide some thoughts on the above-mentioned questions. It first addresses the conceptualisation and operationalisation of the EU's external role, by presenting some achievements of the EU in the field of ESDP. The second part addresses some challenges that the EU is faced with at both the political and operational levels. Finally, the third part draws on these practical achievements and limits to question some of the key characteristics or aspirations of the EU in the security field. In particular, it looks at security actorness, the existence of a strategic culture, and the regional *versus* global debate.

The EU's external role: from conceptualisation to operationalisation

It has become banal to say that the EU has achieved a significant amount since the Saint-Malo Summit. Five years after the coming into force of the Maastricht Treaty establishing the Common Foreign and Security Policy (CFSP), the December 1998 Franco-British Saint-Malo Summit marked the starting point of the European Security and Defense Policy (ESDP). In the midst of the Kosovo crisis and in the context of an absence of the EU in the management of the Yugoslav conflicts, the French and British felt the need to reinvigorate the EU in its security dimension. The final declaration stated that, '[t]he European Union needs to be in a position to play its full role on the international stage', and '[t]o this end, the Union must have the capacity for autonomous action, backed up by credible military forces, the means to decide to use them and a readiness to do so, in order to respond to international crises' (Chirac and Blair 1998).

The Summit led to a series of decisions taken at the EU level (European Councils of Cologne in June 1999, Helsinki in December 1999, and Feira in June 2000), and that were then endorsed in the 2000 Nice Treaty. These decisions were aimed at making ESDP concrete through the establishment of permanent political and military institutions and the definition of Capabilities Headline Goals. In parallel, the EU asserted itself as a security actor by defining its own conceptual framework for security management as well as by institutionalising relations with other security actors.

Institutions, capabilities, operations as evidence of security actorness

Four main ESDP bodies were initially created within the Secretariat of the Council, reporting to the High Representative for CFSP, Javier Solana: a Political and Security Committee (PSC or COPS), a Military Committee, a Military Staff, and a Committee for the Civilian Aspects of Crisis Management (CIVCOM). These institutions were established to enable the EU to decide upon, plan and conduct crisis management operations as defined in article 17§2 of the Amsterdam Treaty, the so-called Petersberg tasks (humanitarian and rescue tasks, peacekeeping tasks, use of combat forces in crisis management, including peacemaking).[1] The scope of ESDP was therefore limited from the outset, and confined to crisis management activities. At the institutional level, the subsequent development of ESDP led to the creation of the European Defence Agency (EDA) in 2004; a civil–military cell as well as an operation centre were also established in 2005/06 within the EU Military Staff, as a response to the need to be able to plan and conduct small-scale crisis management operations autonomously (i.e. without resorting to NATO assets nor calling on states). Finally, in 2007/08 the civilian crisis management structure was developed through the establishment of a Civilian Planning and Conduct Capability (CPCC) to plan and conduct all ESDP civilian operations.

Insofar as capabilities are concerned, the 1999 Helsinki Summit defined a military Headline Goal, according to which 'Member States must be able, by 2003, to deploy within 60 days and sustain for at least one year military forces of up to 50,000–60,000 persons capable of the full range of Petersberg tasks' (European Council 1999). This Headline Goal was declared to be met in May 2003, although 'limited and constrained by recognised shortfalls' (European Council 2003). Shortfalls are particularly noticeable in the field of strategic airlift, logistics, command and control, and operational planning. Subsequently, a new headline goal was defined in 2004 ('Headline Goal 2010'), with a shift from a quantitative approach – with the corps-level target – to a more qualitative approach – through the Battlegroup concept. The Battlegroup is a high-readiness small-size force (approximately 1,500 troops), that shall enable the EU to respond quickly and for short periods (30 to 120 days) to international crisis (Council of the EU 2004a). Battlegroups became operational as of January 2007, with two such units being on standby for six months, with a rotation system agreed upon until 2010.

The EU was initially more discreet in defining its policy towards civilian crisis management. Four 'priority areas' were identified at the Feira Summit of June 2000: police, rule of law, civil administration and civil protection. In the police area, Member States pledged that, by 2003, they would be able to provide 'up to 5,000 police officers for international missions across the range of conflict prevention and crisis management operations', and to 'identify and deploy up to 1,000 police officers within 30 days'. A broader civilian headline goal was then adopted in December 2004, to be met in 2008 (Council of the EU 2004c). It enlarged the scope of EU operations to security sector reform (SSR) and disarmament, demobilisation, and reintegration (DDR) processes, and insisted on integrating civilian and military activities as well as the various EU entities involved in civilian crisis management. The Headline Goal 2008 was declared to be completed and then replaced by a new civilian Headline Goal 2010. Contrary to military crisis management, which falls exclusively within the second pillar (intergovernmental) of the EU structure, civilian crisis management is split between the CFSP framework (second pillar) and first pillar activities. Well before the birth of ESDP and even CFSP, the European Community and its executive body, the European Commission, were involved in conflict prevention or post-conflict reconstruction, which are integral parts of civilian crisis management. The increasing interdependence between development and security makes the role of the Commission in security governance even more obvious, and the chance of overlapping between first and second pillar functions greater.

Following the establishment of the political–military structure, and the signature, in December 2002, of the agreement between the EU and NATO on the implementation of the Berlin Plus arrangement (by which the EU can draw on NATO assets for EU-led operations), ESDP made a leap forward in 2003 with the creation of the first EU-led missions. These began in Bosnia-Herzegovina, with the EU Police Mission deployed in January 2003 as a takeover of the UN Police Mission, and then expanded into Macedonia as of March 2003 with Operation Concordia, the first military operation, and first implementation of the 'Berlin Plus' agreement. That same year, the EU launched its first autonomous military operation, and first mission outside of Europe, with Operation Artemis in the Democratic Republic of the Congo (DRC). These operations fundamentally changed the nature of the debate about the role of the EU in security governance, as they made ESDP tangible. The first missions showed that the EU is capable of going beyond the rhetoric of security actorness by actually becoming present on the ground, i.e. by matching words with deeds. This is reinforced by the adoption in December 2003 of the European Security Strategy (European Council 2003), that *inter alia* defines a theoretical basis for EU action. The following years confirmed the evolution as the EU created and ran 18 more missions (as of October 2008) after the three above-mentioned ones (see Table 1.1). In Europe, the EU has been running its largest military operation in Bosnia-Herzegovina with Operation Althea (following the withdrawal of the NATO operation), and was supposed to deploy its largest and most ambitious civilian operation in Kosovo (EULEX) as of June 2008 (a deployment made, as we write, difficult by the diplomatic battle over the independence of Kosovo); in October 2008, a monitoring mission was also deployed

Table 1.1 EU operations (as of October 2008)

Ongoing	Completed
Europe	*Europe*
• EUFOR Althea, Bosnia-Herzegovina*	• Concordia, FYROM*
• EUPM, Bosnia-Herzegovina	• Proxima, FYROM
• EULEX Kosovo	• EUPAT FYROM (Police
• EUMM, Georgia	Advisory Team)
Middle East – Asia	*Caucasus*
• EUPOL COPPS, Palestinian Territories	• EUJUST Themis Georgia
• EU BAM Rafah, Palestinian Territories	*Africa*
• EUJUST Lex Iraq	• Artemis DRC*
• EUPOL Afghanistan	• EUFOR DRC*
Africa	• EU Support to AMIS, Darfur**
• EUPOL DRC	• EUPOL Kinshasa
• EUSEC DRC	*Asia*
• EUFOR Chad-CAR*	• EU Monitoring Mission, Aceh
• EU SSR Guinea-Bissau	

Source: EU website.

Notes
*military operation.
**with some military elements.

in Georgia. Outside of Europe, the EU has intervened in Asia (one mission in Aceh, Indonesia), in the Middle East (two civilian missions in the Palestinian Territories; one rule of law mission in Iraq (not deployed *in situ*)), and Africa (two civilian, one more military operation in the DRC; one mission in Darfur, one mission in Chad and the Central African Republic, and one security sector reform mission in Guinea-Bissau).

Two remarks can be made about these operations. The first one is that the missions are primarily of a civilian nature (only five of the 21 missions are military), while initially ESDP was fundamentally a military policy. This is the simultaneous result of a deliberate choice and of the fact that the EU responded preferably to the demand it could address, and these were more civilian in nature than military. Second, operations outside Europe are more numerous than the ones in Europe, which seems to indicate the global reach of the EU, or at least a reach 'beyond Europe'. The ability to project security in Asia or Africa through ESDP missions is indeed a demonstration that the EU is no longer only a regional entity but has become global in a way, by its activities if not membership.

A conceptual framework for external action

These operations raise the questions of their purpose and of the extent to which they serve some kind of common EU interests or long-term vision. In other words, it is the question of the conceptual framework of EU external action that is raised. In this respect, the release in December 2003 of the *European Security Strategy* (ESS) (European Council 2003) marked a new step in the quest of security actor status. The ESS was written in 2003, in the midst of one of the most serious political crisis of the EU following the Iraq crisis. Beyond the contextual needs to respond to the US *National Security Strategy* of September 2002 and to rebuild some sort of European collegiality after the Iraq episode, the ESS was also – or primarily – aimed at defining the key elements of a security strategy for the EU. It starts by defining the ambition of the EU to become a global actor, that 'should be ready to share in the responsibility for global security and in building a better world'. With this broad objective stated, the document first looks at global challenges and key threats, identifying terrorism, proliferation of weapons of mass destruction, regional conflicts, state failure, and organised crime as the five key threats faced by the EU. Second, the Strategy defines three strategic objectives: addressing threats; building security in the EU neighbourhood; and building an international order based on 'effective multilateralism'. Third, the Strategy explores some of the policy implications of EU ambition. It fills a gap in the EU effort to theorise its role on the international scene, as well as providing a basis for the development of policy orientations.

The Lisbon Treaty further helped in defining a framework for EU external action (European Council 2007). The Treaty renamed ESDP Common Security and Defence Policy (CSDP), which was upgraded and appeared in an EU Treaty for the first time.

These wide-ranging texts are complemented by a series of documents that define, at different levels, the EU policies. Some of these documents have a geographical approach, such as the EU Neighbourhood Policy (European Commission 2004) or the EU Strategy for Africa (Council of the EU 2005d); some are issue-specific, such as the EU Counter-Terrorism Strategy (Council of the EU 2005c) or the two concepts on security sector reform (Council of the EU 2005a and European Commission 2006). More broadly, EU action is also guided by key texts such as the Convention for the Protection of Human Rights and Fundamental Freedoms or the UN Charter. All together, these documents constitute a conceptual framework for external action that is probably as precise and coherent as many doctrinal texts elaborated at the national level.

Status through partnerships

Finally, the EU quest for global status makes partnerships with other international institutions a necessity. Being a security actor implies that the EU develops relations with other security institutions, but also that it asserts its comparative advantages, its identity as a security institution. Three points can be underlined here. First, the EU has become, through ESDP, an actor in crisis management comparable with other actors such as the UN or NATO. For its member states, this means that the EU has become an option for crisis management operations, as much as NATO or the UN. In practice, the arrival of a new actor in crisis management modifies the environment. The simultaneous presence in the field of the EU and of other actors leads to a redefinition of inter-institutional relationships. Second, in the elaboration of its relationship with other institutions, the EU places a premium on its autonomy of decision and action. This desire has a particular meaning in the context of EU–NATO relations. The whole idea behind ESDP is about autonomy for the EU vis-à-vis NATO, but this autonomy is called into question by EU dependence on NATO assets that makes any kind of truly autonomous EU military operation impossible for the time being. The debate is slightly different in the context of EU–UN relations, where the EU tends to be in a stronger position. The EU is willing to develop linkages with the UN, and has achieved much at both the political level and in the field, but is also adamant that such linkages should not be established at the expense of EU autonomy. Third, over the last decade, the EU has largely developed and institutionalised its links with organisations such as the UN (UNSG and EU Presidency 2003), NATO, the OSCE, and to a lesser extent the African Union. Yet, the nature of the EU–NATO–UN triangular relationship, as well as its policy implications, needs further clarification. At the legal level, the role of the UN Security Council in mandating EU or NATO missions and the proclivity of these regional institutions to seek a UN mandate for their operations are subject to debate. At the political level, the division of tasks among institutions and their respective areas of intervention needs also to be clarified. This is of particular relevance to the debate on EU–NATO cooperation, and on the extent to which the EU should duplicate what already exists within NATO. Finally, inter-institutional cooperation requires better coordination at headquarters and field levels among institutions that increasingly operate simultaneously, as the operations in Kosovo or Chad show.

These different categories of EU development do not necessarily make the EU an efficient and coherent security actor, able to deliver on activities that reflect a well-defined security strategy. However, they do demonstrate a qualitative evolution that makes the EU a very different institution than what it was a decade ago (Cornish and Edwards 2005). The changes are tangible, and most likely irreversible. Yet, these evolutions leave open some key questions as to what the EU is, what it does and why. Two levels of analysis need to be distinguished here. One is about the ability of the EU to deliver ESDP, i.e. primarily crisis management operations. The second level of analysis moves the debate one step higher, and aims at evaluating the impact of ESDP on what the EU is becoming.

A constrained ESDP

The first layer of the debate leads to the conclusion that the EU has still a long way to go before it performs at all levels of the crisis management spectrum. ESDP is a young process (Howorth 2007) and any assessment of achievements and lacunas should be made with some caution. For the time being, it remains that the EU is still a low-key peace implementer, with limited resources and relatively weak political and military clout. It is increasingly active in security governance, but EU missions reveal limited involvement and minimisation of risks as well as a weak strategic vision. Taken together, the five military missions total less than 16,000 troops,[2] which is approximately the strength of the UN operation in the DRC (MONUC: 16,655 as of November 2007) or of the NATO-led KFOR in Kosovo. The largest EU operation, Althea (7,000 when first deployed), represents half the size of UN operations such as UNIFIL in Lebanon or UNMIL in Liberia (respectively 13,264 and 13,322 as of November 2007). Most civilian missions are equally modest in the number of people deployed. The largest one has been the EU Police Mission in Bosnia-Herzegovina, that counted up to 2,000 police officers, and with up to 3,000 personnel, the yet-to-be deployed EULEX Kosovo would mark a quantitative leap. However, most other missions are much smaller, with EUPOL Kinshasa, EUBAM Rafah or EUJUST Themis in Georgia counting fewer than 50. In terms of risks, the missions conducted to date were not particularly ambitious, and those that entailed a certain degree of risk were either backed by NATO (Althea in Bosnia-Herzegovina) or limited in scope and time (Artemis, EUFOR in the DRC, EUFOR Chad). This indicates that the EU has not really been tested as a long-term peace implementer. It is doing a little bit here and there, but has not yet reached the level of operations that the UN or NATO are conducting. Moreover, what the EU does is determined to a large extent by its own capacity rather than by what a particular situation requires. The 'what-can-be-done' approach seems to prevail over the 'what-must-be-done'. This might be a feature of any security actor, but makes particular sense in the case of the EU, that is more obsessed by the fear of failing than the UN or NATO, as UN operations in Africa or the NATO operation in Afghanistan attest.

This situation can be explained by at least five sets of reasons. All impact on EU external action at different levels, but each constitute a key impediment to the further development of ESDP. They are: divergences among member states, lack of capabilities, institutional confusion, disconnect between CFSP and ESDP, and mismatch between ESDP and the key threats to the EU.

National divergences

Divergences among member states on what ESDP is about are consubstantial to the idea of a common security and defence policy. Member states do recognise that the EU should play a role in security affairs, but diverge on the scope and long-term objective of this role. Herd talks about 'four Europes'[3] that may each develop a different conception of what the EU should become. These divergences are well illustrated by the Franco-British divide on the finality of the EU and therefore on the support to be given to ESDP. Intergovernmental by nature, ESDP builds its coherence and political strength primarily on states' cohesion, and therefore also suffers directly from their discrepancies. Issues such as the priority to be given to the EU over NATO, the necessity to provide the EU with permanent planning capabilities and to promote 'permanent structured cooperation' (European Council 2007), or the extent to which the military dimension should be developed are examples of such divergences. The 2004 enlargement made these difficulties even more salient, with the new members being less ESDP-friendly and more NATO-centred.[4] By the same token, divergences on the way the EU should interact with the US impact on the coherence of EU foreign and security policy, as it connects to the very nature of the European project.

Limited resources

Second, the lack of resources impedes the full realisation of EU security policy. Different types of lacunas exist. In financial terms, the constant decrease of defence budgets in Europe since the end of the Cold War has impacted on national capacities, with states often lacking the kind of assets that are demanded by the EU for themselves. Decreasing defence spending in Europe has also deepened the gap with the United States, that spends more on defence than the 27 EU states together.[5] Yet gross financial resources may matter less than the way money is actually spent. Out of 1.8 million troops altogether, EU member states can only deploy about 4 per cent, which is not insignificant but still hard to reconcile with global aspirations served by force projection. As a matter of fact, about 60,000–70,000 troops have been deployed by European states, at all times, in crisis management operations over the last few years (Giegerich and Wallace 2004; Biscop 2007). However, in most cases, these are not EU deployments. In the case of UNIFIL in Lebanon, the participation of EU member states is significant (7,699 out of 13,264 in November 2007), but such contributions remain national and therefore cannot be associated with an EU contribution as it often is (GAERC 2006).

Moreover, beyond the absence of a permanent operational planning structure, capabilities shortfalls are also persistent in the fields of C3I (command, control, communication, and intelligence) strategic mobility (air- and sealift), and logistics (Council of the EU 2006; Howorth 2007: chapter 4), but also in some key areas in the civilian sphere (Council of the EU 2005b; Nowak 2006). Furthermore, when capabilities are put in place, such as the Battlegroups, their utility as crisis management tools and therefore their usage seem to be called into question (Lindstrom 2007). Finally, little integration has taken place. Despite some hopes following the creation of the European Defence Agency, the purpose of which is to rationalise defence spending within the EU, states continue to think in national rather than European terms when it comes to defence procurements, and pooling of resources remain difficult as a consequence.

Institutional confusion

Third, the EU suffers from institutional inertia, which impacts on both its internal and external cohesion. Internally, lack of coordination and tensions between the first and the second pillar of the EU structure, but also between the civilian and the military within the second pillar, are sources of institutional inertia. Externally, problems of EU representation (with the Presidency, the Commission and the High Representative for CFSP all aspiring to talk on behalf of the EU), or of integration in the field of different EU agencies or missions (as in Bosnia-Herzegovina or the Democratic Republic of the Congo), are also negatively impacting on EU visibility and cohesion. The Lisbon Treaty laid out the merger of the positions of Commissioner for External Relations and High Representative for CFSP in a new function of High Representative for Foreign Affairs and Security Policy, who would head a diplomatic service; continuity and visibility would also be assured by a European Council permanent president, as well as the legal personality for the EU (European Council 2007). Yet, given the internal inertia and the different cultures that characterise the EU bodies, not to mention the uncertainty surrounding the future of the Lisbon Treaty, the extent to which these changes would significantly improve the overall cohesion of EU external action remains to be seen.

CFSP–ESDP gap

Fourth, there is a disconnect between the foreign policy level encapsulated by CFSP and the security and defence level contained in ESDP. It follows that ESDP does not always seem to belong to the larger political framework that CFSP is supposed to define. ESDP operations are supposed to 'preserve peace and strengthen international security' and 'to develop and consolidate democracy and the rule of law' (European Council 1992: art.J.1), which are key objectives of CFSP. Yet, the link between the missions in Aceh (Indonesia) or in the DRC with what should be a European common policy vis-à-vis these two countries or the regions they belong to is not clear. In other words, it is the strategic vision that is supposed to underlie ESDP that lacks consistency. Another, more positive, illustration of this disconnect is the fact that ESDP can develop with relative autonomy from the political level, i.e. also from crises that may occur at this level. One example is the launching of the first ESDP operations in 2003 at a time when CFSP was going through one of its major crises, over Iraq. This disconnect may have its advantages; in the long run though, it can only damage the general cohesion of EU external action (Smith, M. 2006). In a way, it is precisely because member states were not in agreement on the bigger strategic picture that ESDP was developed the way it was, i.e. in a way that would avoid the strategic divergences from becoming too apparent.

Mismatch between ESDP and the key threats

Fifth, the ESDP's adequacy with the threats identified by the ESS is being challenged. One central question that the events of 11 September 2001 put to the EU was whether ESDP could provide some response to the threat of terrorism (Bono 2006). That year, the EU was embarked on a process of constituting a corps-level reaction force to be able to manage Balkan-type crises. Yet the relevance of such a force to the fight against terrorism or the proliferation of weapons of mass destruction was far from obvious. Work was then carried out on the contribution of CFSP/ESDP to the fight against terrorism, both in the military and civilian fields, and areas where ESDP operations could support the fight against terrorism were identified (Council of the EU 2004b; European Council 2007[6]). Furthermore, the *European Security Strategy* included 'support for third countries in combating terrorism' into potential ESDP missions (European Council 2003), while a 'solidarity clause' on mutual assistance with any state being the victim of a terrorist attack was inserted in the Lisbon Treaty (European Council 2007: Title VII, art.188 R). Still, the relative narrowness of ESDP is difficult to reconcile with the wide-ranging approach contained in the EU Counter-Terrorism Strategy (Council of the EU 2005b). Beyond ESDP, the question is again that of cross-pillar cohesion. The confinement of CFSP/ESDP to one pillar while the fight against terrorism must draw on all three pillars is problematic.

The EU, a regional security actor, not yet global

This brief overview of some achievements and limitations of ESDP leads us to the kind of security actor that the EU has become. Three issues are analysed: the first is about the meaning of security actorness for the European Union; the second is the emergence of a strategic culture; and the third presents the regional *versus* global reach debate.

Meaning of security actorness

Drawing on Sjöstedt's work (1977: 15–16), Bretherton and Vogler (1999: 20) define an actor of international politics as 'an entity that exhibits a degree of autonomy from its external environment, and indeed from its internal constituents, and which is capable of volition or purpose'. Hill mentions a clear identity, a self-contained decision-making system, and the 'practical capabilities to have effective policies' as defining criteria of actorness (Hill 1996, see also Ginsberg 1999).

Talking about the EU as an actor on the international scene is interesting in at least two respects. At the conceptual/international relations theory level (see Ginsberg 1999), seeing an institution as an actor challenges the traditional/realist approach to the structure of the international system and the nature of its constitutive units, according to which only states can be seen as actors, while international institutions only mirror state policies. In the same vein, trying to locate the EU on the international actors' spectrum is uneasy because of the very nature of the institution, being neither a state nor a conventional international organisation.

Second, characterising the EU as an actor is of relevance because being an actor is indeed an aspiration of the EU. Although CFSP and ESDP remain intergovernmental in nature, both are supposed to make the EU more than the sum of state policies. The 2000 Nice Presidency Report on ESDP stated that

> [t]he aim of the efforts made [...] is to give the European Union the means of playing its role fully on the international stage and of assuming its responsibilities in the face of crises by adding to the range of instruments already at its disposal an autonomous capacity to take decisions and action in the security and defence field.
>
> (European Council 2000)

In the same vein, the ESS presents the EU as being 'inevitably a global player', while '[t]he increasing convergence of European interests and the strengthening of mutual solidarity of the EU makes [it] a more credible and effective actor'.

As the first part of this chapter has tried to show, in the broad security field, criteria such as the existence of the EU as a political entity distinct from its constitutive parts (autonomy), the ability to define strategic and policy orientations, the existence of institutions, resources and operational activities, and the impact on the international security environment are important indicators of EU actorness. To a large extent, the development of ESDP and the subsequent creation of EU-led operations, combined with the role of the Commission in the civilian field, have indeed transformed the EU into a security actor that cannot be solely associated with its member states.

Beyond crisis management, the EU, as a political entity, can also be seen as serving security functions (Wæver 2000), through the integration process and through the liberal model that it represents. One of the original rationales for the creation of the European Community was to prevent the re-emergence of traditional rivalries between France and Germany, and 50 years later, the EU has become a security community, in which resorting to force among its members has become obsolete (Adler and Barnett 1998). Second, the European Union has acted as a stabilising power at the core of Europe, which eventually led to the post-Cold War

enlargements (Wæver 2000). Such enlargements acted as conflict prevention mechanisms.[7] This 'magnetism' did not play any role in the Balkan
region in the early 1990s. Yet after the end of the Yugoslav dislocation,
the prospects for further EU enlargements to Balkan countries are also
aimed at stabilising states after a decade of turmoil.

The question that follows is that of the nature of the actor that the
EU has become. Originally, the EU was fundamentally a civilian power
(Duchêne 1972). However, EU ambition through ESDP has been to move
beyond the civilian sphere, and to make itself a power in all its dimensions.
What this means exactly is still unclear as states diverge on the meaning
of power in the EU context. However, if the EU is acquiring some of
the characteristics of a military power and is, for example, conducting
military operations, then questions about the way such power will be used
and about the compatibility between civilian and military power arise
(Elgström and Smith 2006: Introduction; Whitman 1998; Sjursen 2006).
These questions are nurtured by the assumption that a military dimension
would inevitably alter the EU's conception of its role, in the sense that it
would change its vision of what it can do, and subsequently shape its interests. The EU would move away from its civilian, normative, liberal status
to become a self-interested actor, capable of resorting to force to serve
objectives that were previously not even considered.

An alternative approach is that of an EU conception of power that is
distinct from traditional ways (Manners 2002, 2006; Smith, M. 2006:
49–50). Because the EU does not resemble other security actors and is built
on a series of values, it would be able to combine soft and hard power so
as to behave on the international scene more as a force for good than as
any form of hegemon.

The emergence of a strategic culture

The question of what the EU *is* in the security field leads to that of what it
thinks about security, i.e. the question of the existence of a strategic
culture for the EU. Johnston defines a 'strategic culture' as a 'system of
symbols' which establishes 'strategic preferences by formulating concepts
of the role and efficacy of military force in interstate political affairs'
(Johnston 1995: 46). Strategic culture is about threat assessment and management, and the centrality of the use of force in the latter. Whether such a
culture exists at the EU level begs the question of a Europeanisation of
national cultures. In international relations theory terms, such a process
cannot be contemplated by the realists, while liberals and constructivists
take it as a possibility, though not necessarily a reality.

The ESS states that '[w]e need to develop a strategic culture that fosters
early, rapid, and when necessary, robust intervention' (European Council
2003: 11), insinuating that such a culture does not yet exist. The question
is ultimately that of the use of force by the EU and its member states.

However, one major shortcoming of the ESS is its failure to address the question posed to any security actor, which should be a central theme of any security strategy, i.e. the question of how security can be achieved and the place force may take in achieving it (Heisbourg 2004; Posen 2004). The EU approach to the use of force is indeed noticeably weak in the ESS. The document does not even explicitly refer to the use of force, but instead refers to 'military activities', 'robust intervention', or a 'price to be paid' (European Council 2003: 10–11). This absence reflects the diverging positions of EU member states on the utility of force (Meyer 2006), and therefore sets the limits of the existence of a European strategic culture. If strategic culture is about shared 'basic assumptions about the orderliness of the strategic environment' as well as about 'strategic options that are the most efficacious for dealing with the threat environment' (Johnston 1995), then clarity on the utility of force is a *sine qua non*.

Such a discord on the use of force questions the possibility of a European strategic culture combining soft and hard power (Haarland 2006; Meyer 2006). At the policy level, it makes the concept of 'effective multilateralism' incomplete. As defined in the ESS, 'effective multilateralism' is about the necessity to have functioning international organisations, and also about the readiness 'to act when their rules are broken.' Yet the ambiguity on coercive action begs the question of the meaning of action in response to broken rules, as well as of the implications in operational and possibly military terms. Furthermore, if it is assumed that 'effective multilateralism' may imply the use of force when the 'rules are broken', the way such action would be conditioned to an authorisation of the UN Security Council is unclear. In fact, it is the whole idea of the subordination of the use of force to the UN Charter that is ambiguous. The ESS reasserts that '[t]he fundamental framework for international relations is the United Nations Charter' but refrains from saying that any military operation that the EU might undertake should be formally mandated by the UN Security Council.

Divergences on the use of force are true limitations to the existence of a European strategic culture. The insertion in the Lisbon treaty of a 'solidarity clause' (European Council 2007: Title VII, art.188 R) as well as a defence clause (art.28 A7) may be an indication that things are slowly evolving, but these engagements remain of a rhetorical nature.

However, other signs of convergence seem to attest to the emergence of a common culture of security. Issues such as threat assessment (as defined in the ESS), legitimacy and the virtues of multilateralism in threat management, military and civilian crisis management, are examples where national perceptions and policies tend to converge and where, as a consequence, a European approach is emerging. Cornish and Edwards (2005) and Meyer (2006) point to the socialisation process that takes place within the EU and converge in contending that a strategic culture is indeed in the making. Howorth (2007: 186–187) distances himself from the concept of a European identity, but concludes that 'if the debate is framed less around

issues of identity and more around capacity, objectives and implementation, there are obvious grounds for concluding that such a convergence is
already taking place'. This development may not be complete as long as
clarity on the use of force is absent, but at least the EU has cultivated the
security culture of civilian power, or, as Cornish and Edwards put it
(2001: 588) a 'unique, gendarmerie-style EU strategic culture'.

This leads to a limit of the very concept of strategic culture, that is that
what is scrutinised may prove ill-adapted to what the EU is trying to
develop within the framework of CFSP/ESDP. What 'strategic' refers to for
the EU is not clear, but in any case can hardly be associated with a proper
national defence policy (see for example Rynning, 2003). Because of its
nature, the EU thinks in security terms rather than in strategic terms.
Howorth underlines the limits of applying the concept of strategic culture
to an entity that is not a state, and suggests that the term 'security culture'
may be more appropriate to reflect the 'collective mindset [that] is taking
shape in the EU' (2007: 178). For Javier Solana,

> since the beginning of the European project, [Europeans] have developed
> a specific culture of security, based on conflict-prevention, political
> management of crises and taking account of the economic and social
> root causes of violent action of all kinds. Following the 11 September
> attacks, this practice of 'holistic security' immediately gave rise to a series
> of measures and adjustments to Union policies.
>
> (Solana 2002)

Indeed, the EU is trying to develop a comprehensive security policy that
reflects an emerging common culture of security. This security policy and
this common culture embrace a wide range of issues among which the use
of force may not be central. As a consequence, issues that are relevant to
the security culture of the EU cannot all fall within the narrower concept
of strategic culture.

The EU still a regional actor

Finally, in its aim to play a role in security affairs at a global scale, the EU
has been confronted with the difficulty of reconciling regional capacity and
global requirements. As stated in the *European Security Strategy*, the EU
aspires to be a global actor, that thinks in global terms, and that shapes
the global security agenda. What defines global reach is a combination of
vision, capacity and impact. Few actors (be they state or non-state actors)
of the international system can currently pretend to enjoy such power, and
the bar is therefore set high.

In terms of vision, one could argue that the EU offers a vision of security
management that is EU-specific, based on norms and values and aimed at
promoting a liberal agenda on a global scale. This is developed in the ESS

and in a series of key documents. This 'vision' distinguishes itself from what would be the American vision, and a fortiori from the Chinese or Russian vision.[8] At a more operational level though, when it comes to translate a global project into policy, the European vision is less easily identifiable. Be it in Africa, in the Middle East or in Asia, where the EU is present through many initiatives, action is more event-driven and country-specific rather than the implementation of a strategy.[9] Running ESDP operations in Aceh or the DRC do not necessarily make the EU any more global. Most importantly, if there is a wide consensus within the EU on the necessity to intervene in Europe, there is little agreement on the need to intervene outside. This leads to the question of the possibility for the EU to develop a strategic vision while most of its members lack any strategic vision beyond Europe and do not aspire to develop one. Can the EU think and act in global, strategic terms, when its member states do not? Can the EU play a significant and consistent role in the Middle East or in Africa while quite a few of its member states display either little interest in or little expertise on these regions?

Another limitation to global reach is capacity. The EU is not powerless in this respect, especially insofar as economic assets are concerned, but the shortfalls in capabilities are genuine obstacles to a global role. Capacity is an objective constraint, but it also has a subjective dimension in the sense that, as Kagan put it (2002), capacity may create the will or the vision. And indeed, as said before, what drives EU action is often determined more by its capacity to act and circumstances than by an assessment of what needs to be done, in accordance with a pre-defined strategic vision.

Finally, global reach implies a capacity to influence global affairs. The EU role at the UN provides an example of this influence, or the lack thereof (Tardy 2007). A Communication of the Commission on EU–UN relations (2003: 17) stated that

> All too often the EU's stance in multilateral forums is still a reactive one, with the agenda set by other players. The EU should promote its core objectives in the UN more actively – this would not only further its own interests, but also advance the agenda of the UN overall.

For Laatikainen and Smith (2006: 13–23), the record of EU influence within the UN is indeed mixed. The EU played an instrumental role in the signature of the Kyoto protocol, and is very active in the economic and social fields. It is also the regional organisation that is the most active in the broad field of crisis management, along with the UN. But overall, the EU does not seem to appear as a driving force in many other areas. In particular, it failed to have any significant impact on the 2005 UN reform process (Ortega 2005: 15), has a mixed record in the area of human rights (Smith, K. 2006), and is largely absent from UN-led peace operations.

It follows that the EU has remained primarily a regional security actor, and has demonstrated little capacity to address security issues on a global scale. The EU has started to project security outside Europe, but these activities have not transformed it into a global actor.

Conclusion

What the European Union has achieved in ten years in the security field is undeniable. The EU project was very ambitious, the path was narrow, and the EU was constantly watched, whatever it did or did not do. As of 2003, the EU has started to project security outside its borders through peace missions, which further contribute to its transformation as a security actor.

Yet, what the EU has become remains uncertain. The EU is a civilian power that has taken steps on the way to militarisation, but does not yet qualify as a fully fledged military power. The EU has developed some elements of a strategic culture, or rather a security culture, that is EU-specific, but this security culture is only emerging and needs to be further defined.

In this context, while pursuing its goal of becoming an actor able to shape the international security environment, the EU is facing huge difficulties, some being endogenous (national divergences, lack of resources, institutional confusion, crisis of European integration, etc.), some being exogenous (diversity of threats in a post-Westphalian system, complexity of security governance, competition with other security actors, etc.). At the same time, the EU displays many comparative advantages that theoretically make it an institution uniquely placed to deal with contemporary security threats. Such threats are now primarily of a non-military nature and often emanate from non-state actors. Addressing them requires a multilateral response that is seen as legitimate, that combines military and non-military elements, and that can take place at all stages of the crisis management spectrum. There are not many security actors that even theoretically meet these requirements. The EU does. At a strategic level and in the long run, it may mean that the dynamics of change work in favour of the EU.

Notes

1 The Lisbon Treaty endorsed the extension of the 'Petersberg Tasks', that now include 'joint disarmament operations, humanitarian and rescue tasks, military advice and assistance tasks, conflict prevention and peace-keeping tasks, tasks of combat forces in crisis management, including peace-making and post-conflict stabilisation' (European Council 2007: art.28B).
2 Concordia: 357; Artemis: 1,800; EUFOR DRC: 2,630 (with the reserve force in Gabon); Althea: 7,000; EUFOR Chad-CAR: 4,000.
3 See Herd's chapter in this volume.
4 See Dunay's chapter in this volume.
5 See Lindley-French's chapter in this volume.
6 The Lisbon Treaty established the link between ESDP operations and the fight against terrorism, by stating that '[a]ll these tasks may contribute to the fight against terrorism, including by supporting third countries in combating terrorism in their territories' (European Council 2007: art.28B §1).

7 See Dunay's chapter in this volume.
8 See chapters by Kelleher, Herd and Xiang in this volume.
9 See chapters by Olsen and Dannreuther in this volume.

References

Adler, E. and Barnett, M. (1998) *Security Communities*, Cambridge: Cambridge University Press.
Biscop, S. (2007) 'The Ambiguous Ambition. The Development of the EU Security Architecture', *Studia Diplomatica* (Special Issue), LX(1): 265–78.
Bono, G. (ed.) (2006) *The Impact of 9/11 on European Foreign and Security Policy*, Brussels: Institute for European Studies, Vrije Universiteit Brussel.
Bretherton, C. and Vogler, J. (1999) *The European Union as a Global Actor*, London: Routledge.
Chirac, J. and Blair, T. (1998) 'Joint Declaration on European Defence', Franco-British Summit, Saint-Malo, December.
Cornish, P. and Edwards, G. (2001) 'Beyond the EU/NATO dichotomy: the beginnings of a European strategic culture', *International Affairs*, 77(3): 587–603.
—— (2005) 'The strategic culture of the European Union: a progress report', *International Affairs*, 81(4): 801–820.
Council of the EU (2004a) 'Headline Goal 2010', 15 June.
—— (2004b) 'Conceptual Framework on the ESDP dimension of the fight against terrorism', doc. 14797/04, Brussels, November.
—— (2004c) 'Civilian Headline Goal 2008', Annex to the ESDP Presidency Report, Brussels, December.
—— (2005a) 'EU Concept for ESDP Support to Security Sector Reform', Brussels, October.
—— (2005b) 'Civilian Capabilities Improvement Conference. Ministerial Declaration', 14713/05 (Press 306), Brussels, November.
—— (2005c) 'The European Union Counter-Terrorism Strategy', 14469/4/05 rev.4, Brussels, 30 November.
—— (2005d) 'The EU and Africa: Towards a Strategic Partnership', Brussels, 19 December.
—— (2006) 'Capabilities Improvement Chart I/2006', Brussels.
Duchêne, F. (1972) 'Europe's Role in World Peace', in Mayne, R. (ed.), *Europe Tomorrow: Sixteen Europeans Look Ahead*, London: Fontana.
Elgström, O. and Smith, M. (eds) (2006) *The European Union's Roles in International Politics: Concepts and Analysis*, London: Routledge.
European Commission (2003) 'The European Union and the United Nations: The choice of multilateralism', Communication from the Commission to the Council and the European Parliament, September.
—— (2004) 'European Neighbourhood Policy. Strategy Paper', Communication from the Commission, COM(2004) 373 final, Brussels, May.
—— (2006) 'A Concept for European Community Support for Security Sector Reform', Communication from the Commission, COM(2006) 253 final, Brussels, May.
European Council (1992) Treaty on European Union, Maastricht.
—— (1999) Presidency Conclusions, Helsinki, December.
—— (2000) Presidency Report on ESDP, Nice, December.

—— (2003) 'A Secure Europe in a Better World', European Security Strategy, Brussels, 12 December.

—— (2007) 'Treaty of Lisbon', *Official Journal of the European Union*, C306, vol. 50, 17 December.

General Affairs and External Relations Council (GAERC) (2006) 'Conclusions of the Council on Lebanon', Extraordinary Session, Brussels, 25 August.

Giegerich, B. and Wallace, W. (2004) 'Not such a soft Power: The External Deployment of European Forces', *Survival*, 46(2): 163–182.

Ginsberg, R. (1999) 'Conceptualizing the European Union as an International Actor: Narrowing the Theoretical Capability-Expectations Gap', *Journal of Common Market Studies*, 37(3): 429–454.

Haarland Matlary, J. (2006) 'When Soft Power turns Hard: Is an EU Strategic Culture Possible?' *Security Dialogue*, 37(1): 105–121.

Heisbourg, F. (2004) 'The "European Security Strategy" is not a Security Strategy', *A European Way of War*, London: Centre for European Reform.

Hill, C. (ed.) (1996) *The Actors in Europe's Foreign Policy*, London: Routledge.

Howorth, J. (2007) *Security and Defence Policy in the European Union*, London & New York: Palgrave.

Johnston, A.I. (1995) 'Thinking about Strategic Culture', *International Security*, 19(4): 32–64.

Kagan, R. (2002) 'Power and Weakness', *Policy Review*, 113, June and July.

Laatikainen, K. and Smith, K. (eds) (2006) *The European Union at the United Nations. Intersecting Multilateralisms*, London: Palgrave Macmillan.

Lindstrom, G. (2007) 'Enter the EU Battlegroups', *Chaillot Paper* 97, Paris: EU Institute for Security Studies.

Manners, I. (2002) 'Normative Power Europe: A Contradiction in Terms?', *Journal of Common Market Studies*, 40: 235–258.

—— (2006) 'Normative Power Europe Reconsidered: Beyond the Crossroads', *Journal of European Public Policy*, 13(2): 182–199.

Meyer, C. (2006) 'Do Europeans Think Alike about the Use of Force?' in C. Meyer, *The Quest for a European Strategic Culture. Changing Norms on Security and Defence in the European Union*, London: Palgrave Macmillan.

Nowak, A. (ed.) (2006) 'Civilian Crisis Management within ESDP', in 'Civilian crisis management: the EU way', *Chaillot Paper* 90, Paris: EU Institute for Security Studies.

Ortega, M. (ed.) (2005) 'The European Union and the United Nations. Partners in effective multilateralism', *Chaillot Paper* 78, Paris: EU Institute for Security Studies.

Posen, B. (2004) 'ESDP and the Structure of World Power', *The International Spectator*, 34(1): 5–17.

Rynning, S. (2003) 'The European Union: Towards a Strategic Culture?', *Security Dialogue*, 34(4): 479–496.

Sjöstedt, G. (1977) *The External Role of the European Community*, Farnborough: Saxon House.

Sjursen, H. (2006) 'The EU as a "normative" power: how can this be?', *Journal of European Public Policy*, 13(2): 235–251.

Smith, K. (2006) 'The European Union, Human Rights and the United Nations', in K. Laatikainen and K. Smith (eds), *The European Union at the United Nations. Intersecting Multilateralisms*, London: Palgrave Macmillan.

Smith, M. (2006) 'The Shock of the Real? Trends in European Foreign and Security Policy since September 2001', in G. Bono (ed.), *The Impact of 9/11 on European Foreign and Security Policy*, Brussels: Institute for European Studies, Vrije Universiteit Brussel.

Solana, J. (2002) Speech at the Annual Conference of the EU Institute for Security Studies, Paris, 1 July.

Tardy, T. (2007) 'The European Union and the United Nations: Global *versus* Regional Multilateralism', *Studia Diplomatica*, LX(1): 191–209.

UN Secretary-General and EU Presidency (2003) 'Joint Declaration on UN–EU Cooperation in Crisis Management', 24 September.

Wæver, O. (2000) 'The EU as a security actor. Reflections from a pessimistic constructivist on post-sovereign security orders', in M. Kelstrup and M.C. Williams (eds), *International Relations Theory and the Politics of European Integration*, London: Routledge.

Whitman, R. (1998) *From Civilian Power to Superpower? The International Identity of the European Union*, London: Palgrave.

2 NATO and the search for strategic credibility

Julian Lindley-French

Introduction

Where is NATO going? Such a question pre-supposes from whence NATO came, where it stands today, where the security environment drives it and the member nations agree it should go. There is one simple maxim that can guide the security futurologist: NATO was founded to deal with high politics and big security. It was always thus and given the centrality of American involvement it is always likely to be so. However, the caveat that hangs over NATO concerns the relationship between American grand strategy and the leadership it implies and the extent to which the European Allies agree or not with the objectives, method and conduct of such strategy. Thus, the question that today fixates Europeans and North Americans is whether the change that is ever more apparent in the world will lead to a re-constitution of the strategic mission for which the Alliance was created. The recent behaviour of Russia and the emergence of China suggest that the need for NATO will be greater than for any alternative focus for the grand strategic military–security effort of the partners in the twenty-first century.

There is no easy answer to the vital question posed above because of the many contending views of security within the Alliance and how best to promote it. The Comprehensive Political Guidance (CPG), which was endorsed in November 2006 at the Riga Summit by Alliance Heads of State and Government reflects these tensions. The CPG was designed to enable NATO's military planners to better generate expeditionary, interoperable and flexible forces in pursuit of the full range of Alliance operations over a ten to 15 year period. To that end, the supporting Riga Communiqué proposed a number of important initiatives under the rubric of NATO Transformation. These included a consortium to purchase C-17 strategic airlift, the launch of the Special Operations Forces Transformation Initiative, and the first step towards a NATO Active Layered Theatre Ballistic Missile Defence (ALTBMD) system.

However, implicit in the CPG was the need for member nations to increase defence expenditure in real terms. In fact, by August 2007, expenditures by many members were still falling. Without real improvements, not only concerning how much NATO member nations spend, but also how they spend it, it is difficult to see how the gap can be closed between the aspiration as laid out in the CPG and the defence–economic reality in much of Europe. In other words, if one takes a snapshot of the broad European defence effort as of 2007, the answer to the question 'where is NATO going?' would appear to be down. However, it must be noted that any such weakening of NATO also fundamentally, if not fatally, undermines the EU's European Security and Defence Policy (ESDP), for all the rhetoric in the June 2007 EU Reform Treaty and March 2007 Berlin Declaration.

Consequently, there is a real danger that the European 'pol–mil loop' will be broken as the rhetoric of transformation becomes ever more ambitious and the defence effort becomes ever more parochial, fractured and thus ineffective in today's ever more strategic environment. The figures speak for themselves. According to *The Military Balance 2007*, the British defence budget in 2006 was €40.32 billion or 26 per cent of the total amount spent by NATO Europe. The French budget was €33.15 billion or 21 per cent of the total, whilst the German budget was €26.13 billion or 17 per cent of the total. Thus the biggest three NATO European member-nations spent 64 per cent of all defence expenditure by NATO Europe. In other words, 21 NATO European members are spending an average of €2.6 billion per state per annum on defence which is nothing like enough to generate the capabilities identified as vital by the CPG. Moreover, the majority spend what they spend in an inefficient manner with too much being devoted to personnel and organisational bureaucracies. By contrast, the US defence budget for 2006 was €409.29 billion or 264 per cent of the entire NATO Europe combined defence budget.

Not unlike the European Union, NATO tends to be forced to place institutional reform before capabilities development and as such is a strategic institution in waiting. Not only the pace and change of events, but their rapid transmission from regional to strategic in terms of both scope and challenge demands a wholly new concept of force generation, force structuring, doctrine, the use of technologies, the organisation of support and the pursuit of partners. Indeed, NATO is the only institution capable of coping with the transformation that is taking place in the security landscape. NATO Europe is therefore going to have to engage in both advanced expeditionary 'going in', and advanced expeditionary 'staying put' and that will demand the forging of a new relationship between strategy, force and effect. Preparing to cope with the dark side of globalisation will likely have to be achieved in parallel with the retention of some element of force reconstitution. The steady re-emergence of classical state challengers such as Russia and possibly China is thus reinforcing the Alliance planning dilemma. NATO finds itself at the interface between the regional and the strategic, civil and military, soft and hard power and regular and irregular war and peace. It is an institution of which everything is expected but to which little is given by its members. It is the very antithesis of strategy for which the blame must rest not with the Alliance, but with strategically myopic members.

Replacing strategy with bureaucracy

The capability-capacity crunch

Afghanistan has exposed the many contradictions that blight NATO. With NATO having to undertake Stage 4 operations, i.e. stabilisation and reconstruction operations, across the whole of Afghanistan and organise Provincial Reconstruction Teams (PRTs) under the broad umbrella of the International Security Assistance Force (ISAF) and the more robust British-led NATO Security Force (NSF), Afghanistan is testing to the limit the anaemic defence capabilities and commitment of most NATO members. At the same time, with Europeans also engaged in the continuing mission in Kosovo, supporting the EU's EUFOR Althea in Bosnia and Herzegovina or supporting the UN-led operation UNIFIL2 in Lebanon, NATO and its constituent member nations continue to face a capability-capacity crunch. The need to undertake ever more robust forced entry interventions with small, mobile, lethal professional forces (capability), seemingly contradicts the need for a critical mass of forces able to stabilise and reconstruct (capacity). Nor is the problem of crunch solely a European problem. The Afghanistan and Iraq campaigns have demonstrated the utility of the networked multi-task soldier, rather than the networked combat specialist favoured by the Americans. Consequently, the US Army (less so the US Marines) gets less from its deployed force than the British in terms of generating broad effect per soldier on the ground during complex contingencies, although the British lack the sheer critical mass of force to make the most of their superior counter-insurgency doctrine. The failure to strike a balance between 'going in' and 'staying put' has resulted in NATO forces facing what might be best termed as 'intervention blight'. Highly expensive, professional spearhead forces are being broken by the attrition imposed by stabilisation and reconstruction that uses up both front-line forces and reserves and prevents the proper training, deployment and resting rotation so vital to maintaining a coherent multi-task force that can fight, foray and foster good relations with the Afghan people. Credibility at all levels of effect is the key to mission success and is at risk in this context.

NATO's planning dilemma

Endeavouring to find a mean between what NATO is required to do and what it can do, on 3 March 2006, NATO Secretary-General Jaap de Hoop Scheffer tried to set limits to restore some semblance of balance to NATO's force and operational planning:

40   *J. Lindley-French*

...we are not turning into some form of globocop – ready to deal with emergencies all over the world. We simply do not have that ambition, let alone the necessary means. However, all 26 Allies now look at NATO as a flexible instrument, that we can use wherever our common security interests demand it [...] we need the right mix of forces capable of performing combat tasks and post-conflict reconstruction work.

(de Hoop Scheffer 2006)

Implicit in the Secretary-General's statement is the essential NATO planning dilemma. The nature of the grand strategic environment, the lack of relevant security and defence investment on the part of most members and the absence of any clear political consensus within the Alliance about the means and method of engaging strategic complexity precludes neat strategic choices. As an essentially strategic defence institution NATO must prepare to deal with whatever appears given whatever it possesses and whenever a challenge emerges. Flexibility has thus become the Alliance mantra. However, 'flexibility' is all well and good on paper, but turning it into meaningful military effect is an entirely different matter. 'Flexibility' too often becomes a metaphor for a lack of interoperability between NATO's constituent armed forces as it masks the increasingly divergent levels of capability and capacity from which the Alliance suffers. This problem manifests itself as much between Europeans as between Americans and Europeans. Binnendijk, Gompert and Kugler put the problem succinctly:

At present, much of the HRF [High Readiness Force] is not adequately capable of projecting power swiftly and performing major combat operation missions in distant areas. Reforming these forces is not beyond reach. The NATO Defence Capability Initiative did not achieve this worthy goal because it was scattered across too many forces and measures, and the Prague Capabilities Commitment evidently is encountering similar troubles.

(Binnendijk *et al.* 2005: 8)

The strategic vacuum of bureaucracy

NATO's capabilities conundrum is reinforced by the strategy-vacuum that afflicts most of its members. The absence of grand strategy and the need to 'save' money has seen bureaucracy replace strategy in many NATO (and EU) members. Paradoxically, the very bureaucracy of saving money and maximising effect has made saving money an expensive business, often further reducing the value for money of most defence efforts. The replacement of strategy with bureaucracy is implicit in many NATO declarations of late, particularly those associated with the Comprehensive Approach or Concerted Planning and Action of Civil and Military Activities in International Operations (CPA). This is a bureaucrat's dream come true. The apparent effort to squeeze maximum security effect out of all national (and transnational) military and civilian instruments is fast becoming a refuge for database builders, committee drivers and expenditure checkers as layers of new bureaucracy put ever greater distance between money pumped into security and effect pumped out. NATO insiders will say that the size of the bureaucracy has been reduced since the end of the Cold War and they are correct. However, the enlargements and the need to find personnel from new members posts have still left a command structure that suffers from an at best inappropriate teeth-to-tail ratio, staffed often with inexperienced individuals with a poor command of international military English.

It follows that the temptation is to re-organise system and structure endlessly and then announce it as improvement. In June 2006, as part of an effort to create 'a more expeditionary posture within NATO', the defence ministers of the 25 members of the Defence Planning Committee (DPC) (i.e. excluding France) approved new guidance for the Alliance's force planning process. The new guidelines were designed to shape planning and capabilities developments within the Alliance over the next ten to 15 years. Front and centre was the aim to move NATO away from structures and capabilities associated with static defences or so-called 'in-place' forces to better enable NATO forces to undertake the full spectrum of possible missions. To that end, the objective was to ensure that NATO could conduct a greater number of smaller-scale operations compared with the kind of operations envisaged during the Cold War. The NATO 'idea' is founded on the belief that by changing the planning assumptions with respect to the numbers, size, duration and distance of operations, the forces, assets, facilities and capabilities required to undertake them would over time be made available. Naturally, such changes would also drive the planning at national level and lead to marked changes to the size and shape of the NATO military command structure. Some progress has been made but such are the differences in capability and capacity of the members, not to mention imbalances in quality between the personnel of the contributing states that the Alliance's efforts to confront complexity external to NATO have helped generate complexity within NATO.

Furthermore, if this initiative were blindingly new then one could avoid a certain cynicism about the ability of the Alliance to genuinely shape the defence intentions and commitments of most of its members. It is worth noting the intent of the November 1991 NATO Strategic Concept:

> To protect peace and to prevent war or any kind of coercion, the Alliance will maintain for the foreseeable future an appropriate mix of nuclear and conventional forces based in Europe and kept up to date where necessary, although at a significantly reduced level. Both elements are essential to Alliance security and cannot substitute one for the other. Conventional forces contribute to war prevention by

ensuring that no potential aggressor could contemplate a quick or easy victory, or territorial gains, by conventional means. Taking into account the diversity of risks with which the Alliance could be faced, it must maintain the forces necessary to provide a wide range of conventional response options. But the Alliance's conventional forces alone cannot ensure the prevention of war.

(North Atlantic Council 1991)

Moreover, the 1999 New Strategic Concept stated:

Military capabilities effective under the full range of foreseeable circumstances are also the basis of the Alliance's ability to contribute to conflict prevention and crisis management through non-Article 5 crisis response operations. These missions can be highly demanding and can place a premium on the same political and military qualities, such as cohesion, multinational training, and extensive prior planning, that would be essential in an Article 5 situation. Accordingly, while they may pose special requirements, they will be handled through a common set of Alliance structures and procedures.

(North Atlantic Council 1999)

Therefore, in spite of major efforts by the Alliance over the past eight years in particular, many NATO members still prefer to ignore the changing security environment as the basis of their security and defence planning and choose instead to relegate security and defence to the margins of national expenditure. The 1999 Defence Capabilities Initiative (DCI) and the 2003 Prague Capabilities Commitment (PCC), the two flagship *demarches* chosen by NATO leaders to resolve this fatal flaw in Alliance capabilities have both foundered on the rocks of insufficient defence expenditure.

Negotiating new partnerships

The bureaucratic emphasis upon the importance of NATO having effective working arrangements with other states and international organisations, such as the EU and UN, are important initiatives that should in principle help to create a joined up approach to strategic security. Naturally, in such architecture, NATO would provide the hard military foundation upon which the alchemy of soft security was established – an approach that in theory at least is reinforced by the strong relations that the Alliance seeks with well-respected non-governmental organisations (NGOs). To that end, both the Comprehensive Political Guidance and the Defence Planning Process (DPP) recognise the utility of bringing vital security partners early into NATO planning if effective engagement across the conflict spectrum is to be generated. Moreover, through the work of political NATO in areas such as the Istanbul Co-operation Initiative (ICI) and the NATO–Mediterranean Dialogue it is hoped that a 'holistic approach' to security should be better able to establish stability than un-coordinated national efforts. However, as it is not renowned for its bureaucratic fleet of foot, it is questionable whether NATO can effectively play the role to which it aspires. Not only does such an approach require truly strategic partnerships with those other bureaucratic 'athletes', the EU and UN, without a critical advantage in military capabilities it is hard to see what NATO brings to the table. As bureaucracy grapples with complexity in the absence of strategy the tendency of the big powers, far from working within institutional frameworks, is to step outside them. NATO is no exception.

Therefore, NATO's future much depends on three inter-related but distinct developments. First, a United States that re-engages politically in solutions to international crises through multilateral institutions. Such 'adjustment' to the method and manner of American security policy will take more than a mere change of administration as some Europeans hope. Second, a Europe that finally matches rhetoric with reality when it comes to military investments. There is as yet little evidence of that beyond the British and French.[1] Third, a renovated and re-invigorated Partnership for Peace programme that can muster capable global partners, such as Australia, India, Japan and South Korea, as well as stabilise those less fortunate in Europe's near abroad. Such partnerships will require the newer and smaller members of NATO in Central and Eastern Europe to realise that security is not a one-way street and that they have as much responsibility for the security of their larger, more powerful allies as the latter have for them.

Grand-strategic and regional-strategic dilemmas

Grand strategy

NATO confronts a grand strategic dilemma. NATO was always an essentially simple instrument in which Europeans followed American grand strategy in return for European commitment to American leadership. That basic contract has all but evaporated as a consequence of failure in Iraq and elusive success in Afghanistan. What is still the world's premier military alliance today finds itself having to manage the consequences of a flawed post-9/11 American grand strategy, destructive technology, progressively more capable non-state and state actors and the globalisation of insecurity. Jaap de Hoop Scheffer may hope that the Alliance is not about to become 'Globocop', but if NATO is to do the job for which it was designed over successive strategic concepts, it is hard to see how such a role can be avoided.

Furthermore, Afghanistan and Iraq have demonstrated that intervention, stabilisation and reconstruction are but three intertwined phases of structural engagements to shore up the international system the West created. They are often mistaken for tactical engagements in far away places. Consequently, the mindset of many of the leaders that launch NATO on such missions assumes the need for too little force able to undertake too few tasks, and consequently puts NATO in an almost impossible position. As a result, the Allies are only playing at success in Afghanistan, refusing to commit anything like enough resources, be they military or civil, for mission success. If NATO fails in Afghanistan it will represent the defeat of the strategic West. The consequences of such a world are barely worth thinking about, particularly for NATO.

For the sake of the West's military credibility and by extension that of NATO, it is vital Alliance leaders become tougher about deciding when to intervene, for what strategic reasons to do so, recognise the dangers of open-ended military humanitarian engagements and understand the relationship between the two. If not then NATO will be broken in the space between interest-led and humanitarian-led operations. Equally, NATO's learning lessons from operations is one thing, being in a position to do something about them is entirely another. The theology of the American-led transformation has not helped. The internal political battle that took place between former Secretary of Defense Donald Rumsfeld and the US Army prevented sound 'day after victory' planning, and this has undoubtedly exacerbated the capability-capacity crunch with which even the American armed forces deal with daily in Iraq. If one cannot stabilise much with insufficient peace enforcers, nor can one stabilise much with overly lethal forces.

The post-Cold War hangover in European defence investment has now reached a critical juncture. All European forces are either incapable, i.e. too static, or insufficient or too small whatever the transformation/ modernisation rhetoric. The limited deployability, mobility and usability of European forces, together with the differing rules of engagement imposed by members, has constrained NATO in Afghanistan to the point of failure. For example, it is questionable whether France, Germany, Italy or Spain are any longer indispensable allies of either the Americans or British. Former or part-time allies might be a better description. The Dutch, Canadians and British are stretched whilst the French, Germans, Italians and Spanish are conspicuous by their refusal to properly support their partners. For all the nuances with which Paris, Berlin and Rome endeavour to justify their weakness, the fact is that it is they who are placing the burden on their allies. Whatever the capabilities and however streamlined the structure no Alliance can survive over time a lack of solidarity at the point of sharp contact with the enemy. If NATO fails in Afghanistan, the EU will fail and the three recalcitrant powers might wish to reflect as to whether clever tactical diplomacy to stay out of the fight really is the point. At least they should understand the stakes of the dangerous game they are playing.

Secretary-General de Hoop Scheffer is aware of this dilemma. In 2004 he offered a sobering vision:

> Picture this: NATO's nations take and announce a political decision to undertake a mission. We task the NATO Military Authorities to plan

for it and to resource it. And then we suddenly find out that nations are not prepared to make available the necessary capabilities.

(de Hoop Scheffer 2004)

Faced with the crunch many Europeans effectively absent themselves. Such strategic absenteeism hardly reinforces confidence in the Comprehensive Approach to security which the Alliance is keen to prosecute. Indeed, such a model only makes sense if it is reinforced by a Comprehensive Approach to engagement and an end to the national caveats that have so plagued NATO operations in Afghanistan. If the NATO Partners do not get their collective act together then it is likely the Dutch will face severe problems maintaining their operation in Uruzgan in mid-2008 and over time the British will find it difficult to hold the line virtually alone in Helmand Province in the heart of the critical Pashtun homeland which is the key to success in Afghanistan.

Regional strategy

NATO also faces a regional-strategic dilemma. The July 2007 report by the UK House of Commons Defence Select Committee on the performance of UK forces in Afghanistan is damning.[2] Afghanistan is fast becoming a case study in how not to undertake strategic stabilisation/structural intervention operations. The report identifies six factors for failure that reflect the challenge the Alliance faces as it prepares for a strategic future. First, there are insufficient capabilities on the ground be it troop levels or helicopters. Again, adequate capabilities are the *sine qua non* of mission success. Second, there is a marked lack of Alliance solidarity on the ground. The Americans, British, Dutch and Canadians are bearing a disproportionate amount of risk and cost whilst other NATO Allies effectively hide in less violent parts of Afghanistan. Third, NATO's strategy is in danger of becoming self-defeating. Trying to combat the Taliban and opium production at one and the same time is a contradiction given conditions on the ground as it drives many of the warlords, Pashtun farmers and Taliban into an unlikely alliance. Without a clear operational-strategic concept from the outset, all such missions are doomed to failure. Fourth, too many civilians are dying in NATO operations. In 2007 there was a marked increase in the number of civilian casualties as a result of NATO operations. Such heavy-handedness is not simply the fault of aggressive American doctrine. The Dutch in particular are concerned about the use of such tactics by the British. Over-kill is hardly the most effective way to win hearts and minds and getting the balance right is something that continues to elude NATO force. Fifth, hope that the Afghan National Army and police could take on more of the burden has proved misplaced. Over-optimism as to the utility of local forces in such a society consistently leads to miscalculations as to the extent, scope and duration of NATO operations. Sixth, NATO is losing the media war to the Taliban because it fails to understand the needs, loyalties and culture of the people on the ground.

What is clear is that the further NATO goes beyond its traditional area of operations the more such operations will need regional nation support to legitimise the presence of NATO forces, a clear plan to build up the forces of the host society to which NATO can hand over in time and a willingness of all NATO members to meet the costs of the whole operation. It is self-evident that stability on the ground in Afghanistan will require an immense financial investment, not least to change the behaviour of farmers who now produce some 75 per cent of the world's opium. It is an all too telling and sad irony that the one thing the West could use, economic and financial power, is being constrained by governments unwilling in Europe to explain to their publics the true cost of security and the stakes should NATO fail in Afghanistan. Moreover, the lack of strategic vision has prevented anything like a cogent and coherent regional-strategic solution involving all regional state partners. It is equally self-evident that Afghanistan will only be weaned from extremism over time if powerful states in the region agree to be a full part of the solution to the Afghan question. First and foremost that means a dialogue with three of the regional heavyweights, Russia, China and India and, over time, direct contacts with the fourth, Iran. Here a lesson from history would be useful. The confusion of values with interests that has so complicated NATO's mission in Afghanistan should be replaced by a hard-headed analysis of the West's interests therein and how that translates to policy and practice on the ground. The criteria for withdrawal, with respect, should not be the needs of the Afghan Government or even the people, but rather the security interests of the West and its constituent NATO members.

The basic fissure caused by the unwillingness of some NATO members to carry their share of the burden extends to operational financing. The current system by which costs 'lie where they fall' is not only grossly unfair, but also promotes free-riding (and free-driving). It is a dilemma compounded by the pressure it puts on those willing to take risk and face cost as they are forced to raid capital military modernisation budgets to fund the operations of grossly over-stretched forces. It is this imbalance in the sharing of the cost of operations that threatens to end all pretence to task-sharing upon which the Alliance is supposed to be founded. Indeed, such imbalances are particularly unacceptable when non- or low-effort Allies cite domestic factors as a reason for low security effectiveness. Such sleight of hand leads to a vicious and self-perpetuating cycle of strategic indolence that if not ended will not only destroy NATO as a credible military alliance over time, but any influence Europeans might pretend to have over the strategic environment. The 'we cannot afford it' argument is little more than a form of indirect taxation imposed by the indolent on the committed who are thus forced to pay overly in both lives and gold.

The point is that NATO is being blamed for failings over which it has no control and for which it cannot be blamed. Unfortunately, it is those factors that, if handled badly, could prove crucial in answering the 'whither NATO' question.

The future NATO strategic agenda

The emerging European tragedy is that where NATO goes is not simply a function of the vision and commitment, or otherwise, of its members. Hopefully, the new strategic realities will force NATO member nations to look beyond their domestic issues before it is too late. Or, rather, history suggests that when it is almost too late NATO members will eventually wake up and begin to confront the world as it is, rather than as they would like it to be. The pace of change is such that much of the debate, particularly in Europe, concerning security and defence is bordering on the delusional. No alliance, however well structured, can be protected from the strategically certifiable.

The relevance of the transatlantic relationship

There are many in Europe who dream of an ESDP that can somehow replace not just NATO but the American component within it. Given the political and strategic trajectory of European defence such a dream whilst attractive remains just that – a dream.

Both Europe and the world need a strong transatlantic relationship and NATO is the embodiment of that relationship. First, because it was and is America's first and only truly entangling alliance. Second, a strong transatlantic relationship needs a strong military Europe and Europeans need to stop being so sensitive about that basic reality. In turn that means a Europe with credible and relevant military assets and capabilities. Certainly, European strategy has its limits, be it organised through NATO or the EU. The pace of strategic change is such that without a functioning and credible NATO, European security will become detached from world security as the political correctness that blinds modern Europe prevents it from taking the hard decisions over the need for effective armed forces.

There are, of course, reasons for such limited vision. It is increasingly evident that the centre of gravity of power on this planet is moving inexorably eastward and as it does so the nature of power itself is changing. The Asia-Pacific region brings much that is dynamic and positive to this world, but as yet the rapid change therein is neither stable, nor embedded in stable institutions of the EU-type. Until such a point is reached North Americans and Europeans, together with stable democratic partners such as Australia, Brazil, India, Japan and South Africa, will inevitably be in the lead in the search for strategic stability and NATO must be the hard military-security guarantor that underpins such an effort. Much will depend on the respective attitudes of Russia and China and the role they seek in the world. If both Moscow and Beijing place the fight against systemic instability above state competition then there are reasons for optimism. However, if they adopt an increasingly narrow vision of their national interests, as the recent Georgia crisis showed, then NATO will once again need to re-transform from strategic stabiliser to strategic container as the world enters a new form of cold war. Western leaders need therefore to be clear about the stakes implicit in the shifting centre of gravity and NATO's role therein. For Europeans such thinking is particularly challenging, for leaders, planners and people alike. There is an evident lack of political will to think big about security in Europe, reinforced by an operational tempo on over-stretched and limited armed forces that focuses on what must be done today, thus leaving little room and few resources to consider what next.

Geopolitical realities and NATO's world

All the available economic and political indicators emphasise seismic systemic change and not in the West's favour. In such circumstance tensions will undoubtedly arise between states, and not just between states and non-state actors, and NATO will remain the vital strategic military-security grouping. Indeed, it is the only such grouping. At the very least the competition for energy carries with it the danger of traditional state-to-state competition. Therefore, the world is at a political watershed and whilst few hard planning realities exist at present the need for caution and preparedness is vital. American 'neo-con philosophy' has done little for the idea that there is good and evil in this world, because its clumsiness has undermined both the concept of the Good West and solidarity within it. But those Europeans who equate the absence of the use of force by the democracies with security are taking Europe down a road no less delusional and no less dangerous than British and French appeasers did in the 1930s when they attempted to buy Hitler off. It is the state of NATO that will be the true litmus test of the strategic state of the West's collective security mind.

The shifting centre of gravity of world power is being further complicated by the re-emergence of a systemic balance of power at one and the same time. Consequently, both Europeans and North Americans require a hard-headed analysis of their world, their interests and how best to preserve the system of institutionalised security governance that they constructed. They must do it together. A strong and credible NATO must and will remain the cornerstone of such an effort. Given the broad array of risks and threats, any debate over 'whither NATO' pre-supposes both a transatlantic strategic dialogue and a European strategic dialogue that are as yet still fissured with the residual anger of the Iraq disaster. Sooner rather than later Europeans will need to begin to properly aggregate their own power in pursuit of strategic stability, and not simply disaggregate leadership within Europe as an alternative.

The need for such analysis is reinforced by the briefest of strategic surveys. China is clearly the great agent of systemic change but it would be wrong to assume that Beijing's role constitutes a threat. China could well become a vital partner of the Alliance in promoting strategic stability. Shared concerns over strategic terrorism, the North Korean nuclear programme, as well as piracy suggest much that could inform a proper strategic dialogue between China and the West. Equally, the pace, extent and secrecy of Chinese military modernisation must be of concern to NATO planners.[3] China has put a lot of effort into disruptive offensive electronic warfare and electronic counter-measures that can only be aimed at the US Navy. The effort is similar in nature to that of the Kaiser's Germany in the early years of the twentieth century when Wilhelmine Germany built battleships with a range that could only take them into the North Sea and back. There was clearly only one enemy in mind – the British Royal Navy. To that end China is constructing a navy to deny the US Navy entry to the Sea of Japan for some two to three weeks in the event of a Chinese invasion of Taiwan. Consequently, China's defence spending is at least two to three times officially declared levels. NATO, as the West's strategic alliance, must consider what role the Allies would play in support of the US in the event of such a development.

Security and defence are merging as the dark side of globalisation is reinforced by electronics and instant communications. This is reinforcing both interdependence and mutual vulnerability of all states and peoples. Such is the dependence of systems and societies on virtual infrastructure that disruption of such architectures could well have an effect similar to destruction. This may be the age of the Comprehensive Approach but it must be matched by a comprehensive defence approach as part of new strategic defence architecture that renovates and modernises NATO's Article 5 collective defence clause and that sees all state and trans-state instruments welded into an effective shield. Such a capability will require a total security approach to planning that can only be afforded by a powerful planning instrument such as NATO's Supreme Headquarters Allied Powers Europe (SHAPE).

Updating NATO's strategic concept

It is now over eight years since NATO's Strategic Concept was re-written. Since then the Alliance has witnessed 9/11, the Iraq War, Afghanistan, the Madrid and London bombings, the rise of China and the re-emergence of a prickly Russia. A Strategic Concept distils lessons learned into the 'what', the 'why', the 'where' and the 'when' of NATO action. Although the 2006 Comprehensive Political Guidance (CPG) went some way towards correcting the strategic orientation of the Alliance it is self-evident that if a strategic concept were written today the focus would be far more on strategic effect. This is particularly important in establishing political guidance to planners as they prepare the Alliance to cope with the emerging big world. However, given the breaking of the link between political intent and military capability that has become apparent in the Alliance over the past ten years the challenge will not only be writing what will be in effect a strategic Comprehensive Approach to NATO operations, but convincing national leaders that such a concept informs national planning and investment.

Furthermore, without such a Strategic Concept, underpinned by true political consensus, NATO forces are in danger of becoming unbalanced. Already many of the armed forces of the Alliance are excessively one-dimensional, reflective of planning assumptions based on a limited appreciation of the operational environment. A new Strategic Concept could help to re-establish the transmission between grand strategy, military strategy and military and non-military operations. In addition, such a Strategic Concept should be reinforced by a project that examines Strategic Security Horizons. NATO needs to be preparing for the challenges the Alliance could face 20 to 30 years hence.

Making transformation smart

After a new Strategic Concept the modernisation of NATO's armed forces is the most urgent requirement. The Strategic Concept and force transformation are two sides of the same coin. The political credibility of the transatlantic relationship as the cornerstone of global security is founded necessarily on the twin pillars of the military capability and alleged superiority of the democracies. That might not be politically correct, but it is certainly strategically correct. Yet, NATO's current transformation model is riven with contradictions that lead to capability-capacity crunch. The force planning dilemma implicit therein is undermining the generation of security effect by the Alliance. Both Afghanistan and Iraq have demonstrated the need for a critical mass of forces that can operate across the conflict spectrum and over both time and distance.

In other words, NATO needs both high-end forces, and forces able to stabilise and reconstruct. Some countries are better able than others to enter forcibly, and others more suited to stabilise and re-construct. Such a reality has been lost in the self-defeating and pointless debate over the division of labour between NATO member nations. There is a division of labour within NATO between those countries that can apply robust coercion and those that cannot. Indeed, there are three levels of coercive effect within the Alliance. There are the warfighters, who can undertake forced entry operations, which only includes the US, Britain and France. The second level is the peacekeepers, many of which possess forces with limited offensive or robust military capability, and prominent among which are the Germans and the Italians. Finally, there are the protected states that joined NATO first and foremost as insurance against a revanchist Russia and consequently have little or no expeditionary tradition and little or no interest in wider security issues.

Alliance force transformation is also in danger of stalling in the face of seemingly excuses about pensions, aging populations, shrinking tax bases. Many NATO members continue to afford security insufficient value.

Extending partnership

Europe is by and large free and whole. Partnership for Peace today therefore must mean something different from that of the 1990s. For better or worse the Alliance is called upon to become *the* global hard security hub. However, that does not mean the formation of a global NATO. Such a structure would never work even if emerging powers wanted to join NATO, and most do not. Rather, it is the concept of partnership that must change. In some ways the political importance of partners will increasingly match that of members. Partnership today can no longer simply imply a road to membership, nor indeed a mechanism to include small, instable countries in some form of implicit political relationship with the Alliance. A twenty-first century Partnership for Peace must be seen as part of the architecture to which the Strategic Concept aims and thus a function of grand strategy as much as regional stability. That would necessarily place NATO at the military-strategic centre of a world-wide web of like-minded states, thus better enabling them to work together effectively on operations when they so choose. NATO's priceless assets are its standards and doctrine that can ensure operations are undertaken together efficiently without having to re-invent the operational wheel every time. NATO would thus become central to the orchestration of a form of Society of Strategic Friends organised around the Alliance. That means cultivating ties on a pragmatic basis with the likes of Australia, Brazil, India, Japan, South Africa and South Korea.

Institutions are not ends in themselves, but mechanisms designed to support the needs of the states that created them. NATO and the EU are vital mechanisms, but they are no more than that. Much political energy is consumed by arguments over the relative status of the two organisations. That is placing the institutional cart before the strategic horse. What is needed is a new realism. The new security realm will require a direct US–EU relationship. The civilian component of contemporary security demands it and only the EU can properly co-ordinate essential European civilian resources and capabilities. Indeed, matching the US in this regard will help to legitimise a new transatlantic security partnership. Moreover, Europeans will not project stability if the home base does not become more resilient and given the range of nations, agencies and bodies involved in what is effectively European homeland security, the EU should be in the lead.

Above all, the EU affords the West political options in dealing with political complexity. There will be occasions when neither the United

States nor NATO will be able to lead operations because the identity of an operation will be as important as its strength in achieving mission success. The flag one places on an operation will become as important as the capabilities and capacities, even if EU-led operations rely upon NATO assets and capabilities.

Therefore, a pragmatic relationship is required based on practical co-operation in the field. NATO–EU Crisis Action Teams (CATs) would be such a first step. Second, there is only one set of Europeans, and only one set of capabilities. A closer working relationship is needed between the Prague Capabilities Commitments (PCC) and the European Capabilities Action Plan (ECAP). Third, the relationship between the NATO Response Force and the EU Battle Groups needs to be better established, built around a pool of forces that can be used in either format founded on a strategic reserve comprised of able and capable forces.

Combating terrorism

The so-called 'Global War on Terror' is mutating into 'the Long War'; a systemic conflict that will require sustained vision, strategy, commitment and resilience. Moreover, the nature of the conflict means that it sits on the cusp between counterinsurgency and systemic conflict. Afghanistan and Iraq are evidence of this new interaction between radicalism and power that provide those states seeking to challenge the world order a new form of opposition to Western leadership. Iran's effective and destructive role in supporting the insurgencies in Lebanon, Iraq and Afghanistan attests to this new form of conflict. Consequently, this new Thirty Years War[4] (in which extreme belief systems, old but massively destructive technologies, unstable and intolerant societies, strategic crime and the globalisation of all commodities and communications come into play) will require a multi-dimensional response to a multi-dimensional threat which transcends geography, function and capability. The response of the West and its partners will require a new grand strategy with NATO at its core.

There is a strategic continuum between counter-terrorism, power politics and prayer politics. Counter-terrorism must not, therefore, become the be-all and end-all of Alliance planning nor, indeed, an excuse to focus on tactical terrorism and thus avoid emerging strategic challenges. Alliance strategic thinking and strategic action will require regenerated strategic vision, founded on relevant armed forces capable of managing broad threats in alliance with strategic civil–military capabilities and capacities.

Conclusion

Europeans and North Americans are going to have to think, and ultimately act effectively together in the world beyond the Euro-Atlantic area. That will require a radically overhauled strategic mindset. Europeans are once again going to have to come to terms with military coercion if non-coercive tools are to have a meaningful effect. There is no such thing as soft or hard power, only effect.[5]

Furthermore, the twenty-first century will place a particular premium on credible and effective mechanisms for multiplying security effect, and that means institutions such as NATO and the EU working in harmony for the greater good. Above all, the West needs a NATO able to cope with the undoubted strategic challenges ahead. That does not mean a global NATO but it does mean a NATO able to see, think and act globally. The stakes are high. A lack of strategic vision now will condemn to failure the system of institutionalised balance, legitimacy and stability the West gave the world. The world will be a far more dangerous place as a result. As a consequence, the West will find itself no longer the master of its own security destiny, but buffeted and damaged by the events only it has the collective power to manage and control.

Only a strong West will guarantee a stable twenty-first century and prevent the emergence of global hyper-nationalism and the spread of hyper-fundamentalism, reminiscent of the unstable old Europe that led to NATO. One thing is clear: the need for NATO remains as strong as ever, if not stronger, because it is the one organisation capable of organising truly credible, legitimate and stable coercive power in a world marked by instability and chaos.

There are unlikely to be sufficient funds available for security and defence. Indeed, as Asia booms and America extends, Europeans are in danger of becoming a strategic backwater, all too vulnerable to the tidal wave of change with no breakwater to protect them. NATO was once a systemic alliance necessarily focused on the Euro-Atlantic area, because Europe was at the centre of the world. Today, NATO must become a systemic alliance founded on the Euro-Atlantic area, able to project security beyond its borders, rather than simply ensure it within.

During the interregnum between big worlds from 1990 to 2001, NATO turned away from its grand strategic mission and lost its purpose. However, NATO's destiny is at the strategic level, as a global security mirror of the environment it serves. The Alliance, therefore, must reflect today on the needs of the strategic security environment in which North Americans and Europeans now find themselves. 2016 could well look more like 1956 than 1996.

Notes

1 In July 2007 Britain announced the construction of two super-carriers, HMS *Queen Elizabeth* and HMS *Prince of Wales* as part of a $12 billion investment programme for the Royal Navy. That expenditure is in turn part of a $24 billion overall investment programme in the armed forces.
2 The Report of the House of Commons Defence Select Committee (2007: 19) entitled 'UK Operations in Afghanistan' states that '...we remain deeply

concerned that the reluctance of some NATO members to provide troops for the ISAF mission is undermining NATO's credibility and also ISAF operations'.

3   A note of caution needs to be sounded when discussing the emergence of China as a military peer competitor of the United States. *The Economist* (2007: 11–12) noted that,

> [China's] military budget, in hard currency terms, is not much bigger than France's. It remains decades away from being able to mount a credible military challenge to American pre-eminence. Moreover, whereas conflict remains possible, especially over Taiwan, China's priorities are internal: coping with social and political dislocation that its economic revolution entails.

4   The Thirty Years War took place between 1618 and 1648, principally on the territory of today's Germany. Noted for its savagery, its main contention was a struggle for ascendancy between fundamentalist Catholic and Protestant belief.

5   Effect is the achievement of one's objectives and that means power, i.e. the resources, organisation and application through various means. Max Weber stated that power is the possibility of imposing one's will upon the behaviour of other persons. See Galbraith 1986: 212.

References

Binnendijk, H., Gompert, D.C. and Kugler, R. (2005) 'A New Military Framework for NATO', *Defense Horizons*, 48, May, Washington: NDU.

The Economist (2007) Editorial, 4 August, pp. 11–12.

Galbraith, J.K. (1986) 'Power and Organization', in Lukes, S. (ed.), *Power*, Oxford: Blackwell.

de Hoop Scheffer, J. (2004) 'NATO's Istanbul Summit: New Mission, New Means', speech by NATO Secretary-General to the Royal United Services Institute, London, 18 June. Online, available at www.nato.int/docu/speech/2004/s040618a.htm (accessed 25 May 2008).

—— (2006) 'A New NATO', speech by NATO Secretary-General to the Norwegian Atlantic Committee, Oslo, 3 March. Online, available at www.nato.int/docu/speech/2006/s060303a.htm (accessed 25 May 2008).

House of Commons Defence Select Committee (2007) 'UK Operations in Afghanistan', 3 July, London: The Stationery Office.

IISS (2007) *The Military Balance 2007*, London: Routledge.

North Atlantic Council (1991) The Alliance's New Strategic Concept.

—— (1999) *NATO New Strategic Concept*. Online, available at www.nato.int/docu/pr/1999/p99–065e.htm (accessed 25 May 2008).

3 Where is the OSCE going?

Present role and challenges of a stealth security organisation

Victor-Yves Ghebali

Introduction

Together with NATO, the EU and the Council of Europe, the Organization for Security and Cooperation in Europe (OSCE) forms the quadripartite institutional constellation now operating in the firmament of European security. A direct off-spring of the Helsinki process – the Conference on Security and Cooperation in Europe (CSCE) created in the ultimate period of the Cold War for the management of détente at the multilateral level – the OSCE presents a number of original elements.[1] First, the OSCE's 'Europe' refers to a region encompassing not only the whole continent up to the Caucasus, but also North America and the former Soviet Central Asia – which means that the OSCE provides a forum that is both Euro-Atlantic and Eurasian. Second, the OSCE pursues a global security agenda through a 'cooperative security' approach which prescribes military transparency, excludes coercion, privileges preventative diplomacy, and involves mutual accountability based on the right of friendly interference in internal affairs of states. Third, as a decentralised organisation with an operational focus and light bureaucratic structures, the OSCE has often demonstrated an outstanding capacity for rapid and flexible response to emergency situations. Fourth, the OSCE's decisions and normative instruments, exclusively adopted by consensus, create politically binding commitments whose violation is as inadmissible as that of legal commitments. Fifth, the OSCE, whose membership includes four out of the five permanent members of the United Nations Security Council, is the sole European security body which has officially proclaimed itself a regional agreement under Chapter VIII of the UN Charter.[2]

Against this background, the OSCE operates as a discrete institution, mainly because its comparative advantage lies in preventative action, a function which requires a low-profile and stealth diplomacy posture. Within its niche, it serves as a vehicle for security dialogue, standard-setting and monitoring of commitments, assistance for democratisation and conflict management. Its record can be assessed from the perspective of the three dimensions of its security agenda and the cross-cutting function of conflict management. This chapter offers an overview of the present role of the OSCE and the serious challenges with which it has been confronted since the beginning of the new millennium.

The present role of the OSCE: a three-dimensional security agenda with cross-cutting conflict management functions

Composed of three 'dimensions' (formerly known as the CSCE's 'baskets'), the OSCE's agenda intertwines the 'politico-military' aspects of security with 'economic/environmental' and 'human' dimension matters. The human dimension performs as the most dynamic and high-profile component, the economic/environmental dimension is the least developed; the politico-military dimension occupies a middle-of-the-road position.

Politico-military dimension

The OSCE has developed an impressive array of principles, norms, commitments and best practices related to confidence and security-building measures (CSBMs), arms control, and security sector governance (see Table 3.1).

The OSCE can be credited for having coined, within the 1975 Helsinki Final Act, the concept of military 'Confidence-Building Measures' (CBMs). The concept was expanded, by the 1986 Stockholm Document, into military-significant and verifiable 'Confidence and Security-Building Measures' (CSBMs). A subsequent instrument, the Vienna Document on CSBMs, adopted in 1990 and successively updated in 1992, 1994 and 1999, developed the Stockholm arrangements and introduced fresh measures that now represent the most sophisticated regime of the OSCE politico-military dimension. The 1999 regime provides for information-oriented, communication-oriented, constraining and crisis management CSBMs, as well as mandatory on-site verification by means of observation, inspection and evaluation (Lachowski 2004).

As for the arms control texts, they all concern conventional weapons with one exception, the Principles on Non-Proliferation. Depending on the case, they require reporting on ratification processes of relevant non-OSCE instruments, exchange of information on actual transactions and policies (especially with regards to small arms and light weapons). The most recently adopted text (2003) allows states facing security and environmental risks related to obsolete stockpiles of conventional ammunition to request technical assistance for destruction purposes.

The OSCE has also been active in the cross-cutting field of security sector reform and governance. At the normative level, it adopted a pioneering Code of Conduct on Politico-Military Aspects of Security (1994) whose Sections VII–VIII established a regime which regulates the role and use of armed forces, thus intruding into an area of state power hitherto considered a *sancta sanctorum* (Ghebali and Lambert 2005). Subsequently, after the restructuring of its agenda in the aftermath of the 11

Table 3.1 OSCE texts related to the politico-military dimension

Arms control	CSBMs	Security sector governance
Principles on conventional arms transfers (1993)	Global exchange of military information (1994)	Code of conduct on politico-military aspects of security (1994): sections VII and VIII
Principles on non-proliferation (1994)	Vienna Document on CSBMs (1999 updating)	Vienna Document on CSBMs: Section II (Defence Planning)
Forum for Security Co-operation (FSC)'s decision concerning a questionnaire on the ratification process of the 1993 Chemical Weapons Convention (1996)		OSCE border security and management concept (2005)
FSC's decision on a questionnaire related to anti-personnel landmines (1997 and 2004)		Guidebook on Democratic Policing (2006)
Document on Small Arms and Light Weapons (SALW) (2000), and complementary FSC decisions		High Commissioner on National Minorities' Recommendations on Policing in Multi-Ethnic Societies (2006)
Handbook of Best Practices on SALW (2003)		
Document on Stockpiles of Conventional Ammunition (2003), and complementary FSC decisions		

September terrorist attacks, the OSCE has increasingly addressed matters related to police training and border management, as well as the combating of terrorism, trafficking in human beings and transnational organised crime. However, while the OSCE has accumulated impressive knowledge and experience in many areas of security sector reform, it does not formally acknowledge its relevant activities under that label (Ghebali 2007b).

The development of the politico-military dimension presently faces difficulties raised by Russian grievances about insufficient military–security dialogue within the OSCE, non-updating of the CSBMs regime and the non-ratification of the Adapted Conventional Armed Forces in Europe Treaty (CFE). Moscow deplores the weak involvement of the OSCE in European military affairs – in particular the issue of the deployment of elements of the US anti-missile defense system in Central Europe. It advocates the updating of the 1999 Vienna Document by means of new CSBMs concerning the prior notification of large-scale military transit or deployment of foreign military forces on the territory of any OSCE state, as well as exchange of information on multinational rapid reaction forces. The CFE Treaty, a much more complex issue, has given rise to a growing and bitter debate. Although negotiated under the umbrella of the OSCE, that instrument (currently referred to as the cornerstone of European military security) links 30 out of the 56 OSCE participating states. As long as it remains a non-OSCE regime, the OSCE will only be able to address soft and not hard security issues. Signed on 19 November 1999, an adaptation introduced amendments to the 1990 CFE Treaty and upon entry into force will become accessible to OSCE's non-party states.[3] However, so far, only Russia, Ukraine, Kazakhstan and Belarus have ratified it. NATO state parties subordinate their ratification to the implementation of the Istanbul clauses that provide for the withdrawal of Russian armed forces from Moldova and Georgia. In retaliation for non-ratification (as well as to the projected installation of a US missile shield in Eastern Europe), Moscow has suspended compliance with the CFE Treaty as from 12 December 2007 (Socor 2007). In short, the development of the politico-military dimension is now hostage to the deadlock on the Adapted CFE Treaty, which is itself linked to the twin issues (to be addressed below) of the Istanbul commitments and frozen conflicts.

Human dimension

As a genuine OSCE product, the concept of the human dimension formally appeared in the CSCE Vienna Concluding Document (1989) with a view of merging the Helsinki Final Act's human rights and humanitarian commitments related to a freer flow of persons, information and ideas. Since then, it has considerably expanded, going well beyond standard human rights. It now consists of a complex network of commitments also including the protection of vulnerable groups, the promotion of the rule of law and combating threats to human security (see Table 3.2).

The main human dimension operational tool is the Office for Democratic Institutions and Human Rights (ODIHR) which conducts election monitoring operations, provides democratisation-assistance services and promotes, by means of a dedicated point of contact, the rights of Roma and Sinti. In parallel, a Representative of freedom of the media performs a watchdog function with regards to that specific field. Through the lens of the human dimension, the OSCE appears as a unique organisation. On the one hand, its participating states are *committed* to conduct free and fair elections (expected to meet criteria enumerated in the 1990 Copenhagen Document (CSCE 1990)) and to subject the elections to international monitoring. On the other hand, the human dimension commitments are

Table 3.2 OSCE commitments related to the human dimension (ODIHR 2005)

Human rights and fundamental freedoms	Protection of vulnerable groups	Promotion of the rule of law	Threats to human security
Freedom of thought, conscience, religion or belief (including conscientious objection and alternative service)	National minorities (with particular focus on Roma and Sinti)	Free and fair elections	Prevention of trafficking in human beings
Freedom of expression; free media and information	Refugees, displaced persons, returnees and stateless persons	Impartial operation of the public judicial service; law enforcement	Prevention of gender-based persecution, violence, and exploitation
Freedom of association and the right of peaceful assembly	Children	Treatment of persons deprived of their liberty	Prevention of illicit trafficking in drugs and arms, and other forms of transnational organised crime
Freedom of movement	Women	Respect of equality, tolerance, and non-discrimination	Prevention of terrorism
Freedom from arbitrary arrest or detention; right to a fair trial; right to effective remedies	Victims of trafficking in human beings		Combating acts motivated by prejudice, intolerance, and hatred (aggressive nationalism, racism, chauvinism, xenophobia, anti-Semitism, ethnic cleansing, etc.)
Right to life (abolition of the death penalty)	Migrant workers		
Prohibition of torture and other cruel, inhuman or degrading treatment or punishment	Civilian populations (International Humanitarian Law)		
Respect for private and family life; right to nationality	Persons in detention or prison		
Economic, social, and cultural rights; property rights; workers' rights; freedom of cultural or artistic expression; cultural heritage; right to education	Armed forces personnel		
	Persons with disabilities		
	Indigenous populations		

considered to be a 'source of direct and legitimate concern' to all governments and, as such, do not pertain exclusively to the internal affairs of any
concerned state.[4]

Two problems presently affect the human dimension. The first concerns
ongoing human rights violations by former communist states (especially
Russia, Belarus and the five Central Asian Republics of Kazakhstan,
Kyrgyzstan, Tajikistan, Turkmenistan and Uzbekistan), and – regrettably –
by major Western countries in the context of the fight against transnational terrorism. The other problem is the stonewalling of the ODIHR's
election monitoring activities by Moscow, as part of an overall assault
launched by the Putin administration against the OSCE (see below).

Economic and environmental dimension (EED)

Born as the Cinderella of the CSCE, the EED remains modest, if not
anaemic, because the participating states (with the exception of those
forming the Russian-led bloc of the Collective Security Treaty Organization,
CSTO) view its role as limited to that of political catalyst for the activities of
more specialised and endowed external organisations.[5] Its blatant shortcomings include non-deliverance of operational services, insufficient integration
with conflict management, underdevelopment of the environmental component, and an absence of basic normative instrument setting guidelines for
intergovernmental co-operation, to name a few. The strengthening of the
EED is likely to remain an impossible mission as long as the participating
states stick to the concept of catalyst and do not inject into it a critical mass
of human and financial resources.

The mixed record of conflict management activities

The OSCE disposes of two genuine cross-dimensional tools for conflict management: the High Commissioner on National Minorities (HCNM) and
Long-Term Missions (LTMs), also known as Field Missions. The former is
empowered to act solely for preventative purposes and address only those
conflicts involving ethnic minority issues (Kemp 2001). By contrast, the
latter are mandated to intervene at all phases of the conflict management
cycle and tackle conflicts of any nature. However, a number of non-conflict
management LTMs operate as 'Centres', 'Offices' or 'Missions' and assist
states in matters pertaining to the three dimensions and, especially, to
sustain democratic institution-building (Ghebali 2004). From the outset,
only actual or potential conflicts taking place in the geopolitical space of the
former Soviet Union or in the Western Balkans have been addressed. In most
cases, the OSCE does not act alone. Cooperation with the UN, which is
current, has peaked with the UN Mission in Kosovo (UNMIK), a peace
operation, in which the 'OSCE Mission in Kosovo' with a human dimension
mandate is embedded. At the regional level, partnership on a case-by-case

basis is normal practice with the European Union, NATO and the Council of Europe. It is important to note that the OSCE's conflict management activities include preventative diplomacy, peace-making and peacebuilding (see Table 3.3) – but not peace enforcement, an avenue prohibited by definition for a co-operative security organisation. As for peacekeeping, it is a type of activity performed but not acknowledged as such. Chapter III of the Helsinki Decisions of 1992 (CSCE 1992), whose substance was reaffirmed by paragraph 46 of the 1999 Istanbul Charter for European Security (OSCE 1999), authorises the OSCE to conduct non-coercive peacekeeping operations of its own and also to mandate other European institutions to do so on its behalf. Up to now, the OSCE has not made use of this faculty. However, the OSCE does venture into peacekeeping through such activities as ceasefire monitoring, policing, border monitoring, and others. The Kosovo Verification Mission (1998–99) did perform as a kind of peacekeeping operation, but without the name. Finally, as an integral part of UNMIK, the OSCE Mission in Kosovo is, without a doubt, involved in a multi-functional peace operation.

The major OSCE preventative interventions have occurred in Estonia, Latvia, Macedonia and Ukraine. Conducted by an LTM and the HCNM, they aimed at preventing the worst-case scenario of some form of foreign intervention aggravated by the risk of internal destabilisation stemming from

Table 3.3 Conflict management activities

Conflict prevention	Conflict resolution	Peace-building
Kosovo, Sanjak and Voivodina (Serbia/ Montenegro), 1992–93	Nagorno-Karabakh (Azerbaijan), since 1992	Bosnia and Herzegovina, since 1994
Macedonia, 1992–2000	South Ossetia (Georgia), since 1992	Croatia, since 1996
Estonia, 1993–2001	Transdniestria (Moldova), since 1993	Albania, since 1997
Latvia, 1993–2001	Chechnya (Russia), 1995–2002	Kosovo (Serbia), since 1999
Ukraine, 1994–99		Macedonia, since 2001
Major cases addressed by the HCNM: Russian minorities in Estonia and Latvia; Albanian minorities in Macedonia; Hungarian minorities in Slovakia and Romania; Russian and Crimean Tatar minorities in Ukraine		Tajikistan, since 1994

discontented national minorities. The HCMN also intervened separately to defuse ethnic tensions in a number of other countries (see Table 3.3). As for post-conflict rehabilitation activities, they were and are still undertaken in the Western Balkans and Tajikistan. In all cases, the objective is the reconstruction of a war-torn society in the aftermath of internecine armed confrontation. Interventions have focused on the human dimension aspects of peacebuilding, albeit in a single case, that of Bosnia and Herzegovina, the OSCE reached out to military aspects – through the elaboration (and monitoring the implementation) of specific CSBMs and arms control instruments.[6] While the OSCE has performed rather positively in conflict prevention and unevenly in post-conflict peacebuilding (see Table 3.3), it deserves a failing grade in conflict resolution – as demonstrated by Chechnya and, above all, the so-called frozen conflicts.

After short-lived mediation efforts (1996–97), the OSCE Assistance Group in Chechnya proved unable to prevent Moscow's large-scale military intervention in 1999 or to stop what amounted to a total war against the Chechen population. Following the refusal of the overwhelming majority of other governments to limit the OSCE's role in Chechnya to that of a coordinator of humanitarian assistance (as demanded by the Putin administration), the Assistance Group's mandate was terminated in December 2002. Subsequently, the OSCE ceased adopting any official pronouncements on Chechnya, despite ongoing atrocities committed there by Russian troops.

Since 1992–93, more blatant failure has characterised the management of frozen conflicts in the breakaway regions of Nagorno-Karabakh, Azerbaijan; Transdniestria, Moldova; and South Ossetia, Georgia. Beside the establishment of a dialogue framework between each of the regions and the central state, OSCE attempts for settlement have been thwarted. At first sight, the failure could be attributed to the rejection of all proposed arrangements by the secessionist entities whose respective leaderships reap enormous benefits from large-scale illegal trafficking of all sorts. The real problem stems however from the bare fact that, while being entrusted by the OSCE with an official mediating role, Moscow has been fully backing the Armenians against Azerbaijan and providing political, economic and military support to the self-proclaimed (and unrecognised) breakaway entities.[7] The complacency with which the West treated these flawed mediation processes should also be acknowledged. As from the end of 2003, Moscow overplayed its hand in Moldova through the tabling (as a mediator but without consultation with the OSCE) of a federalisation scheme providing for the exclusive control of Russia on the country (Kozak Memorandum). It also displayed outright opposition to Georgia's Revolution of the Rose, that it considered of having been instigated by the West. As a consequence, Western diplomacy became openly supportive of Moldova and (all the more given the stakes related to the Baku–Tbilisi–Ceyhan pipeline) of Georgia. This shift naturally contributed to anger Moscow further. At the end of the day, it fully exposed the OSCE's impotence in an issue intertwined (as developed below) with an equally protracted issue: the Istanbul Summit military commitments.

The daunting challenges confronting the OSCE: a multifaceted crisis epitomised by Russian grievances

Following its mild institutionalisation through the November 1990 Paris Charter for a New Europe, the CSCE emerged in the post-Cold War setting with a 'fuzzy' security identity (Ghebali 1994). It remained in quest of a specific role and niche until the 1995 Dayton Framework Agreement attributed to it important peacebuilding responsibilities in Bosnia and Herzegovina which, subsequently, enabled it to develop appreciable operational capacities. Since 2000 however, several challenges are casting a shadow of uncertainty on the future of the OSCE. Two of them, the ripple effect of NATO and EU enlargements and the changing parameters of European security, are exogenous causes. All others are of an endogenous nature: the continuing non-resolution of the frozen conflicts, the controversy over the Istanbul military commitments, the unfinished institutionalisation of the OSCE, the dilemma posed by the Kazakh assumption of the OSCE Chairmanship in 2010, and above all Russia's deep dissatisfaction with the OSCE's institutional and political evolution.

The backlash of NATO and EU enlargements

As a result of both NATO and EU enlargements, 36 out of the 56 OSCE participating states have become members of NATO and/or the EU. It is often argued that the latter is now assuming an expanding role in the OSCE area with more resources, effectiveness and credibility, and that its new members have lost interest in the OSCE.[8] Admittedly, the OSCE lacks the military clout of NATO and the EU's politico-economic assets. However, the ripple effects of enlargement should not be over-estimated or over-dramatised for a number of reasons. First, as the expansion of the two bodies has clear geographic or geopolitical limits and constraints, the OSCE will always maintain an edge at the level of membership and continue to be relevant for those states (in the Caucasus, Central Asia and the Balkans) with no predictable future in either or both NATO and the EU. Second, due to overstretch in Afghanistan and the ailing state of transatlantic relations,[9] NATO's continued political ascension can certainly not be taken for granted. Third, because of political divergences among them, EU member states are unable to play a role within the OSCE commensurate with their budgetary contribution, which represents over 70 per cent of OSCE resources. Furthermore, the EU is much less flexible in its *modus operandi* than the OSCE and, furthermore, has no legitimate mandate to operate in the geopolitical area of the former Soviet Union. In fact, asymmetrical capacities between the OSCE and its two partner organisations are offset by complementarities of goals. In other words, the problem is less institutional competition or hegemony than enhanced coordination and synergy.

The changing parameters of European security

In reaction to the 9/11 terrorist attacks against the United States, the OSCE adopted a 'Strategy to Address Threats to Security and Stability in the Twenty-First Century' (OSCE 2003) which focused on terrorism, illegal migration and organised crime linked to illicit trafficking in human beings, drugs, small arms and light weapons. A strategy is normally expected to offer an action plan specifying how, on the basis of given resources and specific means, a number of medium- and long-term objectives are to be achieved with optimal effectiveness and efficiency. However, the 2003 document only offers an inventory of problems to be solved and tools to be possibly used, but no operational guidelines. It actually confirms that coping effectively with the identified threats is beyond the reach of a soft security organisation such as the OSCE. In particular, it comes as no surprise that the OSCE's contribution to the mantra issue of anti-terrorism has brought (despite a host of texts) no practical added value.

The frozen conflicts

The continued non-resolution of frozen conflicts, in particular in Moldova and Georgia, challenges the basic commitments that are the execution of international obligations in *bona fide* (Principle X of the Helsinki Decalogue), the non-stationing of foreign armed forces against the consent of the hosting country (§14 of the Code of Conduct, §3 of Art. I of the Adapted CFE Treaty) and the respect for the territorial integrity of states (Principle IV of the Helsinki Decalogue). As mentioned before, the real source of the problem is that a government fully backing breakaway entities (and hence a de facto party) has been anointed as an official mediator. To put it bluntly, the OSCE is condoning what actually amount to mock negotiations and biased mediations. The most scathing evidence of the erroneous approach adopted by the OSCE vis-à-vis the frozen conflicts for more than a decade is the November 2006 joint declaration through which the leaders of Transnistria, South Ossetia and Abkhazia, heralded from Moscow, that incorporation to Russia was the ultimate aim (Socor 2006). In any case, frozen conflicts continue to heavily damage the credibility of the OSCE.

The 1999 Istanbul military commitments

As part of a package deal agreed at the OSCE Istanbul Summit, and included in the Final Act of the Conference of the State Parties to the CFE

Treaty, Russia contracted two series of commitments with fixed deadlines. The first set was related to the reduction, by the end of 2000, of Russian armaments and equipment limited by the CFE Treaty in Georgia, and the destruction of similar armaments and equipment in Moldova by the end of 2001. More complex, the second set of commitments concerned the completion of negotiations on the duration and functioning modalities of two Russian military bases in Georgia (Batumi, in Azaria, and Akhalkalaki, near the border with Armenia) during 2000, and the disbanding of two other bases (Gudauta, in Abkhazia, and Vaziani, near Tbilisi) by 1 July 2001. While the commitments related to the CFE Treaty were executed in due time (Russia had particular interest in a rapid entry of force of the Adapted Treaty which would introduce legal constraints on NATO's Baltic flanks), the other ones have been honoured selectively. In violation of the principle of sovereignty of states, Russian troops are still present in Moldova and partially in Georgia.[10] In any case, at the 2002 Porto Ministerial Council meeting, the OSCE softened Moscow's obligation to respect the Istanbul commitments by just *taking note* of Russia's intention to achieve withdrawal from Moldova 'provided necessary conditions are in place', as well as of Moscow's and Tbilisi's 'desire' to 'complete negotiations regarding the duration and modalities of the functioning of the Russian military bases at Batumi and Akhalkalaki and the Russian military facilities within the territory of Georgia' (OSCE Ministerial Council 2002: §5, §6, §9). Those formulations contradicted the unconditional character of the Istanbul commitments. The OSCE realised too late that this amounted to condoning Moscow reneging on its commitments with regards to Moldova and Georgia. Ever since, the OSCE has been unable to adopt any ministerial statement rectifying the Porto declaration or even reconfirming the continuing validity of the Istanbul commitments.

The unfinished institutionalisation of the OSCE

The OSCE suffers from a number of obvious dysfunctions due to an insufficient transformation from a conference process to a standard international organisation. It does not have a basic instrument specifying its goals and structures, or the respective attributions of its organs. It also lacks an international legal capacity, an effective financing system, a politically empowered secretary-general, and a political and professional secretariat. These legacies of piecemeal institutionalisation compel the OSCE to operate with low visibility and credibility.

Under pressure from Moscow, the issue of OSCE reform was put on the agenda in 2001. A number of reform measures were then adopted at successive Ministerial Council meetings. In June 2005, the process culminated with a comprehensive report issued by a panel of eminent persons, entitled 'Common Purpose. Towards a More Effective OSCE' (OSCE 2005).

Drawing on the report, the Ljubljana Ministerial Council (2005) adopted a framework decision on 'Strengthening the effectiveness of the OSCE' which tasked the Permanent Council (the OSCE decision-making body) to continue work on a number of items (a reform agenda of sorts) and requested ODIHR to address the issue of election commitments. On that basis, the 2006 Brussels Ministerial Council as well as the Permanent Council agreed on a wide set of measures (concerning OSCE procedures, administration, meetings and executive structures), whose major elements provided for updated rules of procedure and the establishment of a tripartite committee structure (one for each security dimension). However, to Moscow's dismay, the reform process basically resulted in managerial and technical improvements (Dunay 2006; Ghebali 2006 and 2007a). While a solid majority of participating states consider that the Ljubljana reform agenda has practically been exhausted, the members of the CSTO maintain that much remains to be done and, in May 2007, issued an impressive list of still needed reform (OSCE Chairman-in-Office 2007). Of all issues, the most divisive ones are certainly those aimed at turning the OSCE into a full standard international organisation and reforming the ODIHR (Ghebali 2008).

Kazakhstan's bid for the OSCE chairmanship of 2009

Kazakhstan, the most powerful of Central Asia's states, has been seeking the OSCE chair since 2003. Apart from rotating on an annual basis, the OSCE Chairmanship is not subject to any formal eligibility criteria. However, all Chairmanships have hitherto been assumed by states with clearly satisfactory and unchallenged record in human rights and democratic elections – an implicit requirement that Kazakhstan could hardly claim. Furthermore, following its initial bid, Kazakhstan held rigged parliamentary and presidential elections and adopted restrictive legislation on freedom of assembly and expression, free media, etc. (Zagorski 2007). As the United States vetoed Kazakhstan's candidature, the 2006 Ministerial Council Meeting decided to reconsider the issue at the latest during its 2007 session in light of the applicant country having 'committed to a program of political action and reforms and to exercise leadership in upholding OSCE's commitments, norms and values' (OSCE Ministerial Council 2006b; OSCE Permanent Council 2006a, 2006b). In 2007, Kazakhstan did introduce some modest improvements at legislative level, but abstained from amending the most restrictive provisions tainting its election code, criminal code, media law or regulations on religious freedoms. Furthermore, the parliamentary elections of August 2007 clearly failed to meet a number of OSCE commitments. Notwithstanding, Kazakhstan's bid was uncompromisingly supported by Russia and its closest allies which, given a decision taken by the Commonwealth of Independent States (CIS) Kazan Summit of September 2005, consider Astana as a 'collective candidate' (CIS 2006).

The issue was settled in November 2007 at the Madrid session of the Ministerial Council by means of a package deal based on a 'three countries for three years' formula. The Council decided that Greece, Kazakhstan and Lithuania will respectively exercise the Chairmanship in 2009, 2010 and 2011 (OSCE Ministerial Council 2007b). Kazakhstan (for which this was not a trivial matter, but one involving regional and international prestige), declared that it had accepted the compromise as a goodwill gesture (OSCE Ministerial Council 2007b: attachment). Although the exact modalities of the deal arrived at have not been disclosed, it can be surmised (from a letter addressed to the Spanish Chairmanship by Kazakhstan's Minister of Foreign Affairs and confirmed in a speech delivered by him in Madrid) that the price of the Chairmanship entailed two basic concessions. First, Kazakhstan promised to continue democratic reforms for the improvement of legislation on elections, media, the constitution, political parties, local self-government and NGOs – and, in doing so, to duly take into account OSCE recommendations. Second, it pledged to attribute priority attention to the human dimension, to stand for the compliance with the fundamental principles of open participation by NGOs in OSCE events and even – distancing itself from Russia – 'to preserve ODIHR and its existing mandate' [and] 'not support any future efforts to weaken them' (Ministerial Council 2007a). Moscow expressed its frustration in a face-saving statement claiming that the Madrid package deal had not been reached at the expense of its own demands for reforming the ODIHR (OSCE Ministerial Council 2007b, annex).

The Madrid compromise appears reasonable. The rejection of Kazakhstan's candidature would have severely damaged cooperation with the Central Asian participating states. In addition, and as Russia threatened to oppose any other Chairmanship, the compromise avoided a scenario under which the OSCE would have been deprived of Chairmanship from 2009 onwards (see Zagorski 2007). On the other hand, the episode exposed the fundamental dilemma underlying the OSCE Chairmanship. Considering the position as an automatic right (whether under alphabetical order or not) would be consistent with the principle of equality of states, but its flaw is to legitimise any inappropriate candidature, including that of a plain dictatorship (such as Belarus) or microstates with inadequate capabilities. Conversely, reserving the position only for those participating states that meet the basic democratic standards of the OSCE would mean, in practice, attributing it essentially to EU/NATO states.

Russia's dissatisfaction with the OSCE

Being simultaneously connected with the issues of frozen conflicts, Istanbul commitments, and unfinished institutionalisation of the OSCE, the Russian factor constitutes the neuralgic element of the OSCE crisis. Initially, Russia put high expectations on the OSCE, the only European security institution where it occupied a legitimate place. Thus, when NATO envisaged its eastward enlargement, Moscow felt that only the OSCE could provide damage limitation through the establishment of a genuine pan-European security system 'free of geopolitical dividing lines'. However, when its basic reform claims were thwarted and the OSCE proved unable to prevent, stop or simply condemn NATO's military intervention in Kosovo in 1999, the Yeltsin administration considered that the organisation could not preserve, let alone serve, its interests. Soon after taking over, the Putin administration began assaulting the OSCE on the ground of four basic charges (Ghebali 2005; Zellner 2005).

The first grievance concerns double standards: according to Moscow, the OSCE unfairly focuses on countries located 'East of Vienna' (the former Soviet Union and the Balkans), thus creating a fault line between 'state subjects' and 'state objects', as well as between supposedly flawless states and guilty ones. Under a second grievance, that of alleged political self-marginalisation, the OSCE is accused of addressing peripheral issues instead of those actually affecting the landscape of European security – a trend related to its proclivity to act as a sub-contractor (if not a maidservant) of NATO and the EU. A third grievance underscores the unbalanced development of the three dimensions, that is, the outgrowth of the human dimension (with aggressive intrusiveness in the internal affairs of states) at the expense of the two other dimensions. The last major grievance refers to unfinished institutionalisation which leads the OSCE to function with excessively pragmatic and shallow rules. This charge is all-embracing in the sense that incomplete institutionalisation is precisely what, from Moscow's perspective, encourages OSCE's operational institutions to perform with undue autonomy and NATO/EU countries (under the guise of flexibility and pragmatism) to impose their own agenda. Hence the need for an in-depth reform with a view to endow the OSCE with a basic charter and legal personality, limit the excessive political autonomy of the Chairman in Office, the LTMs and especially ODIHR (which is accused of using biased standards when conducting election monitoring operations), and also introduce more transparency and rigor in administrative and budgetary management. In a famous speech, delivered at the forty-third Munich Conference on Security Policy, President Putin reaffirmed the main thrust of that vitriolic indictment (Putin 2007). Anyhow, time and again, Moscow has warned that in the absence of drastic reform, the OSCE would be 'doomed to extinction' (see OSCE Permanent Council 2001a, 2001b, 2005a, 2005b; OSCE Ministerial Council 2006a). As Russian grievances and concomitant demands have been endorsed by some CIS states whose poor human rights record is currently questioned within the OSCE (Belarus, Armenia, and the Central Asian Republics), Moscow does not hesitate to claim that the OSCE is confronted with a 'CIS challenge' (see OSCE Permanent Council 2003, 2004).

Some of the suggested reforms (especially those aimed at completing the transformation of the OSCE into a more standard international organisation) are valid and even overdue. Furthermore, as international institutions are instruments of foreign policy as well as frameworks for multilateral cooperation, it is not illegitimate that Russia seeks to achieve national goals through the OSCE. However, several liabilities prevent Moscow from presenting the best of credentials in support of its case: unpunished atrocities in Chechnya, 'managed democracy' at the domestic level, renegation of the Istanbul commitments, opposition to the spread of democracy in the post-Soviet space, and full-fledged support of breakaway regimes in Transdniestria, Abkhazia and South Ossetia. Furthermore, Russia's mantra reference to sovereign equality of states smacks of double standards: Moscow aims at equality of status among big powers, with no regard for the sovereignty of small states such as Moldova and Georgia, where Russian troops are stationed against the will of the host country. While disregarding basic pan-European commitments, Russia makes the continuation of its co-operation with the OSCE conditional upon the adoption of a reform agenda including elements whose implementation would erode the OSCE's longstanding flexibility and bridle the autonomy of operational institutions. Clearly, the romantic period of Moscow's attachment towards the OSCE is over, all the more that Russian concern with equality of status is now better addressed through bilateral channels, within both NATO and the EU.

Conclusion

The OSCE's track record since the end of the Cold War is globally honourable. As a vehicle for democratisation and conflict management, the organisation has creatively contributed to the consolidation of security and stability in its vast geopolitical area. Its political genetic code, a comprehensive security agenda implemented through a cooperative security approach, remains sound and valid. However, its relevance is now visibly dwindling.

First, the worsening of Russia's relations with the United States, NATO and EU member states has laid bare the limited effectiveness of OSCE's security dialogue function – a fact also eloquently reflected in that no OSCE summit has been held since 1999.

Second, bickering over the meaning and/or assessment of OSCE commitments related to the politico-military dimension (CSBMs and Adapted CFE Treaty) and the human dimension (election standards) is undermining the so-called normative *acquis* of the OSCE.

Third, the old-fashioned Soviet twin arguments of sovereignty and non-interference in internal affairs have resurfaced and are currently invoked by a number of authoritarian regimes opposed to the OSCE's democratisation prescriptions.

Fourth, the conflict management function of the OSCE appears to be winding down. The HCNM is still forbidden to address the ethnic Kurdish issue, due to Turkey's opposition. The case of frozen conflicts put aside, the LTMs' future is not devoid of uncertainty. The Mission in Croatia is to be closed in the near future because of appreciable progress in the process of democratisation made by the host state. In addition, the Mission in Kosovo (OSCE's largest LTM) faces most delicate problems since the province unilateral declaration of independence. Be as it may, given the impact of the war in Afghanistan on the neighbouring OSCE Central Asian states, potential risks to the stability of the OSCE region now emanate from conflicts taking place in adjacent regions. Hence the decision made by the Ministerial Council, in November 2007, to step up the OSCE's engagement with Afghanistan – which presently enjoys the status of 'Asian Partner for Co-operation' (APC) – through support measures in the fields of border security, police training and the fight against drug trafficking (Ministerial Council 2007c). The growing international political and economic weight of China (that shares borders with three OSCE States) is raising the question of whether or not the status of APC should be offered to Beijing (Zellner 2007).[11]

Last but not least, the Russian estrangement from the OSCE could have lethal effects. Indeed, one of the main, although implicit, goals of the post-Cold War OSCE was to encourage the integration of Russia into the democratic community of European nations. Therefore, the OSCE has partly linked its *raison d'être* to a 'Europeanising' and non-hegemonic Russia, while there is now a state whose 'leaders have given up on becoming part of the West and have started creating their own Moscow-centered system' (Trenin 2006). This means that the OSCE has to deal with a new self-assertive Russia claiming free reign in the post-Soviet space and resenting any encroachment, from any quarter, as intolerable. There is little doubt that without Moscow's ongoing support and contributions, the OSCE would lose a large amount of relevance. The trouble is that the accommodation of Russia's basic reform demands can hardly be achieved without devastating consequences – that is, the undermining of OSCE's traditional flexibility and creativity, as well as the downgrading of normative commitments and related monitoring standards.

So far, the OSCE has been responding to the Russian demands through ministerial decisions reflecting makeshift consensus on secondary topics. Political escapism, however, has natural limits. One might fear that those limits have been reached. So, the continued relevance of the OSCE now fully depends on the will of its key actors, namely the EU, the United States and Russia – which actually represent an informal ruling troika. Due to internal divergences, the EU can hardly play a determinant role. Mired in Iraq and Afghanistan, the Bush administration is not likely to attribute high priority to the fate of a soft security organisation.[12] At the same time, it would be unrealistic to expect any toning down of Russian's criticisms or demands. In sum, no breakthrough but rather muddling through seems to be the most likely scenario for the OSCE for the time being.

Notes

1 Institutionalised by the Charter of Paris for a New Europe (November 1990), the CSCE was (retrospectively) re-baptised 'OSCE' as from 1 January 1995.
2 The OSCE issued such proclamation through the Helsinki Decisions 1992 (§2 of Chapter IV) and the 1992 Helsinki Summit Declaration (§25).
3 Noticeably, neutral states whose defense systems rely essentially on non-active armed forces and important depots (Austria, Finland, Sweden and Switzerland) consider that joining the Adapted CFE Treaty would result in constraining the reaction capacity of their forces in time of crisis and entail disclosure of the essential elements of their decentralised defensive systems.
4 See §9 of the preamble of the 'Moscow document on the human dimension of the CSCE' (1991). Comparable provision is included in the Helsinki Summit Declaration of 1992 (§8) and the Report of the 1991 Geneva Expert Meeting on National Minorities (section II, §3).
5 Formally established in 2003, the CSTO presently consists of Russia and six Moscow-leaning members of the Commonwealth of Independent States: Armenia, Belarus and all of the former Soviet Central Asian Republics except Turkmenistan.
6 Namely the Vienna Agreement on CSBMs in Bosnia and Herzegovina (26 January 1996), the Florence Agreement on sub-regional arms control (14 June 1996) and the Vienna Concluding Document on arms control in and around Yugoslavia (18 July 2001).
7 Another so-called frozen conflict in Abkhazia is managed by the UN with some contribution from the OSCE. In all cases, Russia's strategy is to avoid military escalation while maintaining sufficient tension to justify its 'mediation' role and military presence.
8 See Dunay's chapter in this volume.
9 See Herd's chapter in this volume.
10 In Georgia, this refers to the Gudauta base in Abkhazia.
11 The OSCE has granted Partner for Co-operation status, entailing more than a passive observation role, to 11 Mediterranean and Asian States: Algeria, Egypt, Israel, Jordan, Morocco, Tunisia, Afghanistan, Japan, the Republic of Korea, Mongolia and Thailand. For more details, see the Factsheet of the OSCE's External Co-operation Section, available at www.osce.org/ec/item_11_13559.html.
12 Noticeably, the US National Security Strategy of September 2002 and that of March 2006 made no mention of the OSCE.

References

Commonwealth of Independent States (CIS) (2006) SEC.DEL/220/06, Kazan, 20 September.
CSCE (1990) 'Document of the Copenhagen Meeting of the Conference on the Human Dimension of the CSCE', Copenhagen, 29 June, Online. Available at www.osce.org/documents/odihr/1990/06/13992_en.pdf (accessed 6 May 2008).
—— (1992) 'The Challenges of Change', Helsinki Document 1992, Online. Available at www.osce.org/documents/mcs/1992/07/4046_en.pdf (accessed 6 May 2008).
Dunay, P. (2006) 'The OSCE in Crisis', *Chaillot Paper 88*, Paris: EU Institute for Security Study.
Ghebali, V.-Y. (1994) 'The CSCE Process: Bright Past, Fuzzy Present, Uncertain Future', in Clesse, A., Cooper, R. and Sakamoto, Y. (eds) *The International System After the Collapse of the East–West Order*, Dordrecht: Martinus Nijhoff.

—— (2004) 'The OSCE Long-Term Missions: A Creative Tool under Challenge, *Helsinki Monitor*, 15(3): 202–19.

—— (2005) 'Growing Pains at the OSCE: The Rise and Fall of Russia's Pan-European Experience', *Cambridge Review of International Relations*, 18(3): 375–388.

—— (2006) 'The Reform of the OSCE', in Ghebali, V.-Y. and Warner, D. (eds) *The Reform of the OSCE 15 Years After the Charter of Paris for a New Europe: Problems, Challenges and Risks*, Geneva: PSIO/HEI, PSIO Occasional Paper 2.

—— (2007a) 'The 14th session of the OSCE Ministerial Council: Still Addressing the Visible Tips of Political Icebergs', *Helsinki Monitor*, 18(1): 16–45.

—— (2007b) 'The OSCE Involvement in Security Sector Reform: Normative Commitments and Operational Activities Without An Integrated Approach', in Warner, D. (ed.) *The OSCE at a Turning Point: Chairmanship and Other Challenges*, Geneva: PSIO/HEI, PSIO Occasional Paper 4.

—— (2008) 'The 2007 Madrid Ministerial Council Meeting: A Mixed Bag of Non-Decisions and Discrete Set of Measures', *Helsinki Monitor*, 19(1): 82–99.

Ghebali, V.-Y. and Lambert, A. (2005) *The OSCE Code of Conduct on Politico-Military Aspects of Security. Anatomy and Implementation*, Leiden/Boston: Martinus Nijhoff.

Kemp, W. A. (2001) *Quiet Diplomacy in Action. The OSCE High Commissioner on National Minorities*, The Hague: Kluwer Law International.

Lachowski, Z. (2004) *Confidence- and Security-Building Measures in the New Europe*, Oxford: Oxford University Press, SIPRI, Research Report No. 18.

ODIHR (2005) *OSCE Human Dimension Commitments*, Vol. 1: *Thematic Compilation*; vol. 2: *Chronological Compilation*, Warsaw: OSCE/ODIHR.

OSCE (1999) 'Charter for European Security', Istanbul Document 1999, Online. Available at www.osce.org/documents/mcs/1999/11/4050_en.pdf (accessed 6 May 2008).

—— (2003) 'Strategy to Address Threats to Security and Stability in the Twenty-First Century', Annex 3 of MC(11).JOUR/2, 2 December.

—— (2005) *Common Purpose. Towards a More Effective OSCE. Final Report and Recommendations of the Panel of Eminent persons on Strengthening the Effectiveness of the OSCE*, Vienna: OSCE (CIO.GAL/100/05, 27 June 2005).

OSCE Chairman-in-Office (2007) CIO.GAL/78/07, 24 May.

OSCE Ministerial Council (2002) Porto Ministerial Council 'Statements', Porto.

—— (2005) 'Strengthening the effectiveness of the OSCE', Ljubljana, MC.DEC/17/05, 6 December.

—— (2006a) MC.DEL/21/06, 4 December.

—— (2006b) 'Future OSCE Chairmanship', MC.DEC/20/06, 5 December.

—— (2007a) MC.DEL/1/07, 26 November and MC.DEL/38/07, 29 November.

—— (2007b) MC.DEC/11/07, 30 November.

—— (2007c) 'OSCE engagement with Afghanistan', MC.DEC/4/07/Corr.1, 30 November.

OSCE Permanent Council (2001a) PC.DEL/457/01, 22 June.

—— (2001b) PC.DEL/480/01, 28 June.

—— (2003) PC.DEL/986/03, 4 September, ' "Food-for-thought" paper on Long-Term Missions'.

—— (2004) PC.DEL/630, 8 July, Moscow informal Summit Declaration on the state of affairs in the OSCE.

—— (2005a) PC.DEC/775/05, 21 July.

—— (2005b) PC.DEL/905/05, 19 September.

—— (2006a) PC.DEL/830/06, 7 September (Kazakhstan).

—— (2006b) PC.DEL/840/06, 8 September (Russia).

Putin, V. (2007) Speech delivered by President Vladimir Putin at the 43rd Munich Conference on Security Policy, on 10 February 2007, Online. Available at www.securityconference.de/konferenzen/rede.php?sprache=en&id=179 (accessed 6 May 2008).

Socor, V. (2006) 'Moscow Hosts Three Secessionist Leaders', *Eurasia Daily Monitor*, 3(215).

—— (2007) 'Kremlin Would Re-write or Kill CFE Treaty', *Eurasia Daily Monitor*, 4(139).

Trenin, D. (2006) 'Russia Leaves the West', *Foreign Affairs*, July/August, 85(4): 87–96.

Zagorski, A. (2007) 'Kazakhstan's Chairmanship Bid: A Balance Sheet of Pros and Cons', in Warner, D. (ed.) *The OSCE at a Turning Point: Chairmanship and Other Challenges*, Geneva: HEI/PSIO, Occasional Paper 4.

Zellner, W. (2005) 'Russia and the OSCE: From High Hopes to Disillusionment', *Cambridge Review of International Relations*, 18(3): 389–402.

—— (2007) 'Redefining the OSCE's Future: Strategic Uncertainty and Political Contradictions Are Delaying Progress', *Conflicts, Security and Cooperation. Liber Amicorum Victor-Yves Ghebali*, Brussels: Bruylant.

4 The changing political geography of Europe

After EU and NATO enlargements

Pál Dunay

Introduction

Half a generation has passed since the end of the Cold War. All former non-Soviet Warsaw Treaty member-states have joined Western institutions that had not been accessible to them before. Without exception, they have become members of the Council of Europe, NATO and the European Union. Some have also joined the Organization for Economic Cooperation and Development (OECD). With the invitation to Albania and Croatia at the NATO Bucharest Summit (Bucharest 2008: point 2) to negotiate their NATO membership, and the forthcoming accession of Croatia to the EU, the 'extension' process of the West will slow if not fully halt. The 'long decade' that has lasted from 1999 (the first Eastern enlargement of NATO) to 2010 (when Croatia should gain membership in the EU), will come to an end.

The international integration of countries of the former East is only a reflection of their socio-economic and political transformation. The countries of East-central Europe[1] have undergone fundamental change since the end of the East–West conflict. They have established and consolidated multi-party democracies and market economies. In some sense, these countries have gone through rapid modernization and westernization and now increasingly look like their western European homologues as far as their political profile.

However, there are some differences between these two groups of countries. East-central Europeans have had to catch up economically, gain or regain the practice of managing market economies, establish political institutions, provide for their own security, often recognize and integrate national minorities, and find their place on the world political map. What made this all the more demanding was the associated urgency. It is exceptional, in many cases, what these countries have achieved in half a generation.

Nevertheless, the picture is not entirely reassuring. First of all, socio-political and economic transformation is an organic process. Although shortcuts to catch up can be made, and external support can be exploited, the completion of the process is time consuming, nevertheless. There are also a few concrete problems undermining transformation. Namely, corruption continues to be a central problem,[2] and East-central European countries have proven largely unsuccessful in closing a past that continues to interfere with social reconciliation.

Most often the communist history of these countries has been invoked as the prime reason for their attitude to international life. However, it is one of the starting assumptions of this chapter that the role of the East-central European countries is primarily and increasingly determined by their size rather than by their past. The new EU and NATO members are small and medium-size states. Irrespective of their self-assessment, none of these countries are policy-makers. The overwhelming majority of these states were policy-takers during the Cold War, if sovereign at all.

This chapter looks at how eastern enlargements of both the EU and NATO have affected European geopolitics. It also examines the experiences of the new members, as well as their influence on decision-making in the organizations they have joined. Most importantly, this chapter aims to answer the question whether the East-central European countries have moved from the *policy-taker* to the *policy-shaper* category, and whether Eastern enlargements have contributed to the unity of Europe.

NATO and EU roads to enlargement

In both the EU and NATO, it is the founding documents that permit the accession of any European state. Although the boundaries of Europe and 'Europeanness' are largely unsettled,[3] the accession of non-European states is formally excluded in both organizations. In both cases, the state aspiring for membership expresses a willingness to join, and must meet material and procedural conditions. As far as material conditions, both organizations begin with the need of furthering their objectives. NATO requests contributions 'to the security of the North Atlantic area' (NATO 1949: Art.10), and the EU seeks adherence to the 'principles of liberty, democracy, respect for human rights and fundamental freedoms, and the rule of law' (EU 2006: Art.6 and 49). It is a question of interpretation whether a specific country will reinforce security of the Alliance and to what extent, or will respect EU principles. Both institutions have further elaborated the criteria of enlargement in non-legally binding terms, but neither of them have included an exhaustive list of membership criteria. The NATO Enlargement Study openly states that 'there is no fixed or rigid list of criteria for inviting new member states to join the Alliance. Enlargement will be decided on a case-by-case basis and some nations may attain membership before others' (NATO 1995: Ch.1). Although the EU enlargement is more strictly law-based and refers to specific regulations (before the entry into force of the Lisbon Treaty), it is clear that the EU itself does not regard them as exclusive conditions (European Council 1993).

Both organizations have subjected enlargement to a process consisting of three more or less distinct phases: familiarization, stabilization/association and integration. Familiarization started on the day the East-central European states indicated their willingness to leave the communist system behind. Understandably, Western institutions reacted cautiously and waited for evidence of democratic commitment from the countries of the region. During this phase the West offered verbal reassurance of their sympathy to East-central Europeans' efforts (NATO 1990; European Council 1992), cooperative structures that helped build an interactive connection between East and West, and structures to channel resources from West to East.

In the EU, the establishment of cooperative structures started with political dialogue with countries that signed association agreements, while NATO launched the North Atlantic Cooperation Council (NACC) in the last months of 1991. As for channelling resources, there the European Community took the lead with the launch of the PHARE[4] programme that extended to the entire region soon after the velvet revolutions of 1989. The move from familiarization to association followed when the EU published the Copenhagen criteria of enlargement (1993) and NATO launched the Partnership for Peace programme (1994). According to the Copenhagen criteria, aspirant countries were expected to meet political criteria (stability of institutions, guaranteeing democracy, rule of law, respect for human rights and minority rights), economic criteria (the existence of a functioning market economy and the capacity to cope with the competitive pressure and market forces inside the Union), and accept the Community *acquis* (ability to take on the obligations of membership, including adherence to the aims of political, economic and monetary union). Reciprocally, the EU was to be able to absorb new members without endangering the momentum of European integration (European Council 1993). Nine of the ten aspirant countries (Slovakia being the exception) had fairly convincing records as far as meeting political requirements (European Commission 1997: 57).

The criteria did not entail any requirement in the foreign and security policy field, not to mention defence. There were various reasons for this. First and foremost, the Common Foreign and Security Policy (CFSP) was in its infancy (the Maastricht Treaty was not yet in force) and the European Security and Defence Policy (ESDP) was years away from being launched. CFSP furthermore was conceived as an inter-governmental policy based on consensus by the member-states. Between the Copenhagen accession criteria of 1993 and the Agenda 2000 programme of 1997, that first spoke in concrete terms about five East-central European countries that might be prepared for membership in the medium term, the EU had sufficient opportunity to gain evidence about the foreign policy orientation of the East-central European countries. They had no problem with aligning their foreign policies with the EU. The transatlantic orientation of some aspirant countries did not interfere with this as in most cases there was a fair chance that the eventual differences of transatlantic partners could be sorted out amicably. No major strategic discord was in sight between the United States and larger EU member-states that would have obliged the aspirants to take side.

In NATO, it was declared in December 1996 that the Alliance would invite 'one or more of the countries which have expressed interest in joining the Alliance' (NATO 1996). It was followed by an invitation extended to three countries, the Czech Republic, Hungary and Poland, in July 1997. The EU, after having launched Agenda 2000 (European Commission 1997), issued a yearly country report about the performance of the East-central European countries. Although these reports gave valuable insights into the politics and economics of those states, they very seldom raised foreign policy issues, with the exception of the legal status and the treatment of national minorities in some states.

The EU first enlarged to the East in May 2004 with the integration of ten new member-states[5] when NATO was already through two rounds of accessions. Eight of the ten new EU members were also new NATO members,[6] and full overlap between EU and NATO membership in East-central Europe was achieved with the second wave of EU enlargement in 2007, with Bulgaria and Romania joining.

The two enlargement processes were fundamentally different. Whereas it was about political commitment and military preparedness (i.e. largely about the adaptation of one sector) in NATO, it was about socio-political transformation and adaptation in the broadest sense of the word in the EU. NATO enlargement by three in 1999 had one major advantage: the Alliance learned earlier about post-enlargement attitudes and delivery. The EU started to realize how complex and demanding socio-political transformation was only after the big bang enlargement and halfway through to the next.

How new members deliver

Delivering on promises in NATO: performance of the 'new' and the 'old'

The 1999 enlargement of NATO was nearly exclusively a political deed of the Alliance, and military aspects played a marginal role. NATO checked little else than minimum interoperability in hosting aerial reinforcement by the first new members. This enlargement was in a sense the 'working down' of a historical debt for letting East-central Europe fall into the sphere of influence of the Soviet Union in the 1940s. The view is also expressed that 'enlargements have made a traditional large-scale war between European states extremely improbable and have increased the ability of all European states to jointly meet potential future security challenges' (Salonius-Pasternak 2007: 22). The intention was surely not to prevent large-scale war, but the expectation of an increased ability to face challenges together was certainly on the minds of decision-makers.

In fact, the NATO enlargement process has taken place primarily due to the recognition given by the West to the transformation of East-central

Europe and the insistence of these states to provide for their own security inside a strong military alliance.

Political conditions of NATO membership – justice, democracy, economic collaboration and well-being (Bebler 1999: 49) – have been guaranteed then and ever since. Hence post-enlargement attention of the Alliance has turned to military delivery. The record here is mixed, between the view that the new members do their fair share and a sentiment of dissatisfaction with their contribution.

First, European states had to transform their militaries on a number of occasions. They had to move from collective defence, to peace operations, to fighting terrorism and to carrying out counter-insurgency operations. For most of them, the series of changes turned out to be far too demanding. Those who had once been members of the Warsaw Treaty were burdened by an additional round of transformation, from collective offence to a short phase of individual self-defence. Consequently, the new NATO members are lagging behind in their defence transformation compared to their old NATO partners.

Second, on several occasions, the United States has voiced its dissatisfaction with its NATO allies' performance – not only with the new members. The US complained of a divide between its own operational capabilities and load-bearing capacity and that of the rest of the NATO Alliance. Consequently, it is unfounded to pick one poorly performing member-state or the other.[7]

Third, on the ground of operational performance new member-states do not contribute less than the old ones. The new East-central European members are without exception present in the field in the NATO-led force in Kosovo (KFOR), many of them contribute to the International Security Assistance Force (ISAF) in Afghanistan and some are in charge of Provincial Reconstruction Teams (PRTs). In the Afghan theatre of operations, many new member-states confine their contribution geographically or functionally, and tend to avoid dangerous areas. As the foreign minister of Poland put it, 'He who gives without caveats, gives twice' (Sikorski 2008: 1). NATO may need militaries capable of high intensity warfare, but what it needs even more is boots on the ground to sustain field presence in peace operations. In these operations, new members may be just as capable as old ones.

Fourth, as far as defence spending, again the divide is not between new and old members, but between members who spend a higher share of their gross domestic product (GDP) on defence and others. The real problem stems from the fact that many new members have a fairly low GDP and hence the amount they spend on defence is low (NATO 2007: 7). Furthermore, they do not want to jeopardize their socio-economic development for defence spending. Often free of any traditional military threat, these states allocate resources to other areas ranging from fostering development, improving infrastructure or contributing to mitigating social tension.

Fifth, the concern that it would be more difficult to make decisions with more members than with fewer was known before accession. Nevertheless, major operations where consensus was achieved did not provide evidence to this effect (Kamp 2006: 2). Moreover, in some cases where decision-making turned difficult, it was not the new members who caused trouble.

Considering the aforementioned points, no general conclusion can be drawn that new NATO members generally perform worse than the old ones. This being said, it is a fact that many new NATO members have given the impression that they are less performing and committed than some old members of the same size. On the perception side, there has been a concentration of doubts about the performance of a few members, like the Czech Republic or Hungary. In reality, some East-central European states do lag somewhat behind in every category listed above.

Delivering on promises in the European Union: divergences and new solidarities

The situation is more complex insofar as the performance of the new EU member-states is concerned. The EU continues to have a heavy focus upon economic matters. The performance is here overwhelmingly convincing, though with significant variation. The first years of membership for the class of 2004 was characterized by strong economic growth, declining trade deficits, and a continuing rise in foreign direct investment. One of the main concerns of old members, mass movement of labour from new member-states, has remained limited. Despite this fear, most old members – with the notable exception of Austria and Germany – have fully or partially opened their labour market. According to the European Commission (2006: 3), 'The highest percentage of EU-10 nationals is to be found in Ireland, where they account for two per cent of the total population'.

However, the economic performance of new member states has varied. In some cases, GDP growth has significantly slowed down, like in Hungary where it has been approaching zero growth in 2008. Furthermore, the ability to meet the conditions of accession to the monetary union, the so-called Maastricht criteria, is highly imbalanced. Until 2008, only one East-central European country, Slovenia, has been admitted in the Euro-zone, while the application of Lithuania was declined. Slovakia will join the Euro-zone in 2009. The slow alignment with certain macro-economic criteria ranging from the inflation rate to public debt indicate some volatility.

As far as the second pillar of the Union (CFSP) is concerned, the position of candidate countries was extremely brief on chapter 27 of the accession talks.[8] The candidates took note of their obligation to align their foreign policy decision-making structures, including the establishment of the function of political director and the opening of a Political and Security Committee (PSC) mission. It was the general expectation in East-central Europe that this problem-free relationship in CFSP would continue.

Bearing in mind that these countries used to be policy-takers for decades, if sovereign at all, and that they had often closely followed the foreign policies of some large EU member states since the end of the Cold War, there was reason to assume this.

In the field of ESDP, the new members do contribute to EU solidarity by participating in EU military, police and justice missions, and contributing to Battle Groups, with Poland and Romania each being in charge of one.[9] Due to limitations in personnel, expertise and logistics, many new members are mainly active in missions in the Western Balkans. The contribution of the new member-states to EU military missions faces one inherent limitation, that these small and medium-size countries have only one toolbox for international operations, which can be used under either a NATO, EU, or UN flag. Priorities, in spite of the large NATO operation in Afghanistan, have been shifting gradually towards the EU. This will continue with further missions in the Balkans, in the area most easily accessible logistically to most new member-states and least risky to supply. Mission participation further afield understandably presents more of a challenge for the small and medium-size countries of East-central Europe. In Africa in particular, where East-central European countries have not been present for two decades at least, their presence will remain limited, if not exceptional (e.g. Poland in the DRC, Hungary in the Sudan, etc.).

A few years after accession, the new members have moved beyond the disadvantage of not having a global political profile and hence not being familiar with many files on the CFSP agenda. However, catching up has not eliminated the difference between the favourite agenda items of the East-central European countries and those followed less enthusiastically. Their preferences include the eastern neighbourhood and Russia as well as the Western Balkans, while global reach has largely remained alien to the new members, and they continue to play a policy-taker role.

The newly established 'Structured permanent cooperation' is a concern for most smaller EU member countries. It is perceived to carry the danger of a few large members formally and informally determining the EU CFSP agenda. Poland, knowing its own great power nature in strategic terms, does not feel the negative effect of such differentiation whereas Romania is still hopeful that its regional role and particularly its leadership in the Black Sea Cooperation will provide a seat around the table. Some less hopeful countries emphasize that 'Structured permanent cooperation' must not be closed and that it is essential that countries have access to the 'inner circle' dependent on their interest and competence (Gyurcsány 2007).

The Lisbon Treaty has been assessed differently in the new member-states. In several countries (the Czech Republic, Poland and Slovakia) its ratification has fallen into domestic political cross-fire. In Prague, this was due to the strong presence of Euro-scepticism. In Warsaw, the internal division is between the populist right that negotiated the Treaty and the liberal government that signed it. In Bratislava, the government allegedly made arrangements with some elements of the opposition to have the Treaty pass in the Parliament. In other new member-states, the Lisbon Treaty has remained free of controversy and new members would certainly like to have it come into force as soon as possible, also as a symbol that the EU has passed the constitution debacle and is back on track.

If one takes a closer look to the concerns of the new member-states, they clearly centre around institutional matters stemming from the Lisbon Treaty. This is closely linked with the fact that the overwhelming majority of new member-states are small states. They suspect that with further institutionalization of the EU, and of foreign and security policy specifically, the influence of large member-states would increase. That is why the new members advocate that the President of the Council would be a facilitator, rather than a leader of the Council. Furthermore, most new members that have not been in the EU Presidency function would like to see clearly how the Presidency and the President would relate to each other. Will there be harmony or will rivalry prevail? If the first President is a citizen of a large member-state, then many new members would advocate that the first EU 'Foreign Minister' should come from a smaller member. Last, but not least, several new members are concerned about the dominance of some large old members in the newly established External Action Service. Diplomats in East-central Europe speak about 'shady deals' in forming the External Action Service whose staff will arrive from the Council, the Commission and from secondment of member-states. Will most important posts go to citizens of old, and more often than not, large members, thus putting new members into a position of disadvantage?

The new members joined EU consensus and supported the Ahtisaari plan as a basis for the resolution of the pending status of Kosovo. When it became clear that there is no consensus within the EU on the matter, some new members also started to voice their dissenting view. Although East-central European member-states were well aware that both the great powers of the EU and the United States (the two most important points of reference for states of the region) would recognize Kosovo's independence, some of them have given priority to their national interest, and contradicted the mainstream. The debate around Kosovo's independence underlined that only East-central European states that have some similar unresolved concerns, namely Romania and Slovakia, opposed Kosovo recognition. These two states, similarly to Spain, worry about forming states on the basis of ethnicity. As the President of Romania, Traian Basescu said: 'Solutions which grant collective rights to a national minority living on the territory of a sovereign and independent country should not be adopted' (*Kosovo Perspective* 2006: 3). Interestingly enough, although the lack of recognition will be problematic to the international activity of Kosovo, and more specifically for the activity of the EU on the territory of Kosovo, none of those members that oppose recognition have blocked the establishment of the EU rule of law mission (EULEX) in Kosovo. Twenty-two EU members have recognized Kosovo, including eight of the ten East-central European EU members.[10] The new members have thus given an indication that there are instances when they see EU-solidarity and their identified national interests as equally important and take their decision as independently as any other sovereign state.

Expected points of contention

At the time of the enlargements, there were three areas where disagreements were expected between new, East-central European members, and some of the old ones: first, transatlantic relations; second, the former Soviet Union with an emphasis on Russia, Ukraine, Moldova and one day maybe Belarus; and third, human rights with an emphasis on the rights of national minorities. This assumption turned out to be largely correct.

The transatlantic link: between alignment and emancipation

Since the beginning of the 1990s, East-central European countries have been persistent in avoiding having to choose between their mentors, the United States and the EU, including some of its larger members. States with strong threat perception have tended to favour the United States as the ultimate and only credible guarantor of their security. Their balancing attempt has remained successful, with one notable exception, when a political divide dominated the agenda on Iraq.[11] The political conflict emerged over the difference between the position of the United States and some of its European allies in responding to the Iraqi threat (Cottey 2004: 69). In this context, the United States actively sought the support of East-central European countries. At the time of the crisis, only three East-central European countries (the Czech Republic, Hungary and Poland) were members of NATO while no state of the region was a member of the EU, although EU accession talks for eight East-central European countries were concluded in December 2002.

In February 2003, the three East-central European NATO member states joined five older members and issued a statement supporting transatlantic unity (*Wall Street Journal* 2003). The statement resulted in a loss of confidence between the European powers opposed to the US position, and some East-central European states. In the same vein, several other East-central European countries, candidates for EU membership and other states alike (the so-called 'Vilnius Ten'), issued a statement that unequivocally supported the US position (Vilnius Group 2003).

The special circumstances of the case were overwhelming, and it is therefore unlikely that a similar situation could emerge. The conclusions drawn by Vitkus (2006: 120, italics added by author for emphasis) for Lithuania were applicable for other states:

The fact that Lithuania and other CEE states supported Washington was not their infantilism at all, but a result of a complex and even very painful calculation. The calculation was very complicated because this time, as never before, both the general public and many politicians realised that they had to choose from two evils, and all they needed to do was to decide which evil was the lesser one.... But in this concrete case, a greater evil would have been caused by Lithuania and other *countries turning their back on the USA and thus losing USA support for the accession to NATO.*

There is a consensus in East-central Europe about the central role of the United States in the international system. Consequently, none of the East-central European countries see lasting alternatives to the transatlantic link. Beyond this, East-central European countries owe a lot to the United States in fostering their liberation from Soviet rule. It is hence wrong to assume that Europe could be regarded an alternative to the Atlantic commitment.

At the same time, US relations with East-central Europe have evolved significantly since the end of the Cold War. During the two office terms of George W. Bush, relations have not been free of controversial matters. The United States has been quite demanding as far as the development of East-central European armed forces and their commitment to the Iraqi and Afghan theatres.

Since Russia has started to re-emerge in the world political scene, some East-central European countries have faced US pressure in their attitude vis-à-vis Russia. Here ends the commonality of the East-central European position, as some states of the region suffer from a security deficit due to their historical threat perception originating from Russia. Some of the Baltic states and Poland are certainly of the view that the security deficit can be addressed only, if necessary, with the active engagement of the United States. But other East-central European countries without lively threat perception (e.g. the Czech Republic, Hungary, Slovakia and Slovenia), have embarked upon strengthening their pro-European approach simultaneously with a careful distancing from some US positions. This is noticeable when they emphasize shared values rather than shared policies.

Furthermore, one must not underestimate the importance of democratic transformation in the region. Although international matters are far less central to these countries' political discourse than to those of large, well-established European democracies, emerging public opinion on these issues is beginning to influence agendas. The Iraq case and a few others have eroded the popularity of America in East-central Europe, with some impact upon the attitudes of governments. By the same token, a strongly pro-US policy could cause some problems, particularly in states which are lukewarm about US policies, like Bulgaria and Slovakia (German Marshall Fund 2007).

For all the above reasons, the Atlanticism of East-central Europe has become somewhat diluted. To put it differently, East-central Europe's Atlanticism is increasingly Europeanized (Raik and Palosaari 2004: 12–22).

Russia: the changing geopolitical emphasis

Second, through the EU enlargement to East-central Europe and the inclusion of countries familiar with the former Soviet area, the geopolitical emphasis of the EU has changed. The attention to that part of the world has increased in two senses: first, the intensity of reaction to developments perceived as threatening power relations and stability in Europe has been modified; second, the appreciation and support to positive developments, particularly to fostering democratization, has also been altered.

The accession of East-central Europe to the EU coincided with the increasingly self-assertive behaviour of Russia. Russia has been a highly divisive matter for the EU, but the division is not confined to the new members. Positions vary significantly among old member states as well, ranging from Germany to the United Kingdom. The particular importance that European great powers and many new member-states attribute to Moscow keeps the attention of the entire EU focused. It is a shared objective of the EU to avoid a new division of Europe. Some, like Bulgaria, Hungary and Slovakia, are more in favour of socializing Moscow; others, like Estonia, Lithuania and Poland, would rather exert some pressure on it and apply conditionality. The new member-states, of which four share common land borders with the Ukraine, one with Moldova and three with Belarus, are understandably in favour of fostering democratic transformation and development in the western part of the newly independent states. Lithuania and Poland made an exemplary contribution to reconciliation during the 'Orange revolution' in the Ukraine. Since then, and the transformation in Georgia, a number of East-central European countries continue to foster positive processes and contribute to socio-economic development in that region. It is notable, however, that for the new member-states, the European Neighbourhood Policy (ENP) means primarily the eastern dimension of the neighbourhood. This may complicate relations with those old EU members, which intend to pay more attention and allocate larger resources to the North Africa–Middle East dimension of the ENP, not to mention with any country that wants to establish an EU–Mediterranean Union.

Commitment to human rights

Third, the new democracies are committed to the respect for human rights, and do their utmost to avoid any collision concerning national minorities. Those countries, which host national minorities of non-EU nations (like Estonia, Latvia, Poland) are in an easier position than those which host them from other EU member-states (e.g. Romania and Slovakia).

It was the expectation of the EU that new members would not 'import' conflicts into the organization. Yet it would have been an illusion to require that only 'conflict-free' countries could join the EU. It has been expected that peaceful conflict resolution in concord with established international norms be sought. A few years after accession, new members do have a number of pending conflicts. Their causes range from territorial disputes to state recognition, the treatment of national minorities or trade. Although their sources differ, they have one feature in common: namely the fact that the conflicts are not pending with other EU countries but with non-members. Territorial disputes include the one between Slovenia and Croatia as well as between Romania and Ukraine on the continental shelf of the Snake Island (submitted to the International Court of Justice). The question of state recognition, and several matters stemming from it, lies between the Republic of Cyprus and Turkey. A dispute on the treatment of national minorities emerged between Hungary and Serbia. Between 2006 and the beginning of 2008, Poland and the Russian Federation had a highly publicized dispute concerning Russia's ban on importing Polish meat products linked with the application of veterinary standards. The latter dispute had repercussions for the EU as it could not open negotiations with Moscow on the accord to replace the Partnership and Cooperation Agreement. In spite of the complexity of the case and the rhetoric of the Polish leadership, the EU demonstrated solidarity and has indicated to Moscow that member states, old and new alike, can rely on each other and take advantage of it.

The impact of the enlargement on third pillar activities

Finally, one area where eastern enlargement has resulted in major changes is the third pillar of the EU structure, dealing with the area of freedom, security and justice. This is the area where the largest proportion of new *acquis communautaire* has been adopted recently and where approximately twenty per cent of the new rules fall. Enlargement had a major impact in this field with 11 new members controlling parts of the external border of the EU.[12] It was clear in this area that the new members did not intend to spend a long time on the EU periphery and would like the full *acquis* to apply to them. However, bearing in mind the differences in economic development between old and new members, old members felt that the free movement of persons had to remain subject to temporary limitations,[13] and derogations were introduced for the first seven years of membership. Although most old members have lifted or at least eased them, they are still in force in two states (Austria and Germany). The new members could not immediately join the Schengen area, and the so-called Schengen border control was therefore maintained vis-à-vis them until late 2007 (roads and railroads) or early 2008 (air traffic). In 2008, except for three countries (Bulgaria, Romania and Cyprus), the benefits of the Schengen regime apply.

It means, however, that eight new members patrol the external Schengen border. Substantial financial assistance had fostered the new members' preparation for Schengen accession. The allegedly lax control on some new external borders has resulted in a situation that some older members dependent on the border patrol activity of some new members have set up mobile border control units inside their own territory (Williamson 2008). Many of the concerns go back to the high level of corruption endemic in some new member states. This fact will certainly make member states think twice before they extend the Schengen area to Bulgaria and Romania. In Bulgaria, though corruption is on a somewhat lower level than in Romania, the problem is exacerbated by organized crime (European Commission 2007a: 5/13/19). In Romania, the corruption issue, in conjunction with sluggish judicial reform, carries enormous dangers (European Commission 2007b: 2). Experience and data show the difference between various East-central European countries, raising the question whether enlargement can continue irrespective of the further 'gradual' difference in performance.

Looking into the future

Between EU enlargement fatigue and the unreadiness of aspirant countries

Although a large part of EU and NATO eastern enlargement has already taken place, the process is far from complete. The EU has promised prospective enlargement to the Western Balkans. At the Thessaloniki European Summit in 2003, the European Council (2003: point 40) 'reiterated the determination to fully and effectively support the European perspective of the Western Balkan countries, which will become an integral part of the EU, once they meet the established criteria'. Slovenia joined in 2004, Croatia is negotiating its membership, whereas Macedonia has had candidate status since late 2006. Doubts have lately emerged concerning the sincerity of this promise. It would be false to present the perceived slowdown of the enlargement process as hesitation stemming exclusively from the internal problems of the EU. The debacle of the European Constitution, and France's willingness to subject further enlargements to referenda,[14] have contributed to such an impression. However, several countries of the Western Balkans are far from membership. Some of them have unconsolidated statehood, like Bosnia and Herzegovina. Their level of grassroot integration is often far less EU-focused than most members that joined in 2004 and 2007, and their record on corruption and fighting organized crime is unconvincing. This is increasingly scrutinized in light of the poor performance of some recent accession states, like Bulgaria and Romania. In sum, the EU has to contemplate whether it gives priority to stabilization through membership prospects or it leaves more time for some countries of the region to sort their problems and catch up before accession.

Turkey is the country that has the longest lasting record of approaching the European Union. It is a highly complex relationship full of prejudices and not fully pronounced opinions. In this, the performance of Turkey as a candidate country appears less often than it should. It would be premature to conclude whether Turkey will ever become a member of the EU or will have to live with some privileged/special status short of membership. Whether the decision will be based on the dynamism of Turkey's economic and political development or due to the religious and cultural identity of the candidate remains to be seen. It is interesting to see that none of the new EU members speak out against Turkey's membership prospects in the outright negative terms used by members of the German and the French leadership. The new members know that prospective membership was a major boost to their transformation and they do not want Turkey to be deprived of it.

The prospects for NATO enlargement are different. Although NATO has not made a general commitment similar to the EU, its Western Balkans enlargement is well underway. Following the NATO accession of Slovenia, the invitation of Croatia and Albania to negotiate their membership and join the Alliance at the Bucharest Summit was a logical continuation of the process. The fact that Macedonia could not be invited to NATO, due to Greece's veto over the name of its northern neighbour, has demonstrated a reality of post-Cold War international politics. Contrary to the Cold War era, when the antagonism with another alliance created strong cohesion within NATO, it is nowadays possible to sacrifice matters of high importance for a marginal reason.

The issue of further eastern enlargements are just as highly divisive. There is no shortage of EU candidates, although most of them are extremely distant as far as their socio-economic transformation to qualify for membership. NATO is in a different situation as there are only two candidates in the former Soviet area which have indicated their willingness to join the organization. The advancement of both Georgia and Ukraine to join the Membership Action Plan (MAP) and then join the Alliance as members was blocked at the April 2008 Bucharest summit by Germany and France (and tacitly by several other NATO members) (Gebauer 2008a). Even though the matter may be reconsidered, as planned, there is a marked difference of approach between the United States and some European states (Gebauer 2008b). Namely, the United States is still ready to upset the status quo and disregard some opposite interests in these cases, primarily those of Russia who opposes NATO's continued expansion east. More importantly, the United States does not weigh the risk involved in integrating a state, specifically Georgia, experiencing problems of territorial integrity that could implicate Article 5 (collective defence), in the same way as other member states for whom such an accession presents important considerations.

Both institutions react sensitively when faced with hesitation by countries. During the last decade, states that could get closer to EU and NATO were enthusiastic about the prospect of membership. The EU, understandably, reacted strongly when Serbia voiced its reservations concerning a new Stabilization and Association Agreement due to the widespread recognition of the independent statehood of Kosovo. Likewise, some NATO countries have remained hesitant when they noticed the lukewarm domestic support in Ukraine for a possible accession to the Alliance. In sum, it is clear that the enlargement process of the two institutions has not slowed due mainly to the hesitation of their members; the absence of performing and fully committed candidates is also among the reasons. The coincidence of an incomplete transformation of several recent accession countries, the temporary setback in the internal development of the EU, enlargement fatigue due to the often unconvincing performance of new members and the gradual exhaustion of the list of promising candidates taken together seem to have resulted in a loss of early enlargement prospects. It is open to question whether there is a chance to re-energize the process, moreover whether the far-off prospect of membership motivates potential candidates to embark upon or continue painful adaptation.

Conclusion

The post-Cold War enlargements of the European Union and NATO have been the most successful policy of the two institutions. They have changed a region that has been exposed to evolving political agendas and shifting institutional arrangements since the disappearance of the area's empires at the end of World War I. They have anchored East-central Europe in the West. This is a change of historical magnitude.

This change could result in European unification; at least this could be the reasonable expectation of old and new democracies, alike. However, it is clear now that there is at least one state in Europe, which is reluctant to accept post-Cold War power relations and the dominance of the West. Hence that country, the Russian Federation, resists junior partner status and insists on retaining a sphere of influence on its perimeter. As a consequence, European unification will remain partial and there will be two 'centres' with different state-building experiences. This has remained more visible in NATO's extension than in the enlargement of the EU. It is premature to state that this has resulted in a new division of Europe. Russia, despite its current self-perception, is not in the position to challenge the current international system globally or create a systemic division between two parts of Europe.

Furthermore, the enlargement of the EU has somewhat lost its dynamism since the middle of the first decade of the twenty-first century. This has not been due exclusively to internal processes in the European Union but also to the partial transformation of candidate countries, and to the somehow unconvincing performance of some recent accession countries. Consequently, and increasingly, difficult cases appear on the enlargement agenda, and the consensus that once surrounded eastern enlargement in the EU has evaporated.

These two factors could have some bearing upon other organizations of European security, in particular the Organization for Security and Co-operation in Europe (OSCE).[15] The 'Russia factor' has had a much larger impact upon the OSCE than EU and NATO enlargements to the East. Russia's 'going its own way' meant that European unification around EU and NATO will have become impossible for a long time to come. Thus the OSCE could regain its long forgotten role to mediate between groups of countries representing divergent positions. However, this has not been realized, partly due to lukewarm Western interest in that organization. The fact that approximately half of the OSCE's 56 participating states now belong to the EU and NATO has not brought about a fundamental change as the new members have long coordinated their positions with the West at the OSCE. Consequently, the difference is reflected in formal member-ship rather than in change of position on substance in the OSCE.

As far as the performance of new members in the two organizations is concerned, we have seen that it is uneven. New members are not systematic-ally lagging behind their older counterparts, yet their performance has not been sufficiently convincing to boost the continuation of enlargement.

Interestingly, some states are far behind fulfilling the promises made during the accession process, and are certainly less receptive of advice than they were before accession. This may lead both the institutions and their members to conclude that it is preferable for aspirant states to meet most accession requirements before joining.

The enlargements of the EU and NATO have unquestionably and remark-ably affected the geopolitics of Europe. Membership has meant improved security, economic development, alliance building, etc., but has also reflected the vulnerability associated with growing pains – porous borders, discon-tented neighbours, the challenge of increased diversity, power struggles, imbalanced development, etc. The new member states of the EU and NATO have undoubtedly shifted from policy-takers to policy-shapers, some less dra-matically than others, but having gained a place at the table of these organi-zations and hence an increased voice, they confirm that the unification of Europe will continue along its bumpy road for some time to come.

Notes

1 For the purposes of this chapter, the countries of East-central Europe include the Czech Republic, Hungary, Poland, Slovakia, Estonia, Latvia and Lithuania.

2 According to the so-called corruption perception index of Transparency Inter-national (2007), many East-central European EU and NATO members are measurably more corrupt than the 'old' members of the two organizations.

3 This is demonstrated by the repeated appeals of European leaders to discuss the borders of Europe. See Tardy's introduction to this volume; see also Prodi, 2002 and Sarkozy, 2007.

4 The PHARE (Poland and Hungary Assistance with Reconstructing the Economy) programme originally addressed only the two leading reform countries.
5 Among which eight are from Eastern Europe (Czech Republic, Estonia, Hungary, Latvia, Lithuania, Poland, Slovakia, Slovenia), the other two being Malta and Cyprus.
6 Czech Republic, Estonia, Hungary, Latvia, Lithuania, Poland, Slovakia, and Slovenia.
7 Celeste Wallander is of the view that non-performing members of NATO should be obliged to leave the Alliance – certainly a self-defeating idea (Wallander 2002).
8 The position paper of Slovenia consisted of 64 words, including the title.
9 The only new member-state that does not participate in a Battle Group is Malta.
10 For up to date information on the recognition of Kosovo's independence go to www.kosovothanksyou.com/.
11 For the evolution of East-central European attitudes to the Iraq conflict, see Dunay in Giessmann, 2004.
12 The only country that has no external EU border is the Czech Republic which is fully surrounded by other member states.
13 The two eastern extension rounds increased the population of the EU by more than 20 per cent (approximately 105 million persons); the 12 new member states actually added less than 6 per cent to the total combined GDP of the EU.
14 Except for countries which had already embarked upon negotiating their membership at the time the law was modified.
15 See Ghebali's chapter in this volume.

References

Bebler, A. (1999) *The Challenge of NATO Enlargement*, Westport: Praeger Publishers.
Bucharest (2008) 'Summit Declaration issued by the Heads of State and Government participating in the meeting of the North Atlantic Council in Bucharest on 3 April 2008'. Press Release PR/CP(2008)049.
Cottey, A. (2004) 'The Iraq war: the enduring controversies and challenges' in *SIPRI Yearbook 2004: Armaments, Disarmament and International Security*, Oxford: Oxford University Press, pp. 67–93.
Dunay, P. (2004) 'Hungary', in Giessmann (2004), pp. 147–179.
European Commission (1997) 'Agenda 2000: For a stronger and wider Union', *Bulletin of the European Union*, Supplement 5/1997.
—— (2006) 'Enlargement, two years after – an economic success', Communication from the Commission to the Council of 3 May 2006. Online, available at http://europa.eu/scadplus/leg/en/lvb/e50026.htm (accessed 25 May 2008).
—— (2007a) 'Report from the Commission to the European Parliament and the Council on Bulgaria's progress on accompanying measures following accession', COM(2007) 377 final, Brussels, 27 June.
—— (2007b) 'Report from the Commission to the European Parliament and the Council on Romania's progress on accompanying measures following accession', COM(2007) 378 final, Brussels, 27 June.
European Council (1992) Conclusions of the Presidency, Doc/92/3, 27 June. Online, available at http://europa.eu/rapid/pressReleasesAction.do?reference=DOC/92/3&format=HTML&aged=1&language=EN&guiLanguage=en (accessed 25 May 2008).

—— (1993) 'Accession criteria', Copenhagen.

—— (2003) Presidency Conclusions, Thessaloniki, 19 and 20 June, 11638/03.

European Union (2006) 'Consolidated Versions of the Treaty on European Union and of the Treaty Establishing the European Community', *Official Journal of the European Union*, C 321E/1, 29 December.

Gebauer, M. (2008a) 'NATO verspricht Georgien und Ukraine Aufnahme in ferner Zukunft', *Der Spiegel*, 3 April. Online, available at www.spiegel.de/politik/ausland/0,518,545145,00.html (accessed 25 May 2008).

—— (2008b) 'NATO Notrettung für den Gipfelverlierer', *Der Spiegel*, 3 April. Online, available at www.spiegel.de/politik/ausland/0,1518,545178,00.html (accessed 25 May 2008).

German Marshall Fund of the United States (2007) 'Transatlantic Trends: What new democracies share, and don't'. Online, available at http://blog.gmfus.org/2007/09/20/transatlantic-trends-what-new-democracies-share-and-don't (accessed 25 May 2008).

Giessmann, H.-J. (2004) (ed.) *Security Handbook 2004*, Baden-Baden: Nomos Verlag.

Gyurcsány, F. (2007) Address at the Ministry of Foreign Affairs for the Republic of Hungary, 9 May. Online, available at www.miniszterelnok.hu/mss/alpha?do=2&pg=2&st=1&m10_doc=956 (accessed 25 May 2008).

Kamp, K.-H. (2006) 'NATO-Enlargement After the Riga Summit', *Analysen und Argumente aus der Konrad-Adenauer-Stiftung*, No. 32/2006.

Kosovo Perspective (2006) 'Romania for Kosovo within Serbia', 33, 22 December.

Müller-Brandeck-Bocquet, G. (2006) *The Future of the European Foreign, Security and Defence Policy after Enlargement*, Baden-Baden: Nomos.

NATO (1949) *The North Atlantic Treaty*, Washington, D.C., 4 April. Online, available at www.nato.int/docu/basictxt/treaty.htm (accessed 25 May 2008).

—— (1990) 'London Declaration on a Transformed North Atlantic Alliance', issued by the Heads of State and Government participating in the meeting of the North Atlantic Council, London, 5–6 July. Online, available at www.nato.int/docu/comm/49–95/C900706a.htm (accessed 25 May 2008).

—— (1995) 'The Study on NATO Enlargement'. Online, available at www.nato.int/docu/basictxt/enl-9502.htm (accessed 25 May 2008).

—— (1996) 'Final Communiqué issued at the Ministerial Meeting of the North Atlantic Council'. Press Communiqué, M-NAC-2 (96–165). Online, available at www.nato.int/docu/pr/1996/p96–165e.htm (accessed 25 May 2008).

—— (2007) 'Defence expenditures as % of gross domestic product', p. 7. Online, available at www.nato.int/docu/pr/2007/p07–141.pdf (accessed 25 May 2008).

Prodi, R. (2002) 'A Wider Europe – A Proximity Policy as the Key to Stability', Speech. Online, available at http://ec.europa.eu/external_relations/news/prodi/sp02_619.htm (accessed 25 May 2008).

Raik, K. and Palosaari, T. (2004) 'It's the Taking Part that Counts: The New Member States Adapt to EU Foreign and Security Policy', *FIIA Report*, 10/2004.

Salonius-Pasternak, C. (ed.) (2007) 'From Protecting Some to Securing Many: NATO's Journey from a Military Alliance to a Security Manager', *FIIA Report*, 17/2007.

Sarkozy, N. (2007) Visit to Bulgaria by Nicolas Sarkozy, President of France, Sofia, 4 October. Online, available at www.ambafrance-uk.org/President-Sarkozy-in-Sofia.html (accessed 25 May 2008).

Sikorski, R. (2008) Speech at the 44th Munich Conference on Security Policy, 9 February. Online, available at www.securityconference.de/konferenzen/rede.php?menu_2008=&menu_konferenzen=&sprache=en&id=206& (accessed 25 May 2008).

Transparency International (2007) 'Corruption Perception Index 2007'. Online, available at www.transparency.org/policy_research/surveys_indices/cpi/2007 (accessed 25 May 2008).

Vilnius Group (2003) Statement of the Vilnius Group Countries, in 'From Copenhagen to Brussels. European defence: Core documents', *Chaillot Papers 67*, Brussels: EU Institute for Security Studies, p. 345.

Vitkus, G. (2006) 'Three Western Myths about Security and Defence Policy of the EU New Member States: Lithuania's Case', in Müller-Brandeck-Bocquet, G. (ed.), *The Future of ESDP after Enlargement*, Baden Baden: Nomos.

Wall Street Journal (2003) 'United We Stand. Eight European leaders are as one with President Bush', 30 January.

Wallander, C. (2002) 'NATO's Price: Shape Up or Ship Out', *Foreign Affairs*, 81(6): 2–8.

Williamson, H. (2008) 'Illegal migrants surge as border checks are lifted', *Financial Times*, 11 January.

5   Europe and Russia
From strategic dissonance to strategic divorce?

Graeme P. Herd

Introduction

The idea of Europe represents an amalgam of three overlapping but not mutually exclusive notions – as territory, as a set of particular norms and values, and as a post-modern political construct. In territorial terms Europe stretches from the Atlantic to the Urals. At the same time, the majority of states, elites and societies on this territory have assimilated and acculturated democratic liberal norms and values. Third, it can also be considered as an entity that finds expression as the first truly postmodern political form, a new type of polity, a civilian power, 'zone of affluence' instead of 'zone of influence', given full expression through the European Union (EU). Given these overlapping understandings, how does Russia relate to 'Europe'?

Russia represents the largest European state by population and landmass/territory west of the Urals. However, it has constructed its own notion of political and social identity through creation of its own national ideology ('sovereign democracy') and although it has developed 'strategic partnerships' with both the EU and NATO, it has professed little desire to integrate into the EU and perceives NATO to be expansionist, and little removed from the Cold War stereotype of 'aggressive bloc'.

Nevertheless, during the transatlantic trauma of 2002–03 Russia appeared to be a key European voice, playing a leading role as part of the Paris–Berlin–Moscow axis in opposition to military intervention without a UN resolution. This axis made more apparent an emerging trend – Russia's reassertion as an international global player with its United Nations Security Council (UNSC) veto power, G8 membership, independent strategic nuclear deterrent, geographical landmass and 'energy superpower' status.

The transatlantic divisions and tensions were of such a serious nature that analysts and policy-makers warned of the dangers of strategic divorce, and the necessity of strategic renewal. Strategic divorce suggests a Europe in which duplication of functions and confusion over roles, missions and duties within and between NATO and the EU are rampant. Strategic realignment suggests that a complementary division of labour, responsibility and resources has been brokered, allowing the most efficient means to be deployed towards agreed strategic ends. Strategic dissonance appears to fall between these two extremes: the lasting solutions implied by strategic realignment fail to characterise European space, but neither does the complete breakdown engendered by strategic divorce. Instead, post-2003, a fluid environment replete with uneasy compromises has emerged, one that manages rather than addresses the contradictions and tensions between strategic means and ends across the Atlantic and within Europe.

For Russia, transatlantic strategic dissonance looked set to pay dividends, measured in power and influence in and over issues of strategic concern between Europe and Russia: a divided West would by default emphasise a renewed sense of Russian clarity of purpose in international affairs under President Putin. It provided Russia the leverage necessary to maximise efforts to attain its foreign policy goals, not least, the consolidation of Russia as a major power, with a gravitational role in the international system, able to independently determine its direction (Rumer 2007). The very weakness of the concept of a 'global war on terror' becomes its greatest strength for Russia: the inherent ambiguities embodied by this 'war' provided Russia with an ideological pretext for strategic realignment with the United States. At the same time, the disparities within the Euro-Atlantic security community provided an opportunity for President Putin to pick and choose which of the core values and interests of a divided transatlantic community Russia shares. In short, President Putin faced a near perfect strategic context within which to engage with the United States and Europe and reassert Russian national interest. Russia's role as an active rather than passive participant, leader not joiner and a forceful voice on the major strategic issues of the day was best served by such a strategic environment. How, then, have European–Russian relations evolved since 2002–03 and what does this evolution suggest for European security and the state of transatlantic relations?

This chapter argues that Russian relations with Europe prove extremely problematic. In retrospect, while 2002–03 was the low point in transatlantic harmony, it represented the high point in Russian influence in European security affairs. Bilateral relations with the United Kingdom, Germany, France, Lithuania, Estonia and Poland all deteriorated, as did the strategic partnerships with the EU and NATO, even as US popularity also continued its decline. Russia and Europe still cooperated in a number of areas but competition also stiffened, as did issues that could lead to potential conflict. Ballistic Missile Defence (BMD), the status of Kosovo, a moratorium on Russian Conventional Forces in Europe (CFE) obligations, energy dependence, the domestic nature of the Russian regime and the Georgia crisis stand out as milestones in a deteriorating relationship between Russia and Europe. The Georgia crisis in particular managed to fuse political, military and economic sources of insecurity and so represented a more serious divergence in identity, ideas, institutions and interests between Russia and

Europe that suggest European–Russian strategic dissonance has now reached a tipping-point and risks the dangers of strategic divorce.

Deteriorating European–Russian relations after Iraq

Four Europes

The consequences and implications for European security and transatlantic relations of the 2003 Iraq war were more visible than its causes: the transatlantic and intra-European rifts fractured along pre-existing transatlantic fault lines and consolidated realignments around concepts of 'Atlantic Europe', 'Core Europe', 'New Europe', and 'Non-aligned Europe'. These four Europes are not coherent entities, still less consolidated blocs, but rather strategic default positions around which states tended to coalesce depending on which issue the transatlantic security community addresses (Forsberg and Herd 2006). It is within a context of this resultant transatlantic strategic dissonance that Europe now relates to Russia.

The United Kingdom (with the US–UK 'special relationship') can be considered the *primus inter pares* of 'Atlantic Europe', a group that included the Netherlands, Denmark, Spain, Italy and Portugal at the time of the Iraq war. These states were all represented in the coalition of the willing in Iraq, giving political and military support to the US forces that led the invasion. Germany, France, and Belgium are all examples of 'Core Europe' or 'Old Europe': Germany's Chancellor Schroeder articulated an anti-war position earlier than President Chirac of France, despite the fact that it had traditionally aligned itself with the Atlanticist camp. Poland, Romania and Bulgaria and the other post-communist new EU and NATO member states illustrated well the foreign policy perspectives 'New Europe' brought with it.[1] The majority of the 'Vilnius 10' states[2] were prepared to integrate into a common Euro-Atlantic defence culture and give strategic political and military support to the United States alongside 'Atlantic Europe'. They supported the United States primarily because they felt greater dependence on rather than fear of US global hegemony. The events and consequences of 9/11 also impacted on the security strategies of 'Non-aligned Europe', that is, Finland, Sweden, Ireland and Austria. None of these states joined the coalition that invaded Iraq, but neither did they align themselves with 'Core Europe'. Rather, they developed a policy of equidistance between 'Atlantic Europe' and 'Core Europe' in an effort to develop a post-9/11 expression of the concept of non-alignment.

The 'four Europes' against Russia

Russian relations with some individual EU and NATO members deteriorated after the Paris–Berlin–Moscow axis dissolved with the invasion of Iraq. In retrospect, this proved to be the high-point in Russian influence over European responses to US-led strategic gambits. The tit-for-tat expulsions of Russian and then UK diplomats in London and Moscow following the 'Litvinenko Affair' and Russia's refusal to extradite Andrei Lugovoi, accused by British prosecutors of poisoning Alexander Litvinenko in July 2006 (with radioactive polonium-210), signalled the lowest point of UK–Russian relations since the end of the Cold War.[3] Just as Russian relations with 'Atlantic Europe' deteriorated, so too did they with 'Core Europe'. German–Russian relations under Chancellor Angela Merkel are currently more confrontational than under Chancellor Schroeder, who had initiated the St Petersburg Dialogue process in 2000 as part of his *Ostpolitik*, supported pro-Russia economic policy positions within the EU, and who now sits on the board of Gazprom, the Russian energy giant. Chancellor Merkel does still stress the importance of economic interests, but also emphasises human rights, participatory democracy and the rule of law and appears less willing to accept bilateral deals at the perceived expense of new NATO and EU member states. Although President Sarkozy has characterised France as a 'privileged partner of Russia' (Sarkozy 2007) in bilateral relations and described Europe and Russia as 'natural partners', he also condemned Russian 'brutality' in its energy dominance of Central and Eastern Europe and signalled a greater willingness to join NATO military structures, so boosting the transatlantic alliance. In addition, and in contrast to Russia (and China), France has moved closer to the US position on Iran, supporting a harsher UNSC sanctions regime. 'Non-aligned Europe' has fractured in its appreciation of and approach to Russia. Austrian Defence Minister Norbert Darabos joined Moscow in labelling US Ballistic Missile Defence plans a 'provocation' that 'rekindles Cold War debates' (Reuters 2007). By contrast, Finnish Defence Minister Jyri Häkämies delivered a strongly worded speech on Russia: 'The three most important security challenges from Finland's point of view are Russia, Russia and Russia' (Häkämies 2007). 'New Europe' relations with Russia have also suffered post-NATO and EU enlargement in 2004. Polish–Russian relations deteriorated in 2005–07, the period in which Lech and Jaroslaw Kaczynski served as president and prime minister respectively: Russia boycotted Polish meat and plant exports and Poland retaliated by blocking the new EU–Russia Partnership Cooperation Agreement and threatened to veto Russian entry into the World Trade Organization. Following the relocation of a Soviet-era war memorial from central Tallinn in 2007, Kremlin-sponsored youth groups attacked the Estonian Embassy in Moscow and blockaded border posts, while Russia cut oil flows through Estonian transit ports and orchestrated a cyber-attack on Estonian web-sites. Romanian President Basescu somewhat dramatically stated: 'Europe's dependence on Russian gas monopoly Gazprom ... could be the biggest threat to the region since the former Soviet Union's army' (Basescu 2006). Swedish foreign minister Carl Bildt noted that new EU and NATO member states have hardened relations between these two institutions and Russia: 'They are moving towards the mainstream or the mainstream is moving towards them ... And that's been driven by the rhetoric of Moscow to a very large extent' (Dombey 2007: 4).

These examples of deteriorating relations with states from each of the four Europes do not in and of themselves fully explain the current low point in Europe–Russia relations. They do, though, rest on a series of more worrying structural imbalances that are more threatening to the longer term relationship, including fundamental disagreements between Russia and the EU and NATO, as well as EU and NATO member states represented in the OSCE.

Initial hopes with and within NATO

In the early 1990s, the Russia–NATO 'mood music' was in sharp contrast to the discordant claxon Cold War sounds of 'evil empire' and 'aggressive bloc'. However, this optimistic perception of Russia's national interest was undercut by rising Russian nationalism and disillusionment with demo-cratic reforms in the early and middle 1990s. NATO helped to reduce tensions with Russia by establishing the Founding Act of March 1997 and the Permanent Joint Council (PJC). The Founding Act signified 'an endur-ing political commitment undertaken at the highest political level ... [to] build together a lasting and inclusive peace in the Euro-Atlantic area on the principles of democracy and cooperative security' (NATO 1997). Political cooperation between NATO and Russia in the framework of the PJC ulti-mately failed. The PJC consultation process was fragile, functioning as a forum in which Russia was informed about NATO's decisions but had little ability to influence them. In addition, NATO argued that Russia had not explored all possibilities and avenues of cooperation with its programmes. As a result, when Russia froze cooperation with NATO during the Kosovo campaign, many informed analysts predicted that it would take a long time to mend broken relations (Antonenko 1999–2000; Arbatova 2000).

The main impetus for an improved relationship between NATO and Russia was the election of Vladimir Putin as president in 2000 and his readiness to readjust Russia's strategic interests and orientation. The events of 9/11 further consolidated strategic realignment with the West, providing it with substance in the form of partnership in the global anti-terror coalition (Bosworth 2002; Hunter 2003). The NATO–Russia Rome Declaration on a 'New Quality of Relations' (approved 28 May 2002) established the NATO–Russia Council (NRC). The NRC held monthly ambassadorial meetings under the chairmanship of the NATO secretary general, and aimed to 'work out common positions, taking common decisions and carrying common or coordinated actions whenever possible' (Danilov 2005: 80). Cooperation in anti-terrorist efforts and in halting nuclear proliferation, as well as drug trafficking in Afghanistan, has been the result. However, most assessments argue that Russian influence within the NRC is marginal (Adomeit 2007: 31).

For all this positive account, a number of points of tension between NATO and Russia exist. Levels of trust have not increased significantly: Russia's wider national political and military security apparatus and strategic establishment had always perceived NATO as more aggressive than defensive and this attitude is now mainstream, articulated by President Putin himself. Russia perceives that NATO has repeatedly broken a series of promises regarding BMD, CFE and NATO 'expansion', and has since 2003 begun to more forcibly articulate and secure its national interest. The possibility that Ukraine and Georgia would be invited to join the Membership Action Plan at the April 2008 NATO Bucharest Summit drew a sharp response from President Putin, who declared that Russia would be 'forced' to target its missiles at Ukraine were NATO bases to appear on its territory. At Bucharest, despite US pressure, Ukraine and Georgia were not given MAP status – in the words of French Prime Minister Francois Fillon: 'We oppose Georgian and Ukrainian accession [to MAP] because we believe that this is not the right answer in terms of balance of power in Europe and between Europe and Russia' (Fillon 2008).

CFE Treaty and Ballistic Missile Defence (BMD): the broken promises

A very contentious Russia–NATO dispute exists in arms control, the cornerstone of European security in the post-Cold War era. After NATO's enlargement of 2004, it was unclear whether the Baltic states would join the CFE Treaty, a Soviet era treaty signed in 1990, which set equal limits for East and West in Europe from the Atlantic Ocean to the Ural Mountains 'on key conventional armaments essential for conducting surprise attacks or initiating large-scale offensive operations' (CFE 2002). This treaty was revised at the November 1999 Istanbul summit – *Adaptation of the Treaty on Conventional Armed Forces in Europe* (also known as the 'Adapted CFE' treaty). This revision set national rather than bloc-based limits on conventional armed forces, taking into account the different geopolitical realities a decade after the end of the Cold War. However, NATO members would not ratify the adapted treaty until Russia withdrew forces and munitions from Transdniestria and Abkhazia, a condition which Russia found unacceptable (Russian Ministry of Foreign Affairs 2007).

At an Extraordinary Conference of States Parties to the Treaty on Conventional Forces in Europe, a Russian initiative hosted in Vienna in June 2007, Russia demanded the treaty be rewritten, and failing this, President Putin announced the suspension of Russian CFE obligations on 15 July 2007 effective 150 days later (13 December 2007).

In 2002 the United States withdrew from the Anti-Ballistic Missiles treaty to enable the construction of a global missile defence system against the potential threat of limited attacks by 'rogue states' – essentially against possible future intercontinental ballistic missiles from Iran and North Korea.

Plans for a new US 'military footprint' or basing paradigm in Central and Eastern Europe and Central Asia after 9/11, and NATO air patrols over the Baltic states, added to tension in the NATO–Russia relationship.

In May 2007 President Putin had also threatened to target Russian missiles at European cities and on 14 July 2007 Russia then suspended its obligations under CFE, which took effect on 10 December 2007. On 17 August 2007 Putin declared permanent airborne security, following the resumption of TU-95 (strategic bombers) long-range missions skirting NATO airspace around Norway, the United Kingdom and Guam in the Pacific. In addition, Russia has stated its intention of initiating a $200 billion rearmament plan to modernise the Russian military, including developing the next generation of aircraft, a submarine base in the Pacific and new intercontinental missiles.

Russia opposition to proposed US BMD bases in the Czech Republic and Poland has been particularly strong. Russia criticised the unilateral nature of the decision and lack of consultations. It also argues that Iran is ten years from having the missile capability to target the United States and so, in the words of General Yuriy Baluyevskiy, Chief of the General Staff of the Russian Armed Forces: 'The Iranian Missile threat is hypothetical. It's not part of a catastrophic character and it does not require a quick deployment of missile defence sites' (AP 2007). Rather, the proposed anti-ballistic missile shield sites are viewed as Trojan horses aimed at weakening Russia's strategic nuclear deterrent. BMD, Russia argues, changes the strategic nuclear balance in Europe and will result in a loss of strategic parity for Russia. Russian Foreign Minister Sergei Lavrov characterised US plans to build a global missile defence shield an example of 'imperial thinking', and suggested that Washington was using the system to try to encircle Russia (Lavrov 2008).

President Putin at the G8 July 2007 Summit offered to share data collected at Gabala, a Russian early warning station in Azerbaijan, linking it to US systems to increase and expand capability. In response, the United States offered concessions to gain Russian support for the anti-ballistic missile shield. The shield would only be deployed if an Iranian threat, jointly determined, was imminent. Russian liaison officers could carry out inspections of the sites. In addition, the United States linked missile defence issue to two others – the final status of Kosovo and the CFE treaty – presenting Russia with what is, in effect, a grand bargain that would address strategic points of difference between Russia and the United States and Europe. Issues that were primarily addressed by the United States and NATO were now linked to issues which the EU had taken primacy, and this further complicated EU–Russia relations.

German Defence Minister Jung raised the possibility of resolving this dispute: 'we need to combine the US national planning on missile defence capability with NATO. The United States have submitted far-reaching proposals for constructive cooperation with Russia. This is a good basis for discussion' (Jung 2008). However, hopes for a 'Grand Bargain' between

Russia and the West are not likely to succeed. The linkage of the status of Kosovo to BMD, CFE and Iran appears thoughtful but fails on two grounds. If Russia accepts this linkage then it would signal that it privileges the institutions of NATO and EU over strong bilateral relations with key European state actors and the United States – so reversing Russia's preferred modus vivendi with Europe and the United States. If the West can actually link such disparate issues within a 'Grand Bargain', it would indicate that the United States and Europe are much more unified, coherent and realigned around agreed strategic ends and means. This would contradict the current realities of transatlantic and European strategic dissonance.

Russia and the EU: the clash of two diverging models

Historically, Russia's relationship with Europe has been characterised by ambiguity as to its status and identity. After the collapse of the Soviet Union, the desire to 'return to Europe' and westernise according to the prevailing Euro-Atlantic model of market democratic transition and then consolidation was strong, but most were prepared to argue that Russia was both a part of Europe and apart from Europe (Baranovsky 2001). In the 1990s the Europeanisation tendency in Russia became predominant, driven by Russian reliance on Western capital, technology, security, the *'Zapadniki Dreft'* (Western drift) of the Russian population and by the EU's growing energy dependence on Russia.

For Russians, as evidenced by public opinion polling, the EU has had a much more positive image than NATO. Whereas Russia objected to NATO's 'expansion', it welcomed the enlargement of the EU, even when three former Soviet Baltic republics (Estonia, Latvia and Lithuania) were integrated in the 'big bang' enlargement of 2004. The positive image of the EU was driven in part by the perception that it was primarily a civilian power. On balance its growing security role has been evaluated favourably in Moscow. For Russia, promotion of the ESDP was instrumental in its attempt to balance the United States and to fragment NATO's 'hegemony' in security policy. It reflected the continuity of Soviet and post-Soviet Russian foreign policy goals.

However, any prospect of effective EU counterbalance of US power (particularly hard power) would necessitate Russian–EU military, economic and political cooperation, and even integration. A growing number of tensions between Russia and the EU present obstacles to this outcome. The EU's concern at growing authoritarianism in Russia, weak Russia–EU integrative efforts, EU criticism of Russian human rights abuses in Chechnya and divergences in the two sides' understanding of 'Colour Revolutions' in post-Soviet space, as well as Kosovo's final status and EU energy dependence have all impacted negatively on the EU–Russia relationship. These points of conflict are symptomatic of a deeper divergence in Russia–EU relations concerning which values, norms and rules should predominate in what is increasingly becoming a shared neighbourhood. These ideational, identity and interest-based tensions continue to work against the possibility of establishing a wider European bloc, as opposed to simply an EU one, that could exert even a political and economic counterbalance of US power, let alone military counterbalance through Russia's support and promotion of ESDP as an alternative to NATO. Let us examine these points of conflict in greater detail, before addressing the divergent EU and Russian governance systems.

Chechnya as a receding source of tension

A more contentious issue, which has damaged EU–Russia political relations, has been the EU's response to Russian human rights abuses in Chechnya (Forsberg and Herd 2005). Despite the EU's occasional vociferous condemnation and the threatened and actual use of sanctions against Russia, the impact on Russian decision-making appears to have been meagre and to have generated little positive change in behaviour towards the conflict. The EU's policy failure was due to its lack of power resources, will and skill. The EU simply did not have any leverage or 'stick' that would have been big enough to beat Russia into order, nor were the 'carrots' sweet enough to tempt Russia to constrain its behaviour and risk the realisation of de facto Chechen independence. When the EU had to determine its order of priorities in the 1990s, *realpolitik* interests trumped the normative agenda of the Common Foreign and Security Policy. Because the EU wanted to prevent the Chechen issue from spilling over and 'contaminating' the rest of the EU–Russia policy agenda which would disrupt or stall co-operation, all leeway has hitherto been extended to Russia.

This basic approach was driven forward in ways that have generated short-term political capital for particular member states at the expense of undercutting the role, function and integrity of key EU institutions over the longer term. Indeed, the willingness of the EU member states to prioritise their bilateral relations and strategic interests in Russia over the integrity of a common EU approach is a key explanation for the ineffectiveness of EU policy towards Russia. Paradoxically, the very ineffectiveness of the EU policy recommended itself to national leaders. They could continue to promote it for domestic political reasons, safe in the knowledge that their bilateral strategic partnership with Russia would be preserved. In response to domestic pressure and criticism to react to human rights abuses in Chechnya, individual EU member states were able to refer their publics to EU statements of condemnation and concern (Haukkala 2000). As a result, and with the Chechenisation of the conflict under Putin, this issue has receded as a source of tension in EU–Russia relations.

Colour Revolutions: the West accused

Following the 'Rose Revolution' in Georgia (November 2003), the 'Orange Revolution' in Ukraine (November 2004), and the 'Tulip Revolution' in

Kyrgyzstan (March 2005), Russian analysts and politicians accused the United States and the EU (through support for NGOs and the activities of their embassies), as well as the OSCE and the Council of Europe, of 'manufacturing' and 'marketing' or 'exporting' democracy and revolution to the Commonwealth of Independent States (CIS) (Herd 2005). At the November 2004 Russia–EU summit, it was apparent that the two sides did not share the same interpretation of the validity of the electoral process for choosing the president in Ukraine. Visits by Javier Solana and two presidents of new EU member states, Alexander Kwasniewski of Poland and Valdas Adamskus of Lithuania, helped to persuade President Kuchma of Ukraine to allow an unprecedented second-round run-off in December 2004. In this election, the Russian-backed Yanukovych conceded defeat to Yushchenko.

The implications of these events for Russia's power and prestige are not contested. The Ukrainian presidential election has been interpreted in the Russian media in terms of a 'political Stalingrad', Russia's worst foreign policy defeat in the post-Soviet period. Russia's fear of Western-imported revolution, which gathered pace after the 'Orange Revolution' and then the 'Tulip Revolution', has heralded a new crackdown on critics and opponents and helped to justify and accelerate a clampdown on opposition groups in some CIS states, including Russia itself. NGOs, international organisations, diplomatic missions and independent trade unions are increasingly perceived to constitute threats to internal security. President Putin has stated: 'It is bad when such organizations [NGOs] are being used by one state against others to achieve some goals' (Charlton 2007). In response, laws on protest and referendums are being strengthened in Russia and independent trade unions, opposition leaders and their political parties are being squashed.

Russia's foreign and security policy is also influenced by this perception, and US, NATO and PfP military-to-military contacts are now scrutinised to a greater degree than hitherto, and the image of the West as an external enemy has been strengthened. The various revolutions along its periphery have reinforced Russia's criticism of the OSCE as an inherently western-biased organisation, in particular through its promotion of 'human dimension' activities.[4] Russia refuses to pay its share of the OSCE budget, has closed the OSCE assistance group to Chechnya and has broken the OSCE Istanbul Summit commitments agreed in 1999. Its integration, based on shared values, into the Euro-Atlantic security community is thus put into doubt by its responses to regime change, ones at variance with those of central and west European members of the OSCE. In late 2007 Russia significantly curtailed the number of OSCE monitors monitoring the December 2007 Russian Duma elections, as well as the March 2008 Presidential elections.

Energy security: Russia a superpower again

The EU and the United States represent the world's largest energy market, with 40 per cent of the world energy consumption in 2006 and, as such, are dependent on imported energy, much of which comes from Russia (Morelli 2006: 29). The EU Energy Charter Treaty of 1991 represented an attempt to develop a coordinated approach to energy policy and security. As Johnson (2005: 256) put it,

> Energy has long been at the heart of EU–Russian links and it has been a key factor in strengthening their formal and informal ties. This reflects both the EU's deteriorating energy supply situation and Russia's current and future energy supply potential.

Russia's gas giant Gazprom has a stake in 16 of the EU's 27 member states, with direct access to end-consumers in Italy, Germany and France (three of the biggest EU energy markets) and aims to control pipelines, build power plants and gas storage facilities in the EU in order to increase its market dominance from production to the point of sale. However, the reliability of Russian energy supplies has been brought into question by a series of energy-related disruptions over the last two years – from the gas war with Ukraine in 2006 to disruptions of oil supplies via Belarus in 2007 (see below). These events also focused attention on the nature of Russian energy production, and its relationship to Russian state interests and foreign policy. They significantly contributed to a growing western consensus that Russia employs non-transparent, monopolistic, coercive and imperialistic energy politics to expand political leverage over near neighbours and key EU states. Russian energy is now widely perceived to be a tool of Russian foreign and security policy and the issue of energy supplies to Europe firmly securitised (Rice 2006; Smith 2006).

In January 2006 Russia cut gas supplies to Ukraine, a major transit country for Russian gas to Europe, causing a brief drop in supplies. Russia argued that its move to a market-economy entails ending subsidies to Ukraine and charging market prices (Nichol *et al.* 2006). In January 2007 Russia increased the price of oil to Belarus, which again disrupted and jeopardised transit supplies to the EU, as one-fifth of Russian oil passes through Druzhba pipeline (1.8 million-barrels-a-day) connecting Russia to Poland, Germany and Slovakia. In response, the EU demanded an 'urgent and detailed' explanation from Moscow and Minsk. Although EU energy commissioner Andris Piebalgs stated that 'there is no immediate risk' to European consumers (as Germany had 130 days' worth of emergency reserves and Poland 70), unless a resolution was reached shortly, the EU and the International Energy Agency (IEA) would implement 'solidarity mechanisms' to share stocks (European Commission 2007).

These events have caused alarm in Europe and the United States, highlighting European strategic vulnerability and its possible consequences. Russia and the EU have failed to agree to a common strategy that is acceptable to both suppliers and receivers. For Russia 'energy security' means security of demand by foreign customers at high prices. For the EU, particularly Poland and Germany, energy security means dependable energy supplies from multiple and independent sources at low prices. The EU Energy Dialogue and energy review of January 2007 pledged that EU will 'speak with one voice to Russia' (Brower 2007). By the same token, the EU Parliament demanded that the EU speak with one voice on strategic energy matters, avoid bilateral deals and push in its relations with Russia for interdependence, transparency, reciprocity in market access, infrastructure and investment to avoid 'oligopolistic market structures and the political manipulation of the oil and gas supplies' (*European Report* 2007). However, EU energy companies are much more responsive to shareholder and customer pressure than EU directives and communiqués.

Ernest Wyciszkiewicz, energy expert at the Polish Institute for International Affairs, argues that EU energy policy should be coherent enough to prevent one member state posing a threat to another, while '[t]he EU member states differ in their perception of threats in terms of energy' (*European Report* 2007). This absence of shared threat perception amongst EU member states regarding Russian dominance of energy supplies makes it even more difficult to find consensus. As an EU official lamented: 'We know we should do something about Russia, but we don't know what. In the EU we negotiate on rules, whereas Russia wants to do deals' (*The Economist* 2007).

Finally, Russia insists its behaviour reflects normal commercial business practice of selling energy supplies to make money. The need to control pipelines is simply an effort to reduce its strategic vulnerability on unreliable transit states. However, US and European critics understand partly state-owned energy groups, such as Gazprom, as a sinister instrument of the Kremlin's attempts to use energy as a tool of foreign policy. A Swedish defence study argues that since 1991 there have been 55 cut-offs, or explicit threats or coercive price action by Russia. Of the 55 only 11 can be explained in purely market rather than political terms. (*The Economist* 2007) There is at least a visible correlation between the price at which Russia sells gas to its former satellites and their political loyalty to the Kremlin. In other words, access to Russian energy is determined more by support for Russian foreign policy than market forces.

Kosovo's final status: legitimate state versus dangerous precedent

On 17 February 2008 Kosovo unilaterally declared its independence, after a long series of negotiations. The final status of Kosovo had reached a diplomatic impasse in 2007, contributing to strained relations between the United States and the EU on the one hand, Russia on the other. These three together constituted the troika charged by the UN with resolving Kosovo's final status, after the plan by Martti Ahtisaari was presented in March 2007. On 10 December 2007, the troika came to the conclusion that no progress had been made towards an agreement between the Serbs and the Kosovars. Following the declaration of independence, the

United States and most EU member states recognised Kosovo as an independent state. For Russia, this created a dangerous precedent for other breakaway republics and reflected double standards (why would Kosovo be recognised but not Abkhazia, South Ossetia and Transdniestria?) In return and as a consequence, Russia promised to recognise the independence of Abkhazia, South Ossetia and Transdniestria, each of which has held their own referendum for independence. Such an outcome could destabilise the EU's near neighbourhood, including Macedonia and Bosnia and Herzegovina, boost Russian influence in South Eastern Europe, already strengthened by energy pipeline acquisitions, and lead to a crisis in Russia–EU relations.

While it was in Russia's interest to freeze the status quo in Kosovo and other breakaway republics as an additional means of maintaining its geopolitical leverage in post-Soviet space and the Balkans, after the declaration of independence, Russia was joined by Greece, Serbia, Slovakia and Spain, in its refusal to recognise this status. Though in a minority European position, Russia was not isolated, and was able to insist that international law and the sovereignty of the Republic of Serbia be upheld, appealing to international norms and bolstering its own promotion of the notion of 'sovereign democracy'.

The Georgia Crisis: a new Cold War?

On 7 August 2008 President Saakashvili ordered the use of heavy artillery, rockets and ground troops against the breakaway republic of South Ossetia in Georgia, in a bid to unify Georgia by force. Russia, accusing Georgia of 'genocide', declared a responsibility to protect its people, and sent troops, tanks and armoured personnel carriers to occupy both Abkhazia (220,000 people, of whom 70 per cent have Russian passports) and South Ossetia (80,000–90,000 people, of whom 90 per cent have Russian passports). Russian military forces created a buffer or security zone in Georgia proper, and despite an EU negotiated six-point ceasefire, refused to withdraw to pre-7 August positions, or allow OSCE or EU monitors access to the breakaway republics or buffer zones. On 26 August President Medvedev recognised the independence of the two breakaway republics – no European or even former Soviet republic stood with a diplomatically isolated Russia. Disputes over proportionate use of force, regime change and control of energy transit as undeclared strategic objectives, and compliance with UN and EU ceasefire resolutions and agreements, brought Russian–European relations to a new low. NATO froze relations with Russia, while some new NATO members called for rapid NATO membership of both Georgia and Ukraine. The US signed a BMD pact with Poland and reiterated commitments to defend Poland in case of attack. The EU suspended its Partnership Cooperation Agreement and at an emergency summit discussed, though did not institute, sanctions against Russia.

Explaining European–Russian strategic dissonance

EU governance is fundamentally different from that of the Russian Federation, creating not only obstacles to potential functional integration, but also gaps between cooperative capacities and complementarities in policy-implementation. The EU is subject to supranational and sub-national governance dynamics. In terms of economic governance, political processes and external relations, the EU represents a pre-Westphalia order characterised by 'overlapping authorities, divided sovereignty, diversified institutional arrangements, and multiple identities' (Zielonka 2006: 15). This creates a functional challenge for the Russian Federation. EU decisions can be made and implemented at the supranational, sub-state and/or trans-state regional levels, while Russia is wedded to exercising political decision-making in Moscow and to traditional bilateral or interstate relations. Furthermore, the EU's regional policy allows national governments to increase central control over regions in a number of ways: by tightening border accords; by encouraging regional sub-components (such as cities) to become involved in the centralisation process, though promoting Euro-regions; and by creating rapprochement between Russia and the EU. As a result, the Russian and EU systems of governance are at variance in terms of their decision-making process and political culture and also at a conceptual level, with no commonly held definitions of such basic political concepts as 'regions', 'regionalism', 'federalism', 'subsidiarity', 'frontier' and 'sovereignty'. Modern concepts of sovereignty and territorial integrity are much more important in Russia (and the United States) than in the EU.

In addition, the centralisation of political, economic, juridical, military and information power within Russia under Putin is widely perceived by the EU as detrimental to the preservation of democratic values, structures and institutions. President Putin has reversed the process of decentralisation under Yeltsin, which had been characterised by regional bloc formation on an incremental ad hoc basis rather than elite policy choices or strategy. In its place, Putin has instituted a new, vertical hierarchy of power with himself at the apex and power flowing through structures he has created and staffed by personnel he has appointed. Regional governors – and even the mayors of Moscow and St. Petersburg – are now appointed by the president rather than elected. Kremlin-financed, sponsored and orchestrated youth groups attack, bully and intimidate regime opponent and critics, with support of state-controlled media outlets. Estonia, for example, closed its consulate in Moscow after pro-Kremlin youth groups attempted to physically assault its Ambassador in protest at the relocation of a Soviet war memorial in Tallinn (BBC 2007). Strategic assets in Russia have been re-nationalised and are dominated by Putin's appointees. Many of these appointees now embedded in the bureaucracy are, like Putin himself, recruited directly from the opaque military or security services (*siloviki*). Former KGB executives and Presidential Administration officials run Gazprom. Transnefteprodukt (an oil product pipeline company) is run by Vladislav Surkov, Putin's chief advisor, while the new president Dmitry Medvedev remains Gazprom's chairman.

Putin has promoted the notion of 'sovereign democracy' as a means of legitimising the new political order – a regime one prominent critic has characterised as a 'broad anti-democratic counter-revolution' (Kovalev 2007). This doctrine argues that Russian domestic affairs are for Russians themselves to manage, and that external powers attempt to subvert Russian territorial integrity and sovereignty for their own interests and ends. The United States, NATO and the EU represent military attempts to encircle Russia and shift the strategic balance in Europe, as well as political and economic challenges to the independence of Russia as one of the few fully sovereign states in the world. Anti-Americanism, nationalism and social liberalisation plays well to the public gallery and effectively mobilises the population in support of the regime – but regime legitimation through an ability to withstand a combination of apparent indifference, condescension, and machinations of external enemies runs the danger of creating an inward-looking siege mentality in Russia. It also provides a dissonant strategic context that renders cooperative relations with Europe much harder to achieve.

A 'Power Audit of EU–Russia Relations' (Leonard and Popescu 2007) undertaken by the European Council of Foreign Relations (ECFR) argues that the EU lacks unity and as a consequence is unable to translate its comparative power into influence in its dealings with Russia. No single issue encapsulates how inherent weaknesses in EU policy-making process shapes the coherence of EU–Russia strategy, the role of disparate values *and* increasingly interests in shaping relations, and, the extent to which EU–Russian points of tensions become part of the EU–US agenda and help consolidate EU–US relations. The ability of an EU at 27 to establish a coherent policy towards Russia, a common energy strategy, is undercut by the national approach of member states who are willing to carry out bilateral deals with Russia and Russian interest in preventing a more coherent EU from evolving. EU member states understand energy policy to be the preserve and responsibility of member states rather than the EU. However, and paradoxically, securitisation of the energy sector has led to a greater awareness of the weaknesses of member state approaches and the need for a CFSP element in the EU energy policy-making process. Russia and EU policy disagreements extend beyond 'values' to include divergent interests, which are not exclusively mutual but rather can be conflicting. It is now an open question: does the weight of energy ties, geopolitical realities and good-neighbourliness still outweigh conflictual tendencies? Energy, as with Kosovo, CFE and BMD, has become a Euro-Atlantic rather than exclusively EU issue. Strategic energy cooperation was a topic at US–EU summits (e.g. Vienna, June 2006; Washington, April 2007) and as such has strengthened the cooperative transatlantic energy dialogue and helped the United

States and EU in the development of common strategies to provide for security of energy sources and supply. From a US perspective, if EU energy dependency on Russia weakens the EU's ability to deal with Russia on non-energy security issues then this constitutes a long term threat to transatlantic relations.

Conclusion: the failure to anchor European Russia in the political West

European (and US) relations with Russia during the post-Soviet period have been founded on the assumption that Russia's long-term strategic interests, identity and institutional preference is to integrate with the West. Russia was essentially viewed as a nation on a linear pathway 'in transit' to 'normalcy' and 'civilisation'. A progressive rather than 'return to history' narrative shaped European perceptions of Russia's development. Through a process of EU socialisation and with the use of conditionality and monitoring, Russia would gradually become market-democratic: EU and NATO strategic partnerships represented stepping stones to eventual membership of a Euro-Atlantic security community through inclusion into these organisations. As such, Russia would become accommodated to and securely embedded within the liberal international order represented by the political West. This assumption has not only proved false, but Russian relations with the EU, NATO and United States are at their lowest point since the end of the Cold War (Cohen 2007).

By 2008 it is clear that Russia does not wish to integrate into a larger bloc – indeed, 'Russia finally decoupled between 2003 and 2005 from the West in terms of its foreign policy orientation. Russia is now on its own, unashamedly pursuing its self-interest' (Trenin 2007). Russia now seeks to restore its image in the world and adopt a key independent role in international affairs. Russian criticism of 'US imperialism' and 'diktat' in global affairs, and a deliberate distancing of Russia from the West has been one principal means to that end. The strengthening of Russia's military potential in order to maintain a global strategic balance and reasserting its primacy in the security belt around its periphery – its sphere of 'privileged interests' – is another. Russia acknowledges its European cultural heritage, its affinity with the Westphalian model of a Europe of nation states, and seeks greater recognition for its decisive influence over European historical development – critically intervening to save Europe from Mongol invasion, Napoleonic dominance of the European political order and Hitler's 'Thousand Year Reich'. A cognitive dissonance is apparent: Russia relates to an imagined Europe of the past, while the EU has, at least hitherto, related to Russia as a prospective but dependent partner in the future.

However, such perceptions are fading. Individual points of tension between Russia and Europe are not individually critical in shaping the nature of Europe–Russia relations, but the intensity of these points of difference (particularly since 2004) and their cumulative impact have caused the United States and Europe to readjust relations with Russia. A 'new realism' is now notable in EU attitudes towards Russia, with one EU document noting that Russia was 'a strategic partner in many areas of common interest, notably in the economic field, but in others – such as involvement in the post-Soviet space – Russia is likely to remain a competitor or even opponent' (Barber 2007). At the EU–Russia Samara Summit of May 2007 Angela Merkel and European Commission President Jose Manuel Barroso pointedly reminded President Putin that the problems of one member state with Russia were the problems of all 27 member states. Such realism is also prompted by a growing awareness of the implications of European energy dependence on Russia on the coherence of CFSP and EU as a security actor on the global stage. Russia and Europe are thus in the process of reappraising relations, and differences in attitude, perception and goals are more starkly drawn after the Georgia crisis than before. President Medvedev and Prime Minister Putin have noted Western double standards and hypocrisy over the use of force (NATO bombing Kosovo and Belgrade in 1999), regime change (Iraq in 2003) and recognition of statehood (Kosovo in 2008), and internally its dual power structure and 'sovereign democracy' ideology have been massively boosted following its intervention. In Europe there is a growing understanding that Russia does have a different history, political and strategic culture to Europe, that it perceives its near neighbourhood as a legitimate sphere of influence, thinks in pragmatic zero-sum realpolitik and classical realist terms, while the EU focuses on values and process (liberal internationalism).

Already by 2007 some analysts posited a new bipolarity based around an enlarged democratic West (with the incorporation of 'New Europe') and a 'new second world' led by authoritarian capitalist Russia and China, replacing the defeated totalitarian capitalist states of Germany and Japan. (Gat 2007; Kagan 2007) The Georgia crisis has helped consolidate this emergent paradigm and relations between a market-autocratic Russia and market-democratic Europe have become much more tense, with politico-military disputes predominating and cooperation, so far at least, maintained within the economic realm.

However, a temporary freeze in relations with Russia with some concrete medium and long-term consequences, such as damaged investor confidence and investments, does not constitute a new Cold War. This paradigm shift has not occurred primarily because of the need to engage Russia in addressing issues of primary global strategic importance – Iran, North Korea, arms proliferation, terrorism and climate change. In addition, Europe recognises that Russia can act as a spoiler in the international system and has more leverage over Europe than Europe does over Russia.

At present strategic dissonance continues to be the dominant feature of European–Russian relations. However, the trend in these relations is one of gradual deterioration, and the tipping point from strategic dissonance to outright strategic divorce is now closer. Strategic divorce with Russia – disagreement as to what constitutes strategic threats and an inability to cooperate in addressing them – would powerfully strengthen the process of transatlantic strategic realignment, and ultimately, the consolidation of the EU as a global security actor.

Notes

1 See Dunay's chapter in this volume.
2 'Vilnius 10' group consists of the three former Soviet Baltic states, as well as seven post-communist countries: Albania, Bulgaria, Croatia, Estonia, Latvia, Lithuania, Macedonia, Romania, Slovakia and Slovenia.
3 Alexander Litvinenko, a former Lt. Col. in Russia's Federal Security Service, had been granted political asylum and British citizenship before he fell ill and was hospitalised in highly suspicious circumstances.
4 See Ghebali's chapter in this volume.

References

Adomeit, H. (2007) 'Inside or Outside? Russia's Policies Towards NATO', SWP/NUPI Working Paper delivered to the annual Conference of the Centre for Russian Studies at the Norwegian Institute of International Affairs on 'Multilateral Dimension in Russian Foreign Policy', Oslo, 20 October 2006. Online, available at www.swp-berlin.org/common/get_document.php?asset_id=3570 (accessed 26 May 2008).
Antonenko, O. (1999–2000) 'Russia, NATO and European Security after Kosovo', *Survival*, 41(4): 124–144.
Arbatova, N. (2000) 'Russia–NATO Relations after the Kosovo Crisis', in Fedorov, Y. and Nygren, B. (eds), *Russia and NATO*, Stockholm: Försvarshögskolan ACTA B14 Strategiska Institutionen, 43–74.
Associated Press (2007) 'Moscow presses US on Missile Defence Proposals', *International Herald Tribune*, June 22, p. 3.
Baranovsky, V. (2001) 'Russia: A Part of Europe or Apart from Europe', in Brown, A. (ed.), *Contemporary Russian Politics: A Reader*, Oxford: Oxford University Press, 429–442.
Basescu, T. (2006) 'Romania: An Energy Gateway to Western Europe', Speech to the Jamestown Foundation in Washington D.C., 28 July. Online, available at www.jamestown.org/press_details.php?press_id=35 (accessed 26 May 2008).
Barber, T. (2007) 'EU papers reflect new realism on Russia', *Financial Times*, October 24. Online, available at www.ft.com/cms/s/0/34333a0e-826d-11dc-a5ae-0000779fd2ac.html (accessed 26 May 2008).
BBC (2007) 'Estonia shuts consulate in Moscow', BBC News, May 2. Online, available at http://news.bbc.co.uk/2/hi/europe/6615193.stm (accessed 26 May 2008).
Bosworth, K. (2002) 'The Effect of 11 September on Russia–NATO Relations', *Perspectives on European Politics and Society*, 3(3): 361–387.
Brower, D. (2007) 'Checkmate Gazprom', *Prospect*, June 28.
Charlton, A. (2007) 'Putin: No Proof that Iran Seeks Nuclear Arms', *Associated Press*, October 10.

Cohen, A. (2007) 'Domestic Factors Driving Russian Foreign Policy', The Heritage Foundation, Backgrounder No. 2084, November 19. Online, available at www.heritage.org/Research/RussiaandEurasia/bg2084.cfm (accessed 26 May 2008).

CFE (2002) 'Conventional Armed Forces in Europe Treaty', Fact Sheet, Arms Control Bureau, US Department of State, Washington D.C., 18 June. Online, available at www.state.gov/t/ac/rls/fs/11243.htm (accessed 26 May 2008).

Danilov, D. (2005) 'Russia and European Security', in Lynch, D. (ed.), 'What Russia Sees', *Chaillot Paper 74*, Paris: European Union Institute of Strategic Studies, 79–98.

Dombey, D. (2007) 'Old Comrades Harden EU Line against Russia', *Financial Times*, June 28.

The Economist (2007) 'A bear at the throat; European energy security', April 14, p. 37.

European Commission (2007) 'Interruption to EU oil supplies sparks concern', Brussels, January 9. Online, available at www.ec.europa.eu/news/energy/070109_1_en.htm (accessed 26 May 2008).

European Report (2007) 'EU/Russia/Ukraine/Belarus: EP Delegations Set Out Common External Energy Policy', *European Report*, 3295, April 26.

—— (2007) 'EU/Russia: Experts Urge EU To Develop Common Energy Policy', *European Report*, 3313, May 25.

Fillon, F. (2008) 'Press statement on the occasion of the NATO Bucharest summit', Agence France Presse, April 1.

Forsberg, T. and Herd, G.P. (2005) 'The EU, Human Rights and the Russo-Chechen Conflict', *Political Science Quarterly*, Fall, 120(3): 1–24.

—— (2006) *Divided West: European Security and the Transatlantic Relationship*, London: Blackwell.

Gat, A. (2007) 'The Return of Authoritarian Great Powers', *Foreign Affairs*, July/August, 86(4): 59–69.

Häkämies, J. (2007) Speech at the Center for Strategic and International Studies, Washington, D.C., accessed at Finnish Ministry of Defence website, September 6. Online, available at www.defmin.fi/speeches?663_m=3335 (accessed 26 May 2008).

Haukkala, H. (2000) 'The Making of the European Union's Common Strategy on Russia', *Working Paper No. 28*, Helsinki: The Finnish Institute of International Affairs.

Herd, G.P. (2005) 'Colourful Revolutions and the CIS: "Manufactured" versus "Managed" Democracy?', *Problems of Post-Communism*, March/April, 52(2): 3–17.

Hunter, R. (2003) 'NATO–Russia Relations after 11 September', *Journal of South-east European and Black Sea Studies*, 3(3): 28–54.

Johnson, D. (2005) 'EU-Russian *Energy* Links: A Marriage of Convenience?', *Government & Opposition*, Spring, 40(2): 256–277.

Jung, F.-J. (2008) 'The World in Disarray – Shifting Powers, Lack of Strategies', Speech during the 44th Munich Conference on Security Policy, 8 February. Online, available at www.securityconference.de/konferenzen/rede.php?menu_2008=&menu_konferenzen=&sprache=en&id=203& (accessed 26 May 2008).

Kagan, R. (2007) 'End of Dreams, Return of History', *Policy Review*, 143, June/July. Online, available at www.hoover.org/publications/policyreview/8552512.html (accessed 26 May 2008).

Kovalev, S. (2007) 'Why Putin Wins', *New York Review of Books*, 54(18), November 22. Online, available at www.nybooks.com/articles/20836 (accessed 26 May 2008).

Lavrov, S. (2008) Speech given as a Myrdal Lecture in Geneva on 7 February 2008, published on the website of the Russian Ministry of Foreign Affairs, 12 February.

Leonard, M. and Popescu, N. (2007) *A Power Audit of EU–Russia Relations*. Policy Paper, London: European Council on Foreign Relations.

Morelli, V. (2006) 'The European Union's Energy Security Challenges', CRS Report for Congress, RL336336, Library of Congress, Washington D.C., September 11. Online, available at http://fas.org/sgp/crs/row/RL33636.pdf (accessed 26 May 2008).

NATO (1997) 'Founding Act on Mutual Relations, Cooperation and Security between NATO and the Russian Federation', Paris, 27 May. Online, available at www.nato.int/docu/basictxt/fndact-a.htm (accessed 26 May 2008).

Nichol, J., Woehrel, S. and Gelb, B.A. (2006) 'Russia's Cutoff of Natural Gas to Ukraine: Context and Implications', CRS Report for Congress, RS22378, Library of Congress, Washington D.C., February 15. Online, available at http://opencrs.cdt.org/rpts/RS22378_20060215.pdf (accessed 26 May 2008).

Reuters (2007) 'Austrian Minister: US missile threat is a provocation', August 23.

Rice, C. (2006) Remarks at the State Department Correspondents Association's Inaugural Newsmaker Breakfast, Fairmont Hotel, Washington, D.C., January 5. Online, available at www.state.gov/secretary/rm/2006/58725.htm (accessed 26 May 2008).

Rumer, E.B. (2007) 'Russian Foreign Policy Beyond Putin', *Adelphi Paper*, 390, London: International Institute for Strategic Studies, 1–86.

Russian Ministry of Foreign Affairs (2007) 'Regarding suspension by the Russian Federation of the Treaty on CFE, 12 December 2007', Website of the Russian Ministry of Foreign Affairs. Online, available at www.mid.ru/brp_4.nsf/e78a48070f128a7b43256999005bcbb3/10da6dd509e4d164c32573af004cc4be?OpenDocument (accessed 26 May 2008).

Sarkozy, N. (2007) Joint Press Conference with the President of France Nicolas Sarkozy on the Results of Russian-French Talks, President of Russia Official Web Portal, Moscow, 10 October. Online, available at www.kremlin.ru/eng/text/speeches/2007/10/10/1431_type82914type82915_147984.shtml (accessed 26 May 2008).

Smith, K. (2006) Statement Before the House Government Reform Subcommittee on Energy Resources and the Subcommittee on National Security, Emerging Threats, and International Relations, May 16. Online, available at www.csis.org/media/csis/congress/ts060516smith.pdf (accessed 26 May 2008).

Trenin, D. (2007) 'Kosovo: A Case for a European DAYTON', *Frankfurter Allgemeine Zeitung*, 20 November.

Zielonka, J. (2006) *Europe as Empire: the Nature of the Enlarged European Union*, Oxford: Oxford University Press.

Part II

European security

External dynamics

6 The United States and Europe
Waiting to exhale

Catherine McArdle Kelleher

Introduction

'It was the best of times. It was the worst of times.' Dickens's paradox at the
start of *A Tale of Two Cities* may be the best summation of the present state
of the transatlantic relationship. Viewed in terms of the raging emotional
debates of 2002–03 over the US decision to invade Iraq, the level of cooperation and rhetoric now seems relatively positive. In its second term, the Bush
Administration has pursued a more conciliatory tone and has paid far more
attention to European concerns on preserving the environment, the security
impact of climate change, and the challenges in energy security. Those allies
in Europe who opposed US action in Iraq have agreed to disagree about past
decisions and present consequences, to complain off-line, and to discover
benefits and virtue in the rich range of other common activities and convergent policies, economic, political and military. Every European poll shows
unparalleled public criticism of President Bush and of the United States, yet
there is far less anti-Americanism evident at elite levels. There is even a
purportedly pro-American French president, Nicolas Sarkozy; a skilled and
somewhat pro-American German Chancellor, Angela Merkel; and a British
Prime Minister, Gordon Brown who, still in Tony Blair's shadow, at least
avers his support of a 'principal' US–UK link.

Yet, there remains a cloud of uncertainty, a widely shared perception that
all is not well in the transatlantic framework. To be sure, transatlantic malaise
is hardly unique in postwar history. The 'death' of NATO, the primary multilateral expression of commitment, has been confidently predicted for years.
However, NATO has survived, and has undergone major restructuring and
reorientation since the end of the Cold War. Its forces are on the line in
Afghanistan, the first non-European, anti-terrorism conflict of its history. Are
these changes and new commitments enough to overcome the strategic
divides revealed by Iraq in 2003 and Iran now? Or will they be sufficient to
secure future ties beyond institutional inertia? Have not NATO and the
transatlantic bond lost a unique rationale, one that might still command in its
member states the political support and the resources necessary to the new
security agenda?

The predominant mood on both sides of the Atlantic now is one of expecting decisive events or changes that will follow the settling in of the new American president. These will mesh with the programmes of the new generation of European leadership, and the shape of the post-Iraq shakeout in the Middle East and elsewhere. There is also an urgent present test: the outcome of the purportedly failing NATO-led effort to stabilise and reconstruct Afghanistan. Long-term forecasts about the future of the transatlantic relationship may simply be too hard to make. As throughout much of the post-Second World War period, the key variables will almost certainly be the direction of American policy and its allocation of resources and attention.

This chapter will touch on the fundamentals of the present transatlantic strategic quandary as seen by groups of both Americans and Europeans. We will then turn to three critical tests for transatlantic commitment: joint military efforts in the 'new warfare' in Afghanistan; the fight against terrorism and Weapons of Mass Destruction (WMD) proliferation globally; and the strategic divides between Europe and the United States revealed in the latest 'crisis', the Missile Defense (MD) debate, as well as Russia's role in the latter. Success or failure in each area will be key to the future of the transatlantic tie, to the prospects for NATO or a NATO-like organisation to survive, and to stability in the medium term in the international community.

The transatlantic strategic quandary

The strategic quandary is how to define a transatlantic future that both fits the security challenges of the present and allows for the greatest amount of flexibility for the future at a time of strategic uncertainty. Clearly, the transatlantic tie is today about choosing and advancing a strategic framework that meets the political and military requirements both within the region and elsewhere.

Alternative transatlantic frameworks: does Europe still matter?

Following in the lines of traditional transatlantic analysis, there are at least four alternative ways to define dominant transatlantic interactions in the longer-term future. First is a 'traditional model' – a combination of predominantly bilateral ties and NATO or NATO/EU dialogues within a strong commitment framework – that would constitute the primary forum for the hammering out of transatlantic cooperation. Second, the 'transatlantic pool', favoured more often in the first Bush Administration, from which 'coalitions of the willing' might be drawn on an ad hoc basis, with NATO assets as the 'toolbox' to provide capabilities and support. Third, the 'Riga network', essentially as proposed by the Bush Administration at the Riga NATO Summit in 2006, would be a somewhat looser transatlantic alliance network linked through US leadership to cooperation with other like-minded states and groups throughout the world (e.g. Japan, Australia). Fourth, the 'core of a global coalition of democracies', in which transatlantic identification and treaty arrangements would be decreasingly important and the global agenda for multilateral action in terms of common goals and values, more predominant.

The base assumptions of these models would be of continuing transatlantic consensus on the need for transparency and stability, on the values and goals that have served the West well, and the habit of continuing cooperation to mutual benefit. The choice would be about a framework and the form of political and military commitment. If sufficiently attractive, one of these alternatives might come to replace or enhance the scenarios of NATO or NATO/EU evolution that have characterised transatlantic debate since the end of the Cold War.[1]

Viewed in the context of a shooting war, and in the midst of the squabbles over rights and obligations, all but the first alternative seem somewhat academic or far-fetched. However, it is instructive to look at how different yet convergent some discussions of these alternatives on both sides of the Atlantic have been.

For a number of officials and strategists in the United States, and not just those close to the Bush Administration, it is hard to imagine that a version of alternative number one will be a primary cornerstone of American foreign policy in twenty or perhaps even ten years. A number of these actors see this as America's 'Asian century', dominated certainly in its first decades by the fast-moving political and military emergence of Asian powers, and most especially China and India, to levels matching their present economic prowess. Europe, they believe, is not central to facing these challenges, both because of its relative decline in power and resources but also because it has only secondary contributions to make to the American agenda. In this view, which echoes the thrust of the National Security Strategies of both 2002 and 2006, Europeans are only beginning to comprehend the Asian challenge beyond economics or to see any necessary security role for themselves in potential turbulence. The tools they fashioned to help end the Cold War conflict and stalemate in Europe – engaging civil society, multilateral human rights protection, and imposed transparency – may not be immediately relevant to the potential for conflicts in Asia. Moreover, these instruments will provide only second order help in confronting the challenges of terrorist violence and WMD proliferation.

An even larger group of Americans also questions whether formal multilateral frameworks based on consensus pose particular challenges for a dominant power that believes in its global reach. Organisational procedures are slow; consensus-building is often hard and imperfect, and political constraints lead at best to lowest-common denominator decisions when the asymmetries of power and interest are not taken into account. This has been a favorite theme of some in the Bush Administration (particularly regarding formal treaties and the divisive debate over Iraq), but is hardly a new theme in American foreign policy.

For both Americans and many Europeans, the operational significance of these asymmetries in power registered forcefully first in Kosovo and then in the Gulf War. Before the Bush decisions of 2003, some conservative American critics went a step further and argued the United States would be better off fighting alone given the 'unbridgeable' gap in transatlantic military capabilities (BBC 2002). Europeans, with the possible exception of the British, the French, and maybe the Germans, were simply too far behind to catch up. They could at best attain 'niche' capabilities and the traditional ideas of transatlantic burden-sharing had not survived even a neighborhood test, in the Balkans.

Many Europeans read Kosovo differently, i.e. as an inability to affect the outcome or even the course of action given their weakness and lack of national or European capability. Some vowed privately never to allow this again, whether through the development of a European autonomous capability or through exploring options for at least a 'soft balancing' of the United States and its penchant for unilateral decisions.

Both American and European leaders have also come to recognise one major stumbling block in the march towards any of these alternatives: the dramatic decline in the US image and its desirability as a partner among domestic populations in Europe and throughout the world. Poll after poll reflects the popular European disapproval of the United States in Iraq, and specifically of the Bush Administration (ranging as high as 80 per cent in the cases of France, Germany and Spain) (US German Marshall Fund 2005). But poll data also suggest that, for most Americans, the calculus that has sustained a relatively unique transatlantic framework and will continue to do so in the future still holds (Pew Research Center 2005). Americans still tend – albeit in somewhat smaller numbers – to see the Europeans as 'like us'. They expect Europeans, regardless of whether there is any confirming evidence, to have the same values, to assess the emerging threats the same way, to be spurred by the same convictions to promote democracy and a just international order. Europeans are the most intertwined and trusted allies, even the often-maligned French, and Americans expect them to cooperate.

There are less sentimental parallels in elite opinions. Particularly after the last decade, American elites are far less confident that they can bear the burdens of global leadership on their own. Europeans have taken over political responsibilities that are significant and not easily accessible to Washington – such as the negotiation of the European Three (France, Germany and Great Britain) with Iran over Iranian enrichment facilities, or the years-long drive to persuade Libya to give up its long-hidden nuclear capabilities. EU forces have also assumed a number of low-end political military tasks under UN mandates in Africa.

In the broadly-supported American image of the preferred international order, Europe will continue to be a zone of peace and prosperity. Yet Europe is now challenged by several internal security issues. Europe's energy vulnerability looms ever larger; the need, especially for the smaller and Central and Eastern European (CEE) states, for assured supplies and relatively equitable access to resources remain pressure points for Russia's oil diplomacy. There are still lingering hot spots and points of potential flare-up for civil wars or terrorist incursions: Georgia of course, but also Ukraine, Belarus, the Caucasus and the several 'frozen conflicts' along the southern periphery of Russia. More urgently, there is the complex security status of Turkey, in terms both of civil unrest and the demands of domestic Islamists, and of its potential ambitions for dominance vis-à-vis the northern Middle East in general and the Iraqi Kurds in particular. Europe, Americans conclude, must come to understand new European security needs.

European positions: diverging threat assessment and management

Europeans share a similar level of ambivalence about the transatlantic future and their preferences for a future framework for security cooperation. The strongest surface indicators are the depth of present domestic unhappiness with the United States. The strongest disapproval is reserved for what is seen as the unchanging American penchant for the use of military force, and American unwillingness to abide by the traditions of international law. Most prominent are the high numbers of Europeans who rank the United States as the primary present threat to global stability (Pew Research Center 2006). This level of resentment is particularly strong among youth populations, whose memories of Cold War partnership are vague, if they exist at all (Glenn 2007; Marquand 2007). It is reassuring that since 2005, this type of condemnation has rarely been echoed in elite and governmental rhetoric in Europe. Hope for popular improvement, however, is assessed in years, not months, although there are strong indicators that this populist anti-Americanism is specifically tied to the Iraq war and to President Bush himself (US German Marshall Fund 2005).

Few of the smaller democracies in 'New Europe' are interested in, or willing to support, a global network or partnership for security; their sights are set at the European level and even North Africa or the Middle East seem to pose only faraway threats. Even the dispatch of peacekeeping forces on UN missions is debated; and provision made for speedy withdrawal if conflict or acute threat looms. Military deaths for those who contributed to the American coalition in Iraq have been a new experience for the domestic political scene. Few CEE leaders seem anxious to contemplate another contribution even on a small scale in the foreseeable future. Some domestic critics indeed challenge the price/benefit ratio involved: was the cost of this out-of-region support for the United States actually appreciated or compensated? How have alliance membership and the resulting obligations actually benefited national security in recent years? (Pew Research Center 2007).

In this broad context, Britain, France, and increasingly Italy and Germany present a more engaged agenda nationally, with NATO, and within the European Union, for security tasks up to and including the use of military force as a last resort (e.g. the European Security Strategy of 2003). These states have a more global scope, and have been clear leaders in the fight against terrorism and in the efforts to limit WMD proliferation.

However, even for these states, national security interests and European regional interests, especially as expressed within future European Union security competencies, have priority.

Two contrasting fears plague most centrist European elites. First, the experience of the post-Cold War era suggests it is difficult to avoid sharing the risk of American use of military power. Despite recent cuts, American forces are still deployed from Europe; American tactical nuclear weapons are still in Europe in small numbers, and soon to be joined by the 'independent' plan for anti-missile defenses. European sites under broad prior bilateral agreements with the United States are still used for intelligence, planning, and even extraordinary rendition and secret detention (Marty 2007). NATO as an organisational framework means at least a continuing political forum in which the United States regularly participates. Paradoxically, and second, as the current MD debate shows, the fear of being left out of a decision critical to the security of their populations reflects the other side of their fear that American unilateralism will drag them into a conflict that does not match their priorities.

Yet, America is still a welcome makeweight, and in some of the new CEE democracies, is still trusted more as a partner that will take their national interests into account than some partners in Western Europe. Few have forgotten the lukewarm reaction of many Europeans to the pro-democracy 'color revolutions' in Ukraine and Georgia. Even more dramatic recent examples have been the disappointing range of European responses to the cyberspace attacks on Estonia, or to the blockading of the Polish meat trade by Russia, or Russian pressure on energy supplies to all its former Warsaw Pact allies and a few of its West European clients. For these countries, the bilateral relationship with the United States is still a closely-held insurance policy.

In sum, the search for a new framework of the transatlantic bond is long not resolved and may never explicitly involve any of the four alternative frameworks discussed above. The global network or the linking of other democracies seems most remote now in any practical or operational security terms. Yet simply clinging to structures and patterns of the past seems equally unlikely.

An urgent present test: Afghanistan

Unquestionably, one of the critical tests that will define new security collaboration is the outcome of transatlantic efforts within the International

Security Assistance Force (ISAF) in Afghanistan. Led by NATO since 2003, its mission is to support the Afghan government led by Hamid Karzai, and to provide both security and reconstruction assistance throughout Afghanistan (NATO 2007a, 2007b, 2007c). ISAF is the largest NATO mission ever undertaken outside of Europe, involving 34,000 military from 26 allied and 11 non-allied countries linked to 8,000 (down from 23,000 in 2006) separately commanded American forces under the counter-Taliban Operation Enduring Freedom (OEF). Moreover, it is an explicitly mixed force – involving not only traditional defensive and police functions and training for Afghan units, but also capacities to support rebuilding, counternarcotics, and regional development. At the outset it was a firmly 'hearts and minds' campaign but with the increase in terrorist and Taliban violence, it has had to undertake more combat functions. At its heart are the Provincial Reconstruction Teams (PRTs) of military working with civilian officials and specialists with all 25 PRTs now under NATO leadership (Caan and Scott 2007; US Department of State 2006).

The risk of failure: American and European responsibilities

The problem is that, in the view of a number of key leaders, this is a test the transatlantic community is about to fail. The operation in Afghanistan has always come a poor second to the efforts in Iraq in both attention and resources (*NavyTimes* 2008).[2] Critics see the risk of failure as stemming from mismanagement, inattention, poor coordination, and the collective inability to provide or sustain the forces needed for this challenge. The impact of failure in Afghanistan could be enormous within NATO and across the region. Privately, European military leaders interviewed in 2007 argued that this will mean the end of any NATO effort to transform its security capacity to meet the pressing security challenges of terrorism and insurgency (see also Watt and Temko 2007).

One problem is a concatenation of events that led to delayed reactions to events outside Kabul and allowed the Taliban to regroup in their traditional Pashtun-dominated southern strongholds along the Pakistan border. Part of this certainly must be laid on the Bush team's determination for a rapid, national response to 9/11. The allied invocation of NATO's Article V commitments on collective defence was not welcome, and genuine offers of help from Europe were put aside. The campaign against the Taliban was to be American. In the initial stages the CIA was largely in charge. American military forces were designated as the 'offensive' elements from the first in the OEF that also included some allied combat forces. It is only since 2003 that the ISAF 'hearts and minds' push has been a critically linked element. Even now, there is close coordination between the two forces but no unity of command.

The result was to amplify European tendency to start slow and sure, and a reluctance to take on combat roles. ISAF was first confined to stability in Kabul, and only slowly extended to the non-Pashtun northern and western provinces where essentially NATO forces replaced OEF forces. EU financing and European national aid poured in, but not a greater number of European forces or development teams. Only in 2006 was the ISAF mission extended to the southern areas bordering Pakistan and then to the eastern areas. This completed the circle and NATO assumed responsibility for security throughout Afghanistan in October 2006. This has also meant considerable escalation in combat and death.

Criticism of the more 'offensive' American approach reveals a deep and continuing allied division over the strategy and tactics to be used. There are the usual discontinuities of coalition warfare, observed from the Second World War to NATO operations in the Balkans but made more dramatic by the counterinsurgency anti-Taliban backdrop. Many of the forces from the new democracies have not been trained or initially equipped for this type of mission. This has meant delays and gaps, which meant some nations – especially the Canadians, the Americans, the Dutch, and the British – have borne the brunt of the expansion and the greatest burden of death and injury (US Department of Defense 2007).[3]

Far more important divisions concern the political willingness to use force as reflected in different rules of engagement (ROEs, i.e. how national contingents may be used and what kinds of equipment they must have) and in the many 'national caveats' that have been imposed by contributing countries on these rules. NATO sources reported 26,000 of the target goal of 32,000 forces would operate without caveats. This has meant an unevenness in the functions of the NATO-led PRTs as well as inefficiencies in operations (e.g. against warlords, against poppy farmers, reconnaissance against possible Taliban staging areas).

Furthermore, a number of the contributing partners believe the American 'offensive' approach leads inevitably to an emphasis on 'force protection' (where every Afghan is a potential enemy) rather than promoting democracy and stabilisation (where every Afghan is a potential partner or ally). Some even argue that this may have a boomerang effect in terms of creating more sympathy and recruits for the Taliban cause. The number of civilian casualties resulting from what European and especially British military critics believe is an excessive American reliance on airpower has a similar impact.

Official American responses have been muted. But informal statements often reflect equally bitter American criticisms and deep dissatisfaction with the efforts of its allies. American critics fault the significant lags by a number of European states in fulfilling their manpower and equipment pledges.[4] The 2008 Bucharest Summit again framed promises to provide more combat capable troops (at least 90 per cent of the target goals), including more French troops in the north. But the increase in flow is only relative with modest increase.

There is no question of the seriousness of the test NATO faces in Afghanistan. Only the distraction of the bigger challenges the United

States faces in Iraq explain why there has been relatively little attention in Washington to the problems perceived in Afghanistan. The ISAF command remains publicly positive as do the civilian and military figures at NATO headquarters. But they are very worried, and admittedly surprised by the intensity and the scale of the fighting and Taliban growth over the last two years. Assessed at this point, there is still much to do even if the NATO political process has begun to supply many of the right answers. Reconstruction is slow, and slower when run in parallel with combat.

In sum, there has been a steep allied learning curve with considerable success in the North and in the West. On most measures, forces are now more capable and more agile. Alternatives to coalition forces are non-existent or worse. But despite brave rhetoric at Bucharest, there is no new high point in political consensus. Force numbers are still insufficient and implementation is still uneven. Most important of all, the firm political will necessary for sustained deployments are somewhat elusive even among the strongest contributing states, as the recurring Dutch and Canadian parliamentary debates have shown.

Longer-term transatlantic tests: counterterrorism and counterproliferation

Bilateral cooperation, transatlantic priorities and political constraints

Better evidence of transatlantic determination and cohesion exists on two longer-term policy priorities: counterterrorism and counterproliferation. These both represent core goals for most allied governments, with considerable popular understanding and support behind them. The continuing series of terrorist attacks in Europe itself – Madrid (March 2004) and London (July 2005) most horribly – undergird the sense of solidarity. Even those who blame the violence against European innocents on US actions in Iraq have come to see the immediate threat as urgent and societal. The consensus has already led to significant new action and cooperation at every level; national, transatlantic, global, and at the United Nations. Most takes place in bilateral or functional channels, not within the NATO organisational framework.

In a similar way to actions in Afghanistan, the open questions concern transatlantic priorities and political constraints. On terrorism, most effective cooperation is among the larger countries. This takes place out of the public view and through established intelligence channels, and has been considerably enriched by agreements and understandings expanded after 9/11. Consultations are regular and frequent at all levels: not just reactive, as in the use of Interpol, and not only when judicial action according to national procedures has taken place. Within the EU, the rights of pursuit across borders have been sanctioned and there is far better data exchange than at any time in the past.

Little of this takes place in standard military arenas and indeed military action is less welcome and needed than highly trained, skilled police, gendarmerie, and coast guard units. The exceptions are in policy areas where Washington has viewed allied agreement as unachievable, as in its turning a blind eye to an Israeli military strike in 2007 against a supposed reactor built in Syria with North Korean help.

Perhaps the greatest immediate successes have come in the area of terrorist financing. The transatlantic consensus in NATO and beyond has been instrumental in establishing new international underpinnings at the United Nations, the Organisation for Economic Cooperation and Development, and through national banking measures for the monitoring and constraint of flows of terrorist funds and goods. The net is not exhaustive or always effective, but it clearly has forced more narrow channeling and new incentives for coordinated national actions, if not common action.

The proliferation security initiative; towards a broad transatlantic consensus

Coordination is primary in an activity which blends the two policy goals of counterterrorism and counterproliferation, the Bush Administration's Proliferation Security Initiative (PSI).[5] This is not true for all the states that have declared interest in PSI. A number see counterterrorism as having no place in PSI efforts. But from the Bush viewpoint, a major new contribution has been made towards counter-proliferation.

Crafted specifically to avoid a formal organisational structure and the constraints of 'a lowest common denominator' treaty, PSI involves no new authorities or broad commitments – true to the Bush Administration's admitted preferences. Rather, it focuses on a statement of interdiction principles adhered to by a core group of about eighteen states, with unannounced general support from another 60 or so countries (Winner 2005). The goal is to stop the flow of material (related to weapons or launching vehicles) by air, sea, or land to terrorist groups or rogue states that would allow them to create or use WMD. The principal instrument, intelligence, drives enforcement of national law and regulations. Regular exercises have been held, primarily at sea in the Mediterranean, the Atlantic, and the Pacific (Byers 2004). There is thus a premium on bilateral intelligence cooperation and trust in a known network of officials and observers. No public figures are available: unofficial reports suggest more than 20 interceptions have already taken place in the almost five years of operation.

PSI does reflect a broad transatlantic consensus on both principle and operations. Most of the NATO allies and littoral Partnership for Peace (PfP) countries are public adherents or unannounced supporters. A number have taken leadership roles in some of the more public exercises or actual incidences – Spain, Italy, Germany, France, Poland, and the United Kingdom in addition to the United States. It is the United States that has been most pro-active in pushing this non-treaty based activity to its limits. It has signed agreements with all the flagging (registry) states to ease boarding inspections at sea, away from territorial waters. It has pushed new technologies and techniques, often in conjunction with application within domestic Homeland Security Department programs. It has pushed for increasing transparency and common operational pictures, to ensure timely interdiction and the 'creative' use of national regulations to ensnare cargoes and ships. In the Bush doctrine, the need for continuous real-time surveillance trumps many established rights including the right of privacy of communication and the usual evidentiary requirements.

How deep the political gap

The significant transatlantic differences in both areas however lie in the details and the perspectives about political priorities. The United States, Britain, France and increasingly Germany have been the most pro-active on the terrorism threat and the most willing to increase activity and policy pressure on countries or individuals who harbour or support terrorists. The United States and Britain have also been perhaps the most active and the most willing, not surprisingly, to cite the post-9/11 threat as the basis for overturning customary legal regulations or to create new restrictive measures. The French in their national realm have been almost as pro-active, operating from a different legal and regulatory base.

But in the past, most of the European states and especially Schroeder's Germany balked at full support for the ideas of initiatives proposed by the United States and to a lesser extent by the United Kingdom. There is the overhang of public negative views about Iraq, and the Abu Ghraib fall-out. It is Guantanamo however, that throughout Europe has become a potent political symbol, particularly the refusal of the United States to observe the Geneva Convention, or for a long time to repatriate even those European or allied nationals who had been imprisoned so that they could be tried according to national laws. Disclosures of national collusion with extraordinary rendition, in the transport of CIA prisoners, or in the establishment of secret American holding pens in Central and Eastern Europe have only reinforced these views. Allied governments are embarrassed; parliaments are outraged and political opponents increasingly assertive. On a more practical level, national participation in any new initiative – American or European – is therefore now subject to even greater popular scrutiny and demands for reassurance that national judicial procedures and rights will be safeguarded. Few American guarantees in this area are accepted as credible.

There is also a fundamental difference in perspective among the transatlantic states. The United States and the larger European states, often backed by the Central and Eastern European states, see the need to combat terrorism within the transatlantic realm but also outside it. The United States is the most active globally, most determined to cap the Al-Qaeda/militant Islamist/copycat terrorist threat outside of its national domain. American military and economic capabilities give it the choice to do so; indeed at a critical level the wars in Iraq and Afghanistan are being justified in terms domestically not only by the slogan 'war on terror' but also the determination 'to defeat them over there before they come over here'. It is the ultimate nationalist goal but carried out far from the national political framework.

Most of the European states face a different policy reality. The terrorist threat, if they see it as serious at all, exists within the national or neighborhood borders, visible and related to national legislation and judicial procedures. There are constraints on aggressive pursuit, on imprisonment, on interrogation methods. Moreover, some states give credibility to both inside and outside threats – Britain and France, as perhaps the strongest examples. Their policy choices are subject to greater national scrutiny from the outset.

In sum, however, the transatlantic record of adjusting to the twin challenges of terrorism and proliferation shows considerable success. The consensus-building has been relatively straightforward; the operational restrictions have been put in place with considerable ease and little opposition. The range of efforts is impressive: from the negotiation work of the European Three vis-à-vis Iran to the national prosecution of money launderers for terrorist groups or businessmen attempting to circumvent the export restrictions on WMD-related materials. There are still domestic debates and legal questions to be addressed, such as the acceptable limits to be placed on the right of privacy or the scope and methods of scholarly inquiry in the interests of national security. Iranian cheating on its Non-Proliferation Treaty (NPT) obligations has also sharpened debate about the range of legitimate international responses beyond sanctions. The challenge will be to widen and deepen the consensus for action, for broader areas of export control and surveillance, for earlier detections and constraint of terrorist cells and terrorism sympathisers, but the progress thus far is promising.

The medium-run challenge: missile defense and the Russian policy

By far the most challenging medium-range transatlantic debates have focused on MD, specifically the Bush plan for a small MD system, sited under bilateral agreements in Poland and the Czech Republic, to complement MD deployments in Alaska and California. Its announced target would be missiles launched by Iran and other rogue states, aimed at the United States.

The transatlantic debate has largely been sparked by the strong Russian reactions and couched in political, not technical, terms.[6] Is the real target of the American MD system in Europe Russian offensive capability? Does this deployment not violate the spirit, if not the letter, of the informal US–Russian agreements about the conditions for German unification and perhaps NATO expansion as well? Does it not constitute a plan for permanent NATO forces deployed in states 'of concern' to Russia, in the former Warsaw Pact allies and within 'Russian space' around its borders? Have the NATO allies beyond the host countries, the Czech Republic and Poland, really been consulted or just informed about American actions?

Somewhat surprisingly, mixed into the heated exchanges and impassioned rhetoric seem to be options for significant Russian–American co-operation as well. President Putin has suggested the inclusion/substitution of MD radar sites in Azerbaijan (Garbala) and in southeastern Russia (Armavir) and the establishment of joint data exchange centres in Moscow and Brussels.[7] In their series of Moscow visits in 2007 and 2008, Secretaries Rice and Gates raised the prospect of the participation of Russian officials at all the MD nodes, with full transparency. American and Russian experts have also suggested areas of complementarity in present Russian and American technical expertise if there were to be agreement on developing future joint systems.

Contrary to public belief in both Europe and the United States, the present MD plans have a lineage reaching back to before the Bush Administration. Technical cooperation in MD between Russia and the United States has been discussed since the mid-1990s. The program gained attention early in the Bush Administration, as plans went forward toward fulfilling the Bush 2000 campaign pledge to get 'serious' about MD.[8]

Discussions with the eastern Europeans began as early as 2002, in parallel with renegotiation of usage agreements for the existing British and Danish–Greenland radar sites. But in public reports, all these plans seemed to gain momentum in 2005 and 2006, as Washington stepped up its opposition to Iran. Russian critique has been low-level but continuous throughout, taking on new drama first in President Putin's confrontational address in February 2007 at the *Wehrkunde* gathering in Munich and then throughout 2007 and early 2008.

Criticisms in Europe about the lack of transparency and consultations in these decisions are questionable in light of the regular press coverage these conversations have had. The North Atlantic Council itself recognised the significance of this dialogue at the Prague Summit in 2002, when it decided to commission a study on the feasibility of a full-spectrum multilateral MD architecture to protect Alliance territory, forces, and population centres against the full range of missile threats, a study completed in 2006.[9] At the Istanbul Summit in 2004, it called for joint NATO–Russia cooperation in MD in crisis response situations as well as generally in the development of short and mid-range MD in Europe. Although they have moved glacially in recent years towards any operational steps, NATO MD efforts are always described, at least by the United States, as 'complementary' to the goals of the longer-range US-only proposal.

Washington's views on the present debate

Debate in 2007 and 2008 has taken a number of surprising turns,[10] most dramatically in terms of Putin's decision to revive earlier options for MD cooperation. The offer at the G-8 summit in spring 2007 to make the Garbala radar available (purportedly without prior notification to the Azeri government) was a surprise. Most of the hard-core MD supporters in the Pentagon and in Eastern Europe dismissed the offer as 'theater'[11] or claimed that it would not and should not substitute for the CEE sites. Putin, however, soon followed with a second offer at the Kennebunkport meeting in July 2007 not only for site visits and expert discussions, but also to make data available from Armavir, a more attractive radar in southeast Russia, providing an unprecedented view from Russian territory into Iranian airspace and elsewhere. He continued to insist that these sites would substitute for the CEE sites and that the United States should cease negotiations with the CEE states and take active cooperative steps to ensure that the MD in Europe would not be the basis for active defensive shield against Russian forces.

Putin's bombast is seen in many Washington circles as part of his increasing reliance on the nationalist 'Russia as victim of the West' theme that has come to characterise many areas of Russian foreign policy over the past two years and revisited during the Georgia crisis. The *Wehrkunde* speech in February 2007 was as much about Russia declaring 'we're back and you had better pay attention to us' as it was about specific policies or charges.[12] It reflected actions in other areas, as in oil and gas resource ownership.

Russian threats about targeting the MD sites and withdrawing from key arms control agreements (Intermediate-range Nuclear Forces (INF), Conventional Armed Forces in Europe (CFE), and even the broader OSCE) in retaliation were generally dismissed by Bush Administration insiders. Positions are also coloured by a related, larger area of concern, the expiration of the START I regime in 2009, and the announced intention of the Bush Administration, despite relatively recent Russian requests for a formal, legal successor regime, to do nothing to extend it.

One clear message from the US Congress, however, is worth noting. The House has refused to authorise MD funds for a 'third' MD site (after sites 1 and 2 in California and Alaska) unless and until there are formal agreements signed with both the Czech Republic and Poland governing US use of their territory. An agreement with Prague was reached in April 2008, and with Warsaw in August 2008 in the midst of the Georgia crisis. The House–Senate conference may lead to a different outcome but it is by no means certain in light of substantial opposition within the Democratic ranks. Given elite approval but significant popular disapproval of the MD plans in both European countries, formal bilateral agreements may take considerably more time.

The transatlantic debate and the Russian factor

The debates of both the US and Russia with Europeans on this issue take a very different tone. Many European conservative critics echo their American colleagues and assert that this is just a familiar Russian tactic, to divide the NATO allies from the United States and from one another to maximise its influence and opportunities. Russia has followed similar tactics in marketing its oil and gas on which Europe is so dependent. Those who opposed Russia's wishes are at least leaned upon heavily; Russia has wielded its new economic role repeatedly towards its former allies and made access and trade as well as oil and gas supplies far more difficult for them. The lack of NATO and European solidarity with the targets just makes it more likely that a Russia that pursues an increasingly assertive brand of nationalism will try again.

There are clear differences in the discourse in what Donald Rumsfeld once called 'Old' versus 'New' Europe. Many European observers privately argue there are parallels in the unilateral MD actions by the United States designed to divide Europe in its own interest just as in 2002–03 (Leonard and Popescu 2007: 26–27). Initial Russian approaches were targeted at Germany, stressing the failure of the United States to consult, and the breaking of the informal understanding surrounding Russian agreement to German unification. In contrast to Schroeder, Chancellor Angela Merkel has been somewhat less impressed by Russian claims of a direct threat to them.[13] She has reportedly been angered by the proposed bilateral deals, and has publicly and privately chided the United States, Poland and the Czech Republic for the lack of consultation. She is aware of the popular opposition to MD in Europe of well over 50 per cent, as well as expert fears within her security bureaucracies about MD viability, given US–Russian tensions, of the entire arms control and European stability regimes (Pullinger *et al.* 2007). In France, Nicolas Sarkozy has been more supportive of the US approach, reflecting his distance from the positions of Jacques Chirac and in his first visit to Moscow gave far more approval to the general concept of MD. Popular sentiment is divided although there is surprising sympathy for a multilateral European solution.

The generally negative turn in British–Russian relations over the last three years has meant little elite discomfort with the MD proposal and indeed some enthusiasm for participation in production at the cutting edge of technology that British MD systems contributions seem to promise. Popular opinion is mixed, with a majority seemingly more concerned by increasing Russian authoritarianism and rampant nationalism than the details of the MD in Europe programme.

The clearest contrast to the more sympathetic German, Italian and Spanish reactions to Russian complaints has been the strong approval of the MD in Europe plans in the Polish and Czech governments. Strong majorities (more than 60 per cent) in their populations do oppose the deployments or express fear that the Russians will make good their threats and re-target Polish and Czech cities in retaliation. Both governments, however, can count on some domestic political bonuses for their positive positions and an affirmation of the strong anti-Russian sentiments that still run deep. The Polish case has reached significant proportions with the long-lasting Russian prohibitions on Polish meat exports to Russia and the claims of Polish attempts to undermine existing Russian legal rights. The Czechs, on the other hand, were initially responsive to Russian requests that they delay their decision but have indicated government willingness to go ahead with Washington.

Perhaps the more fundamental issue is Polish and Czech resentment of Russian efforts to define their territory as subject to a Russian '*droit de regard*' (Peel and Wagstyl 2007). Neither state accepts the designation that it is or should be part of 'Russia's near abroad'. That ended, they argue, with their entry into both NATO and the EU as full members. Their choices regarding MD in Europe are their sovereign right, not part of some informal understanding about 'NATO expansion'. Was this not the kind of protection for which they had wanted to join NATO, and enter close partnership with the United States, up to and including sending contingents to Iraq?

NATO at Bucharest supported what was reported as a German-proposed 'interim' MD solution that buys everyone time. The final communiqué 'recognised' the 'significant contribution' of the potential US system but also urged more cooperation with the Russians and a 'buckling' together with any future Europe-wide NATO system. NATO would undertake a year-long study to develop options for such a systemic architecture. This leaves room not only for debate and compromise but also a different decision by a new US president.

Beyond these immediate security concerns, the more fundamental questions raised have yet to be addressed. What kind of role does the United States and Europe wish Russia to play in the European security system? How will the Georgia crisis impact on such a role? How truly equal will they allow any strategic partnership to be and how significant? In a post-Georgia crisis context, how willing is the United States or are the Europeans to establish a joint project or joint development plan with the Russians, one that might focus on a blending of strengths rather than the hostilities of the past? And under what international, rather than national, chapeau are efforts to avoid the threat of rogue launches to be constrained and if necessary challenged?

Conclusion

Long-term forecasts about the Atlantic future may simply be too hard to make. As throughout much of the post-Second World War period, the key variables will almost certainly be the direction of American policy and its allocation of resources and attention.

As we have seen in each of the three cases we have reviewed, there is a wide range of possible change and no reason to expect that American political outcomes will necessarily respond to European and American hopes about the post-Bush era. Expectations may indeed run too high on both sides of the Atlantic. Europe should be more central to US interests, European critics obviously think. Certainly Bush's successor will handle foreign policy differently given the miniscule attention Bush paid to it in general (Iraq excepted) and to Europe in particular. Facing a post-Iraq world, will he not be given to more political engagement, to consultations before action and to understand the core benefits of multilateralism and the rule of law? Europeans are descendents of Venus, American neo-con populists still write, unable or unwilling to do anything but unduly constrain US freedom of action. But with renewal now in train, will the EU not be on track to become a net security provider especially outside of Europe? And where, if anywhere, does a stridently renationalising and aggressive Russia fit?

It is prudent not to substitute hope for experience, to comprehend the need for sober readjustment of the metrics of the Bush years. The new US president inherits a number of key challenges – the winding down of Iraq, the proliferation challenges in Iran and North Korea, the continuing and sharpening economic bills, and the foreseeable list of intense intractable conflicts. Change will more likely be incremental and too slow for many; the euphoria of governing will soon give way to the problems of a United States now confronting a vast social and economic agenda at home, postponed by the discredited war on terror.

Notes

1 See Lindley-French's chapter in this volume.
2 In a congressional testimony in December 2007, chairman of the Joint Chiefs Administration Mike Mullen stated: 'In Afghanistan, we do what we can. In Iraq, we do what we must'. Additionally, Admiral William Fallon, CENTCOM commander, suggested in the *New York Times* (2008) that 'the United States had taken its eye off the military mission in Afghanistan'.
3 Unofficial figures tabulated by Iraq Coalition Casualties Count (www.icasualties.org) in April 2008 indicate that of the 792 deaths in Afghanistan so far, the Americans (492) and the British (91) have had the largest number of deaths, followed by the Canadians (82), the Germans (25), the Spanish (23), the Dutch (14) and the French (12).
4 Prior to the December NATO meeting in Scotland, Secretary of Defense Gates was particularly pointed internally but also publicly in his criticism of allied efforts. Both he and Admiral Mullen testified to Congress to this end in *the Washington Post*, December 11, 12 and 13, 2007.

5 The Proliferation Security Initiative (PSI) was launched in May 2003 and stems from the National Strategy to Combat Weapons of Mass Destruction of December 2002. It is aimed at

> stopping shipments of weapons of mass destruction (WMD), their delivery systems, and related materials worldwide. The goal of PSI is to create a more dynamic, creative, and proactive approach to preventing proliferation to or from nation states and non-state actors of proliferation concern.
>
> (US Department of State 2004; see also Boese 2005)

6 See Herd's chapter in this volume.
7 Lewis and Postol (2007) report that Putin also said Russia would have no objections to US missile defense interceptors being stationed in Iraq or Turkey or other appropriate southern European locations, or to the United States using Aegis ship-based interceptors as part of a missile defense for Europe.
8 A number of analysts point to a core memo by Secretary of Defense Rumsfeld to the Missile Defense Agency (MDA) in January 2002, reinforced by the National Security Presidential Directive 23 (NSPD-23), signed by President George W. Bush on December 6, 2002.
9 The study and its follow-on were done by a transatlantic consortium led by US-based Science Applications International Corporation (SAIC).
10 Some of those interviewed for this essay suggested that the specific announcement of the CEE sites (presumably the announcements in early 2007), while generally approved earlier at the highest levels, seemed to come as somewhat of a surprise since the discussions had not been closely monitored above the working level. Secretary Gates is said to have been the one to actually approve the programme in its entirety given Secretary Rumsfeld's decision to 'leave that to his successor'.
11 See former Ambassador Bob Joseph's comment on this as a 'trick' made at the Army conference 'Celebrating 50 Years of Space and Missile Defense', 13–17 August, 2007, quoted by Jack Mendelsohn (2007).
12 See Herd's chapter in this volume.
13 See, for example, the debate featured on the *Deutsche Gesellschaft fur Auswaertige Politik* webpage. Among the participants, Admiral Ulrich Weisser (former head of the Defense Planning Staff), and Ambassador Frank Ebele (formerly Foreign Office and unification negotiator).

References

BBC (2002) 'US "ready to go it alone", 2 February. Online, available at http://news.bbc.co.uk/2/hi/europe/1798132.stm (accessed 26 May 2008).

Boese, W. (2005) 'Arms Control Association Fact Sheet: The Proliferation Security Initiative (PSI) At a Glance', *Arms Control Association*, September. Online, available at www.armscontrol.org/factsheets/PSI.asp (accessed 26 May 2008).

Bucharest Summit Declaration (2008) Issued by the Heads of State and Government participating in the meeting of the North Atlantic Council in Bucharest, 3 April. Online, available at www.nato.int/docu/pr/2008/p08-049e.html (accessed 26 May 2008).

Byers, M. (2004) 'Policing the High Seas: The Proliferation Security Initiative', *The American Journal of International Law*, 98(3): 526–545.

Caan, C. and Scott, W. (2007) 'Rebuilding Civil Society in Afghanistan: Fragile Progress and Formidable Obstacles', Washington, DC: United States Institute of

Peace. Online, available at www.usip.org/pubs/usipeace_briefings/2007/0710_civil_society_afghanistan.html (accessed 26 May 2008).

Glenn, J.K. (2007) Testimony, US House of Representatives, 23 March. Online, available at www.gmfus.org//doc/House%20Testimony%203–07%20with%20Charts.pdf (accessed 26 May 2008).

Leonard, M. and Popescu, N. (2007) *A Power Audit of EU-Russian Relations*, Brussels: European Council on Foreign Relations.

Lewis, G. and Postol, T. (2007) 'European Missile Defense: The Technological Basis of Russian Concerns', *Arms Control Today*, October.

Marquand, R. (2007) 'Europe's youth take complex view of US', *Christian Science Monitor*, 13 August. Online, available at www.csmonitor.com/2007/0813/p01s04-woeu.html (accessed 26 May 2008).

Marty, D. (2007) 'Alleged Secret Detentions in CoE member states', Council of Europe. Online, available at www.coe.int/T/E/Com/Files/Events/2006-cia/ (accessed 26 May 2008).

Mendelsohn, J. (2007) 'European Missile Defense: Strategic Imperative or Business as Usual', *Arms Control Today*, October.

NATO (2007a), 'Afghanistan: Reconstruction and Development', June. Online, available at www.nato.int/issues/afghanistan/factsheets/reconst_develop.html (accessed 26 May 2008).

—— (2007b) 'NATO support to Afghan National Army (ANA)', June. Online, available at www.nato.int/issues/afghanistan/factsheets/ana-support.html (accessed 26 May 2008).

—— (2007c) 'NATO Topics – NATO in Afghanistan', 13 July. Online, available at www.nato.int/issues/afghanistan/index.html (accessed 26 May 2008).

NavyTimes (2008) 'Troops face long road ahead in Afghanistan', 25 January. Online, available at www.navytimes.com/news/2008/01/military_nextafghan_080125w/ (accessed 26 May 2008).

New York Times (2008) 'Mideast Commander Retires After Irking Bosses', 12 March. Online, available at www.nytimes.com/2008/03/12/washington/12military.html?_r=1&adxnnl=1&adxnnlx=1211807769-pUhnIyIPDn8v4Sd83A7KCg&oref=slogin (accessed 26 May 2008).

Peel, Q. and Wagstyl, S. (2007) 'Prague warns of Kremlin ambition', *Financial Times*, 20 July.

Pew Research Center (2005) 'US–European Alliance', *Pew Global Attitudes Project*, 23 June.

—— (2006) 'Table: Dangers to World Peace', in 'America's Image Slips, But Allies Share U.S. Concerns Over Iran', *Pew Global Attitudes Project*, 13 June. Online, available at http://pewglobal.org/reports/display.php?ReportID=252 (accessed 26 May 2008).

—— (2007) 'Global Unease With Major World Powers', *Pew Global Attitudes Project*, 27 June. Online, available at http://pewglobal.org/reports/display.php?ReportID=256 (accessed 26 May 2008).

Pullinger, S., Gasparini, G., Neuneck, G. and Pasco, X. (2007) *Missile Defence and European Security*, European Parliament, Policy Department External Policies, November.

US Department of Defense (2007) 'Military Casualty Information', Personnel and Procurement Statistics, 14 July. Online, available at http://siadapp.dmdc.osd.mil/personnel/CASUALTY/castop.htm (accessed 26 May 2008).

US Department of State (2004) 'The Proliferation Security Initiative', June. Online, available at http://usinfo.state.gov/products/pubs/proliferation/ (accessed 26 May 2008).

US Department of State (2006) 'Provincial Reconstruction Teams', 31 January. Online, available at www.state.gov/r/pa/prs/ps/2006/60085.htm (accessed 26 May 2008).

US German Marshall Fund (2005) 'Disapproval of President Bush's International Policies vs. Undesirability of US Global Leadership', *Transatlantic Trends*, 7 September.

Watt, N. and Temko, N. (2007) 'Failure in Afghanistan risks rise in terror, say generals', *Guardian/Observer* (interview, online edition), 15 July. Online, available at www.guardian.co.uk/uk/2007/jul/15/world.afghanistan (accessed 26 May 2008).

Winner, A. (2005) 'The Proliferation Security Initiative: The New Face of Interdiction', *Washington Quarterly*, Spring, 2(28): 129–143.

7 Europe and the Middle East
Attempting to bridge the divide

Roland Dannreuther

Introduction

History, colonial legacies, religion and culture all contribute to make Europe's relations with the Middle East and North Africa particularly complex and sensitive.[1] The Middle East is the most direct neighbour of Europe, with the physical distance at times only a few kilometres (Morocco and Spain) or even within the borders of one country (Turkey). But, the cultural distance is far greater with Europe's Christian legacy and the Middle East's Islamic inheritance continuing to define and express mutual perceptions of difference and otherness. Turkey's candidature for the European Union directly confronts the question of whether the European integration process can overcome or will only exacerbate this sense of a civilisational divide. History also provides similar dynamics of connectedness and distance. The region, with the exception of Turkey, Iran and Saudi Arabia, experienced European colonial rule and has continuing social, cultural and economic ties with European countries. But, the colonial period is also remembered as a time of humiliation and damaging legacies, the most critical and long-lasting of which is the Arab–Israeli conflict where all parties of the dispute at least agree that they were betrayed by the British. France's complex and conflict-ridden history of occupation and colonisation of Algeria is another key and highly sensitive historical legacy.

The more strictly material power relations between Europe and the Middle East are almost as complex as the cultural and historical. Europe as represented through the EU and NATO is, at least from the Middle East perspective, a regional economic, political and military behemoth. Europe's economic prosperity contrasts with the relative poverty of most Middle Eastern states, with Israel being the one major exception. Europe's political integration also contrasts with the chronic political disunity in the Middle East, including among the linguistically unified Arab states. The military might of NATO has been shown to be of a different qualitative order to the nominally large but generally inept armed forces of the Arab region, again with the notable exceptions of Turkey and Israel. For its part, the European Union is keen to promote an image of itself as an ethical and post-imperial multilateralist actor, whose engagement with the external world is based on liberal internationalist rather than realist or geostrategic objectives. This promotes an explicit European ambition to be a 'normative power', which sets high standards in relation to such issues as democratic freedoms, human rights, the rule of law, civil society, and social equality (Manners 2002, 2008; Youngs 2004).

But, Europe can also appear weak and less than the sum of its parts, consistently demonstrating a certain impotence when faced directly with the multiple security challenges of the Middle East. Its much heralded normative agenda, with its ambitions for the political transformation in the region, can often appear as more rhetoric rather than substance. When it comes to the crunch, the far-reaching ambition for socio-political transformation holds a secondary place to the more immediate security-driven concerns, such as the perceived threats of international terrorism, uncontrolled migration, transnational organised crime and the spread of regional conflicts. All too often Europe is seen as meekly caving in to the interests of the Middle East's authoritarian regimes, who can offer reassurances over Europe's security concerns but at the expense of any real commitment to permit domestic economic and political reforms. Overall, Europe's interactions with the Middle East do not generally reveal it in the best of lights. Those who argue for the EU's emerging great power status rarely highlight the EU's policies in the Middle East, but rather tend to focus on the EU's eastward enlargement and the EU's involvement in the Balkans (Manners 2002; Zielonka 2006).

This chapter has two main sections. The first identifies the opportunities in the Middle East that the end of the Cold War have opened up for Europe. It highlights that these opportunities have been matched and also somewhat negated by an increased perception of threat, not just of a direct physical nature, such as the rise of international terrorism, but also to the domestic solidarity within Europe, as experienced with the divisions during the second Gulf War. These fears and concerns have led to significant frustration of European ambitions to project its normative agenda in the region. This section also explores Middle Eastern perceptions of Europe's role in the region, with a similar mix of expectation and frustration. The second section first examines the institutionalised policy responses of the EU to the Middle East, focusing in particular on the Euro-Mediterranean Partnership (EMP or 'Barcelona Process') and the European Neighbourhood Policy (ENP). The section then addresses less formally institutionalised European engagement, where the specific role of individual European states are more visible, and where the engagement deals with the more military-security aspects, such as peace support operations in Lebanon and Afghanistan and the Middle East Peace Process. It is argued here that one can realistically expect a rather limited role to be played by the principal European military-security organisations, most notably NATO and the EU.

Mutual perceptions and the end of the Cold War

The end of the Cold War provided Europe with an opportunity to regain a degree of influence in the Middle East which would match its economic and political power and its geographical propinquity. The Suez Crisis in 1956 had marked the point where the major European powers – Britain and France – essentially withdrew from the Middle East to be replaced by the two new superpowers of the United States and the Soviet Union. The emergent European Community sought a Middle Eastern role from its very earliest attempts to develop a foreign policy during the 1970s, which culminated in the Venice Declaration in 1980 supporting a Palestinian state and recognition of the Palestine Liberation Organization. However, this tentative European demarche was vigorously rebuffed by the United States (and even more strongly by Israel), resulting in a perception in Washington and Tel Aviv that Europe was potentially as problematic, if not more so, than the Soviet Union as a partner in the Middle East peace process (MEPP) (Greilsammer 1984; Hollis 1994).

This suspicion of the perceived partiality of Europe continued into the post-Cold war period. The Madrid Summit in 1991, which was convened after the liberation of Kuwait so as to promote the Arab–Israeli peace process, was co-chaired by the United States and the Soviet Union. From this initial exclusion, Europe's position was to be gradually enhanced. The EU capitalised on the role that it was given in the multilateral track of the Madrid process to promote a constructive image of its activity and to emphasise the substantive contribution that it was playing in the peace process. By the late 1990s, the EU had assumed a critical role as the key financial supporter for the emergent Palestinian Authority. In the same period, the EU's ambition to be a serious foreign policy actor, as institutionalised through the Common Foreign and Security Policy (CFSP), was translated in 1995 into an ambitious strategy for the Middle East in the form of the EMP or Barcelona Process.[2] By the same token, the evident failure of the US attempt to reconfigure the Middle East through the invasion of Iraq after 2003 appeared to offer Europe a further opportunity to fill the strategic vacuum (Diamond 2005).

Threat perceptions and missed opportunities

However, European perceptions of the Middle East as an opportunity for great power projection are constrained by perceptions of threats emanating from the region. The general rule is the greater the threat perception for Europeans, the more timid and constrained is Europe's strategic response. There are three main reasons for this. First, there is an acute sense that events in the Middle East can have threatening spillover effects in Europe. As former French foreign minister, Hervé de Charrette (1997), noted 'when violence returns to the Middle East, sooner or later it will show up in Paris'. France had its own intimation of the post-9/11 security environment when domestic Algerian terrorism was translated into a series of terrorist attacks on the Paris metro in 1995/96. Similar fears have been expressed with the rise of North African immigration into Europe, which particularly affect the Southern European countries. But Europe's response to such perception of threat is not, as with the US post-9/11, one of strategic ambition and a radical drive to transform the region. Rather it is one of retrenchment and a strategy of containment. This recognises that security is best left in the hands of the existing governments, however authoritarian or repressive they may be; that the risks, for instance, of inclusion of Islamist parties in the political process are too great to be supported; and that the formal commitment to economic and political transformation of EU's foreign policy should be limited to the strictly economic rather than the social and political (Tanner 2004; Youngs 2001).

A second factor behind this inhibiting sense of threat is more internally driven. This is that the Middle East threatens the internal solidarity of the EU. The classic recent case for this was over the US-led intervention into Iraq in 2003 which divided Britain, Spain and Italy from the other core EU states, most notably France and Germany, and which further created a fissure between the 'old' and the 'new' Europe. In 2007, a similar if less critical division emerged over President Sarkozy's proposal for a Mediterranean Union, which angered Germany since it appeared to relegate German involvement to a position of 'silent observer' along with other non-Mediterranean EU member states. It also upset Turkey whose consistent fear is that the French ambition is to obstruct Turkish EU membership. The issue of Turkey's candidacy is probably the most critical source of internal EU tension, where differing European perspectives threaten the very constitutional identity of the European Union. The growing sense that the EU has reached its geographical and cultural limits, and that Turkey should be excluded from the European family of nations, potentially entrenches the sense that Europe is defined by its Judaeo-Christian roots, despite the formal commitment to the Enlightenment and secular universalist values as set out in the preamble of the rejected Constitutional Treaty. Scepticism of Turkey's credibility as a candidate member only perpetuates the perception that it is an Islamic inheritance which is incompatible with a European identity (Rumelili 2003). The paradox is that it is the moderate Islamist party in Turkey, the Justice and Development Party (AKP), which has moved furthest in promoting European integration, precisely so as to encourage the religious and political freedoms which the Kemalist secular nationalist establishment is reluctant to permit (Onis 2006). Yet, the more that Turkey moves towards an Islamic identity, even of a moderate and democratic nature, the more the EU expresses its reservations of its potential accession. As such, Turkey brings to the fore the internal but unresolved European debate about the relationship between religion, secularism and political culture (Neumann 1998).

The Israel/Palestine problem contributes a further critical fissure in European unity. It is notable that the EU is most confident and pro-active when there is progress being made in the Middle East Peace process (MEPP). It was precisely at this juncture in 1995, when the prospects for peace appeared most favourable, that the EU unveiled its ambitious EMP and initiated the Barcelona Process. However, once Israel and its Arab Palestinian neighbours reverted to violent confrontation, the internal divisions within the EU became increasingly apparent. The underlying structural differences between European states over their basic approaches to Israel contribute to uneasy compromises in EU policy towards Israel/Palestine. On the one hand, EU policy incorporates the interests of countries like Germany and the Netherlands, who are conscious of the European reasons for the creation of the state of Israel – European complicity in the Holocaust – and who wish to recognise Israel's status as an advanced industrial economy and a modern democracy. On the other hand, the EU has to be sensitive to the more pro-Arab stance of countries like France, Italy and Greece, with their geographical proximity and social links to the Arab world, and who wish to punish Israel for its actions in the West Bank and Gaza Strip. The resulting compromises in EU policies manage ultimately to satisfy neither side in the conflict (Dannreuther 2004: 162–165; Haas 1997: 61–62).

This leads to the third factor which contributes to the sense of the Middle East as a threat to European interests and solidarity. This threat is linked to the internal solidarity between EU member states but involves the broader transatlantic dimension of this solidarity. Compared to other regions where the United States and Europe cooperate, such as Russia, Africa or East Asia, the Middle East has consistently proved to be the most difficult area in which to ensure a durable convergence of transatlantic interests. It is notable that the Middle East is a region where collective action through the Atlantic Alliance has been almost completely absent, despite regular attempts during both the Cold War and post-Cold War period to promote the Middle East as a natural site for transatlantic intervention. This is not to say that the benefits for such collective action, for the United States and Europe to play 'complementary' roles in promoting their common interests in the region, are not recognised or acted upon (Gordon 1998; Perthes 1999). In most instances, even where the differences can be significant, such as in confronting Iran's nuclear ambition, Europe and the United States do act to support each other's mutual interests. The crunch comes when interests diverge to an extent where such common action becomes impossible. It is at such junctures that the fissures within Europe about the meaning and substance of the transatlantic relationship become transparently evident.

Again, the European response to the US objective to dislodge Saddam Hussein brought this out with all of its damaging consequences for intra-European solidarity. For British prime minister Tony Blair, the virtues of transatlantic solidarity demanded subordination to US leadership. Without such immediate support, Blair (2003) argued, the consequence would be a transatlantic relationship based upon 'rivalry rather than partnership', making it more difficult to confront the common threats that both Europe and the United States face in the post-9/11 security environment. For French president Jacques Chirac, it was the fact that US policies towards Iraq were so damaging to European interests in a number of critical areas, not just for the Middle East but more broadly, that it would be an abdication of Europe's vocation if it did not seek to defend these interests in its diplomacy. In the end, there was neither sufficient European engagement to provide legitimacy for the intervention and to contain the damaging longer-term consequences, nor sufficient European solidarity to counterbalance and subvert US ambitions. The consequence was a Europe which was both divided and paralysed (Gordon and Shapiro 2004; Haine 2004).

Perceptions from the Middle East

The perceptions of Middle Eastern countries and peoples with regards to Europe reflect, in many ways, the complex mix of European hopes and fears. There are admittedly significant divergences between the states of the Middle East, given their different interests and diverging external relations and orientations. There is, though, a generally positive regional support for an enhanced European engagement. This is evident even among the most traditionally pro-American Middle East countries. In Israel there is a commonly expressed, if highly unrealistic, hope that membership of the EU might ultimately provide an exit-route from Israel's geopolitical fate to be surrounded by hostile Arab states. Turkey, a similarly traditionally pro-American country, has, as noted above, embraced its potential EU membership with a series of reforms which have fundamentally changed the nature and face of Turkey. Amongst the Arab Gulf states, also closely tied to the strategic relationship with the United States, Europe is welcomed as a force which can help to balance a perceived overpowering US hegemony.

Similar hopes are found even more strongly among the Arab states which have traditionally had a more tense relationship with the United States. The general perception amongst these states is that the post-Cold War US hegemony has been a negative development for the Middle East. The hopeful expectation is that Europe, even if in a more limited way, might be able to restore a degree of regional balance and help offset the dominance of the United States. There is, therefore, a generally favourable attitude to the greater prominence and diplomatic activism of the European states and the EU, with the hope of some 'soft balancing' against US–Israeli dominance. More generally, there is also recognition that Europe offers a number of benefits, such as opportunities for economic trade and the prospects for immigration and social mobility.

However, these hopes and expectations are counterbalanced by a number of factors which dampen any prospective enthusiasm that Europe will be able to deliver on its putative promises. There is, first, the deeply ingrained suspicion of European strategic objectives. This is, in part, driven by the cumulative inheritance of the past, most notably the colonial legacies which continue to be perceived to frustrate the social and political aspirations of the region. Although almost a century has passed since the dissolution of the Ottoman empire, the consequences of Europe's 'original sin' of the political demarcation of the Middle East state system is viewed locally as the root cause of the dysfunctionality of states such as Iraq, Lebanon and Israel/Palestine. Europe is still viewed, whether fairly or not, as seeking to perpetuate this unjust political order, as suspicions of British intentions in Iraq and Afghanistan in its military deployments, or Syrian suspicions of French support for the Lebanese anti-Syrian bloc, continue to demonstrate. The suspicion also has a strong cultural dimension, with echoes back to the crusades, where Europe is seen as promoting Western values which are inimical to the cultural inheritance of the Islamic world. Europe's self-confident normative agenda tends to accentuate these cultural tensions. This is found even in Israel, where the commitment to a Jewish state for the Jewish people contrasts with the European integrative process which seeks to transcend such ethnic exclusivity (Dror and Pardo 2006: 31).

Second, Europe suffers from the perception of its intrinsic weakness. In a region where military force is still perceived, in the classic realist sense, to be the *ultima ratio* of international politics, the military weakness of the EU is viewed as a critical deficiency (Cooper 2003; Kagan 2003). Even after the debacle in post-2003 Iraq, the United States remains the power to which the countries of the region instinctively turn to deliver their key political objectives. There is little expectation that the EU will have either the capacity or the will to challenge the asymmetrical power balance which is constitutive of the perceived US–Israeli regional hegemony.

This finally feeds into a perception of European hypocrisy in its dealings with the Middle East. This is particularly felt among those groups which seek to challenge the authoritarianism of the ruling governments of the region. To these emergent civil society groups, there appears to be a critical disjuncture between the rhetoric of economic and political transformation and the reality of European support of the existing governments – the perceived best guarantors of the security and energy interests of Europe. The sense of double standards is particularly evident in Europe's ambivalence over the emergence of populist Islamist movements, which generally flourish in conditions of political liberalisation, and the subsequent European tendency to support repressive anti-democratic measures to contain such Islamist-inspired movements. Similarly, the rhetoric of European integration comes against the hard constraints of agricultural protectionism and anti-immigration measures. For the many farmers in the southern Mediterranean, who find that European markets remained closed despite all the talk of trade liberalisation, and for the thousands of unemployed youth who dream of working in the EU and find themselves unable to get a visa, Europe appears an exclusionary rather than inclusionary neighbour. This sense of exclusion was perhaps most asserted in relation to Morocco, which is so close physically to Europe, but which was bluntly told when it tried to present itself as an EU candidate that it was simply not eligible. Although geographically so close, it was also a world apart.

Limits to external influence

Dwelling on the many aspects which divide Europe from its Middle Eastern neighbours, and the multiple sources of mutual incomprehension which underlie this should not though be taken so far as to present an unbridgeable chasm. There is a tendency in the academic literature to conclude on such an unqualifiedly pessimistic note. Frustration is widely expressed by such academic commentators at Europe's consistent inability to translate its rhetorical commitments into effective and durable policies (see, for example, Keinle 1998; Gillespie and Youngs 2002; Phillipart 2003).

These perceived failures need to be placed in context. It is not as though the comparative advantage of the United States as an actor with abundant 'hard' power assets has been translated into a durable transformation of the region. Admittedly, the United States did make significant progress in the 1990s towards promoting a settlement of the Arab–Israeli conflict. However, once the United States became frustrated with such labour-intensive diplomatic processes and reverted to a much greater concentration on its military capabilities in the aftermath of 9/11, the results have hardly resulted in success. The post-2003 Iraq has descended into anarchy and civil war and the Middle East as a whole appears more unstable than ever before. This does not mean that Europe has a magic 'soft power' formula for dealing with the Middle East, which makes it somehow more competent than the US, but that both the US and Europe have considerable difficulties in fashioning policies towards the region that contribute to sustained change.

In this regard, some recognition also needs to be accorded to the limits of external power projection in the Middle East. The region is not a strategic vacuum where external powers, along the lines of their earlier colonial counterparts, can act without taking into account the local structures of power (Yapp 1991: 5). The Middle Eastern states do have considerable powers of retaining and perpetuating their rule, relying on various forms of economic rent, such as their oil wealth, and on deeply penetrated neo-patrimonial systems of legitimation. Middle Eastern ruling regimes are also highly experienced in playing off external powers to their strategic advantage and in presenting themselves as the least worst alternative to the instability which would ensue from their deposition (Karsh 2003: ch.5).

All external powers are constrained by these countervailing structures of power. Europe and the EU are no exception to this strategic reality.

Influence through institutionalisation

Acceptance and recognition of the existing power structures of the Middle East is a better starting point when seeking what is possible rather than what is desirable. One of the comparative strengths of the EU as a foreign policy actor is that it generally does not seek to impose change but rather to provide a structured set of incentives which are designed to encourage others to change themselves willingly. The EU is also structurally and culturally predisposed to establish frameworks within which these desired processes of transformation are expected to develop. It is this ambition to promote 'effective multilateralism', as set out in the European Security Strategy (ESS) in 2003, which is one of the key differentiating features of the EU's ambitions to be taken seriously as a global actor (European Council 2003; Biscop 2005; Dannreuther and Peterson 2006; Tardy in this volume). The ESS also recognised that it was especially in its immediate neighbourhood that the EU should concentrate its efforts so as to 'promote a ring of well-governed countries to the East of the European Union and on the borders of the Mediterranean with whom we can enjoy close and cooperative relations'. The EU also has a relatively well-developed experience of seeking to establish such institutionalised frameworks of cooperation in the Middle East. Indeed, three dimensions can be identified to the EU's structured relations with the region: the EMP or Barcelona Process; the European Neighbourhood Policy (ENP); and, more recently and tentatively, the makings of a more integrated engagement with the greater Middle East.

One advantage of such frameworks is that they can provide longer-term mechanisms for adaptation even when they fail to achieve their original objectives. This is notably the case with the Barcelona Process, which was established in 1995, and where the general consensus is that it has failed to live up to its expectations. The factors behind this failure have been, though, instructive and have fed into the institutional design of the ENP and to Europe's broader engagement with the greater Middle East.

The Barcelona process: an instructive failure?

There are a number of factors behind the relative lack of success of the EMP and which have provided instructive lessons. The first is that the EMP was originally designed on the assumption of progress being made on the Arab–Israeli front, seeking to generate a broader OSCE-style dynamic of economic, political and social transformation.[3] Indeed, the EMP was set out as a process separate to and hopefully insulated from the MEPP. In reality, as noted above, such insulation was not possible once the MEPP faltered, severely circumscribing the effectiveness of the EMP. A second factor is that the EMP was also originally designed as a counterpart and a parallel process to the EU's eastern European engagement. In practice, once agreement on the future accession of the East-central European (ECE) countries to the EU became unavoidable, the EU's attention became much more focused on the negotiations and support required for eastward enlargement (Mair and Zielonka 2002; Vacudova 2005). At the same time, the EU's ambition to develop a security and defence capability, which was only in an embryonic form at the time of the initiation of the Barcelona Process, was developed through the European engagement in the multiple crises in the Balkans. Overall, these factors meant that the EMP never enjoyed the political attention that it was promised.

One further problematic design flaw in the EMP was the attempt to use the initiative to engineer and 'construct' a pan-Mediterranean region as a deliberate counterpoint to the traditional strategic map of the region, which posits a Europe distinct from a predominantly Arab and Muslim world. Implicit within this design was an expectation that such an experiment would itself contribute to the desired process of economic and political transformation, even without sufficiently compelling direct material incentives (Calleya 1997; Volpi 2004). In practice, this rhetorical commitment to a Mediterranean regionalism contributed to some counter-productive results. From the Southern Mediterranean perspective, the European commitment to regionalism lacked substance when the reality appears to conform to a series of EU bilateral relations, where the EU deals separately with each of the partners. For the EU, the collective regional ambitions were seen to hinder more intensive bilateral relations, resulting in those countries which genuinely sought to forge closer ties with the EU being slowed down by their more recalcitrant partners. In addition, the artificial separation of the Arab Mediterranean countries from the rest of the Middle East tended to contribute to strategic frustration and regional disintegration rather than the hoped-for dynamic of regional integration.

The ENP: towards a more strategic engagement

The European Neighbourhood Policy (ENP), which was unveiled in 2004, was at least in part designed to correct some of the flaws in the EMP and, though not set up to supplant the EMP, to provide a distinctive second overarching dimension to European strategic engagement with the Middle East. The ENP was itself, as compared to the EMP, a reflection of the very different foreign policy actor that the EU was in the mid-2000s as compared to the mid-1990s. The enlarged EU of 25 member states was not only a larger but also a more self-confident actor in international affairs. In addition, the shock of 9/11 and the increased anxieties over the international security environment finally galvanised the EU to admit that it had clear security interests and to identify and prioritise the principal security threats facing Europe. This resulted in the unveiling of the European Security Strategy in 2003, which was inevitably coloured by the perception of the threats emerging from the Middle East.

The Europe of the ENP is, therefore, a more openly strategic power, which is also more settled in its territorial configuration, than was the case in the mid-1990s when the Barcelona Process was initiated. This is most notably reflected in the way that the ENP downplays the EMP's identification of a common Mediterranean vocation of the Southern Mediterranean countries, and instead places these countries as part of a European border region stretching from Morocco in the West to Belarus in the North-East, passing through the Mashreq and the Caucasus.[4] This extensive border region is conceptualised in much the same way as the border regions or marches of traditional empires, where a principal concern is with security and in ensuring that instability flowing from the outside should not undermine internal imperial security. The ENP represents, in this regard, a new East–South parallelism where it is now the western Newly Independent States (Belarus, Ukraine and Moldova) and the South Caucasian states, rather than the ECE accession countries, who are the parallel 'Eastern' partners to the Mediterranean countries. And, in contrast to the earlier parallel tracks, where the standards demanded of the ECE countries were always more rigorous and politically conditioned than for the Mediterranean countries, there is at least a theoretically greater expectation of similar standards for the new East and the South. Democracy, human rights and the rule of law are accorded a more prominent place in the ENP Action Plans than they enjoyed in the EMP Association Agreements (Smith 2005: 764; Dannreuther 2006: 194).

The ENP's strategic orientation also accords less attention in the idealist expectations of the type of Mediterranean regionalism promoted by the EMP. The ENP mantra is that 'no one size fits all' and that, instead of blindly promoting collective regional objectives, the policy will be more carefully differentiated and calibrated to the conditions in each country. The ENP was itself designed by the officials who were responsible for eastward enlargement and therefore the strategic emphasis is on positive conditionality, whereby the EU rewards partners who conform most fully to its minutely ascribed preferences and expectations (Kelley 2006). This shift in emphasis in the ENP has been warmly received by those EMP countries which have so far been most successful in meeting EU ambitions, such as Morocco and Tunisia and, rather more controversially, Israel.

The change in emphasis in the ENP from free trade, which is the principal goal of the Barcelona Process, to offering partners a 'stake in the internal market' is a further reflection of this shift away from a regionalist paradigm. This change is based on the realisation that trade openness is not, in itself, a sufficient generator of reform and that a deeper overhaul of practices is required. For the EU of the mid-2000s, the message is that the way forward is to be actively socialised in European practices of doing things, in particular learning to conform with EU standards and regulatory norms. In other words, increased integration with Europe will bring its rewards, not least in providing greater access to European markets. In addition, there are encouraging signs that the EU increasingly recognises that agricultural free trade and greater prospects for inward migration must also be included within the overall incentive structure. However, this must be counterbalanced by continuing European security concerns, most notably over energy security, uncontrolled migration and international terrorism.

Beyond the ENP to the greater Middle East

One problem with the ENP is that it does not seek to project institutionalised European cooperation beyond the EMP countries of the Southern Mediterranean, which as was noted earlier can be seen as a weakness in the earlier design for the EMP. It remains the case that the European engagement among the Gulf States, Iran, Iraq and the greater Middle East is considerably less defined and institutionalised and, apart from the embryonic EU–GCC[5] framework, lacks the legal contractual arrangements which generally give substance to the external activity of the EU. Nevertheless, there is increasing evidence of growing European presence in this broader region, which provides some grounds for treating this engagement as the third dimension of Europe's Middle East policy framework.

The shifting context for this is linked to the aftermath of the 2003 intervention into Iraq, which had initially so exposed European divisions and internal paralysis. However, European fortunes have arguably considerably improved with the United States bogged down in counter-insurgency and civil war within Iraq (Diamond 2005). As a consequence, although European states have not taken on a greater role in Iraq – once the British presence is excluded – Europe has generally assumed a greater prominence in practically every other area of strategic concern in the Middle East (Biscop 2007). In Afghanistan, European states, working collectively through NATO, have taken on a significant responsibility for entrenching stability, extending NATO's 'out-of-area' operations into Asia for the first time. This is a major test for NATO's continued post-Cold War relevance and for the seriousness of European intentions to play a global role. In Lebanon where, after the failed attempt by Israel to obliterate Hizbullah by force in 2006, the Europeans were almost automatically seen as possessing the military credibility and political legitimacy to manage the delicate task of strengthening the UN force in Southern Lebanon. As a consequence, in 2007, there were 8,000 Europeans out of a force of 13,000 for the UN operation (UNIFIL) (Gowan 2007). In Iran, it is the Europeans who have been the most significant negotiators over the nuclear question, though these efforts have yet to bear significant fruits (Everts 2004; Smeland 2004). And the EU has been the leading actor within the quartet supporting the Palestinians in the context of the MEPP (Dannreuther 2004). In the background is the most ambitious attempt at European social engineering: the intensive accession negotiations between the EU and Turkey. These promise to bring Turkey into Europe and Europe into the heart of the Middle East and all its insecurities, not least those of Turkey's neighbours – Iraq, Iran and Syria.

This greater European engagement remains piecemeal and lacks the formal institutionalisation which characterises Europe's presence elsewhere in the Middle East. In general, individual European states, such as France, the UK, Germany and Italy, play a more visible and substantive role than the EU itself, reflecting the fact that many EU states lack the experience or historic engagement with the region. Nevertheless, what is discernable is that Europe has gained an enhanced credibility as a result of the damaging consequences of the United States treating the Middle East as the experimental testing ground for a unipolar exercise of power and hegemony. Europe/EU has certainly, as a result, profited from becoming the 'acceptable face of the West'. Europe's ambitions do not, though, seek to counterbalance the United States in any meaningful way or deliberately to reduce US influence. Rather, the implicit logic of Europe's greater engagement is to establish an alternative set of norms and principles, which reflect European experiences of integration, as the foundation blocks for breeding the mutual respect and trust amongst Middle Eastern states which is the essential pre-condition for peace.

The core elements of these underlying norms and principles can be understood to include at least four key aspects. First, there is the primacy given by Europe to a resolution of the Israel/Palestine problem based on the two-state solution. Ever since the 1980 Venice Declaration, Europe has been consistent in emphasising that this conflict holds the key to peace in the broader region. Second, there is the emphasis on the local and regional roots of instability in contrast to the tendency, evident in much US and Israeli strategic thought, to view the problems of the region through the prism of external global forces, such as global terrorism (or Soviet penetration in an earlier period). This informs, for example, European policies towards Israel/Palestine, Lebanon and Iran and, in the Iranian case, an implicit recognition that the root causes of Iran's nuclear ambitions lie ultimately in its sense of regional and international insecurity. Third, there is what might be called the John Stuart Mill approach to democratisation, where liberal self-determination is seen as something which can only be generated from within rather than imposed from without. The final element in this distinctive European approach is the conviction that intensive dialogue, ideally institutionalised, with a carefully balanced set of incentive structures, is the most effective approach for generating change. It is such a conviction which has seen the EU and European member states consistently promoting dialogue with so-called 'rogue states', such as Iran and Libya, as the main way to reintegrate them into the international system.

This combined set of norms and values which might be considered to represent a cohesive European 'regime' for defining relations with the Middle East is, though, yet to be fully tested. The challenges are multifold. In Afghanistan, the solidarity between the European NATO states and the United States is considerably strained, particularly over European reservations regarding continued autonomous US counter-terrorist action in Operation *Enduring Freedom*, as well as US anxieties that European states are not providing sufficient resources for their activities within the NATO-led International Security Assistance Force (ISAF).[6] Even between European NATO members, tensions remain high over national caveats which mean that certain countries, such as Germany and the Netherlands, are precluded, unlike the British, Canadian and French forces, from combat operations (Gallis 2006). In Lebanon, the continued presence of substantial European forces goes against the urgent need to see a longer-term resolution of the political problems within the country (Gowan 2007). In both Iran and Israel/Palestine, where the EU and EU states have expended much diplomatic activity, there remains the question of whether concrete achievements will actually emerge from these endeavours (Biscop 2007).

Is there a role for NATO and ESDP in the region?

It is also evident from this preceding analysis that Europe/EU's preferences remain primarily focused on a longer-term framework for transformation which relies primarily on non-military instruments and incentives. There is, as a consequence, a rather limited role generally seen by Europe for the engagement of 'hard security' European institutions, such as NATO and the EU through the European Security and Defence Policy (ESDP). For the ESDP, this is in part driven by the limited capabilities for autonomous military action, where the principal focus of such action is constrained to peace operations in the Balkans and in sub-Saharan Africa. There is little appetite to extend such action into the more complex strategic environment of the Middle East, despite the establishment of two small civilian ESDP missions in the Palestinian Territories. For NATO, the constraint is driven more by the limits of solidarity and the fact that it is still suffering from its enforced marginalisation after the high-point of its engagement in Kosovo, as well as through the subsequent period of transatlantic disunity during the crisis and war in Iraq. As noted above, it is in Afghanistan, on the periphery of the Middle East, that NATO is seeking to resurrect its institutional credibility and where it is finding many difficulties. Given the problems facing this operation, there is limited transatlantic will for the Atlantic Alliance to assume a more prominent role in the heart of the Middle East.

There are other factors which limit the potential for NATO or the ESDP in the Middle East. The ambivalent position of Turkey, a member of NATO but not of the EU and thus not taking part in the ESDP, complicates any putative direct intervention of either institution into the Middle East. Given the strained relationship between Turkey and the Arab world, Turkey's prominence in NATO is an additional element in the more general Arab distrust of the Atlantic Alliance that is considered more threatening to than supportive of Arab interests. The identification of NATO with US hegemony adds to the regional unease in attitudes towards NATO. More generally, the European members of NATO have consistently resisted incorporating the Middle East into NATO's theatre of operations. During the Cold War, there was a vigorous campaign, spearheaded by US policy-makers and analysts, promoting the Middle East as an arena in which NATO could and should act 'out-of-area' so as to provide a European contribution to US responsibilities in the region. European NATO members resisted this, fearing that it would lead to European entanglement with US actions and thus erode NATO solidarity. There is little evidence that this European perception of the Middle East being a de facto 'exclusion zone' for NATO activities has significantly changed. There are from time to time indications of a willingness to see NATO take on a peacekeeping role for an Israel–Palestinian settlement, but this can be taken to be primarily rhetorical in nature while no settlement is thought to be imminent.

There are, nevertheless, opportunities for both NATO and ESDP to adopt a more low-key posture of fostering dialogue and mutual cooperation with their Mediterranean and Middle Eastern counterparts. Both NATO and ESDP have developed institutionalised dialogues with a number of the southern Mediterranean countries. At its 2004 Summit, NATO unveiled the Istanbul Cooperation Initiative which extended such mutual cooperation to the broader Middle East with a particular focus on the GCC countries. Finally, NATO also has a limited presence in Iraq with a training mission. However, it would be unrealistic to expect that such cooperative measures will achieve the same positive results as with a number of European states involved in the Partnership for Peace (PfP) Programme. The most significant contribution of the PfP Programme has been in encouraging security sector reform and the institutionalisation of greater democratic control of the military. It is, though, this area where most Middle Eastern states are most vehemently opposed to such external intervention, since one of the principal pillars of their rule relies on direct personalised control of the armed forces and security services.

This is not to say that a prospective role for NATO and/or the ESDP cannot be envisaged for the future. However, this would depend on significant advances in the peace process and in the general stabilisation of the region, with a consequent lessening of anti-Western sentiments and views. For instance, if a NATO/ESDP peacekeeping force could be one potential scenario for an eventual peace agreement between Israel and Palestine, at the current time, it does appear to be a distant prospect.

Conclusion

This chapter has sought to provide an overview of European interactions with the Middle East which reflects underlying realities and which presents a sanguine assessment of the complex mutual perceptions which are constitutive of this relationship. This includes the recognition that, with the partial exception of Turkey, the Middle East is not part of Europe and that the sense of difference and otherness is an integral element of the relationship. It also recognises that Europe does have critical security interests in the Middle East and that such security concerns will, at times, have a greater salience than the normative agenda of promoting social and political reforms. It is therefore safer not to exaggerate the 'normative' identity of the EU, which can lead to the expectation that the EU acts in ethical and moral ways which are radically different from other great powers. To do so, particularly in the Middle Eastern context, is to constantly highlight the ineluctable security interests that Europe has in the region and its primary duties to its citizens to ensure their security from external threats. Despite these concerns, it appears unlikely that Europe, particularly as expressed through the EU, will seek to become a 'hard power' actor in the Middle East and will thus rely primarily on its broader instruments for gaining influence.

Such a perspective on the realities of political power in the Middle East also involves a recognition of the intrinsic limits of external influence in promoting change in the region. Ultimately, reforms will have to be generated domestically from the governments and peoples of the Middle East. It is also the case that, though such reforms might be desired by the EU and other external powers, there is often a lack of will on the part of governments and critical domestic constituencies within such states for such changes. The critical challenge for interested external powers is, therefore, not one of simple power projection but of designing the most appropriate structures for encouraging reform. This is the area where the EU has in particular gained considerable experience, if not necessarily much immediate success.

The chapter has argued that the EU has also learnt from some of the lessons of its institutionalised engagement over time, as expressed in the shift in policies and orientation from the EMP to the ENP. Europe has sought to articulate a distinctive and alternative conceptualisation, based on its own experiences of integration, on how to overcome the sources of conflict in the broader Middle East. The hope is that lessons can be learnt from this experience which would bring stability to the Middle East. The key issue is whether such attempts will be sufficient to overcome the inherited tensions in European–Middle Eastern relations and to generate a positive response to the need for reforms from the governments and peoples of the region. Ultimately, though, the future prosperity and peace of the Middle East is dependent on the region engaging with the global processes of integration which have been so critical for the economic transformation of other extra-European regions.

Notes

1 The Middle East is an artificial and constructed geographical term and is variously understood. For the purposes of this chapter, the Middle East will be taken to include North Africa, as well as the Arabian Peninsula, the Eastern Mediterranean, Iraq and Iran. The Greater Middle East will refer to a larger region which also includes Afghanistan, Pakistan and Central Asia.
2 The countries of the EMP included initially 12 members – Algeria, Cyprus, Egypt, Israel, Jordan, Lebanon, Malta, Morocco, the Palestinian Authority, Syria, Tunisia and Turkey. The main aim of the EMP was to encourage cross-Mediterranean trade and social and political engagement.
3 See Ghebali's chapter in this volume.
4 The ENP countries include those in Eastern Europe, Ukraine and Moldova; the South Caucasus, Armenia, Georgia and Azerbaijan; as well as the Southern Mediterranean, Algeria, Egypt, Israel, Jordan, Lebanon, Libya, Morocco, Syria, Tunisia and the Palestinian Authority.
5 Gulf Cooperation Council member states include Bahrain, Kuwait, Oman, Qatar, Saudi Arabia, United Arab Emirates. The EU signed a Cooperation Agreement with the GCC in 1988.
6 See Lindley-French's chapter in this volume.

References

Biscop, S. (2005) *The European Security Strategy: A Global Agenda for Positive Power*, Abingdon: Ashgate.
—— (2007) 'For a "More Active" EU in the Middle East. Transatlantic Relations and the Strategic Implications of Europe's Engagement with Iran, Lebanon and Israel-Palestine', *Egmont Paper 13*, Brussels: Royal Institute for International Relations.
Blair, A. (2003) Interview, *Financial Times*, 27 April.
Calleya, S.C. (1997) *Navigating Regional Dynamics in the post-Cold War World: Patterns of Relations in the Mediterranean Area*, Aldershot: Dartmouth Publishers.
Cooper, R. (2003) *The Breaking of Nations: Order and Chaos in the Twenty-First Century*, London: Atlantic Books.
Dannreuther, R. (2004) 'The Middle East: towards a substantive European role in the peace process' in Dannreuther, R. (ed.), *European Union Foreign and Security Policy: Towards a Neighbourhood Strategy*, London: Routledge.
Dannreuther, R. (2006) 'Developing the Alternative to Enlargement: The European Neighbourhood Policy', *European Foreign Affairs Review*, 11: 183–201.
Dannreuther, R. and Peterson, J. (eds) (2006) *Security Strategy and Transatlantic Relations*, London: Routledge.
Diamond, L. (2005) *Squandered Victory: The American Occupation and the Bungled Effort to bring Democracy to Iraq*, New York: Holt.
de Charrette, H. (1997) Interview, *Les Echos*, 8 April.

Dror, Y. and Pardo, S. (2006) 'Approaches and Principles for an Israeli Grand Strategy towards the European Union', *European Foreign Affairs Review*, 11(1): 17–44.

European Council (2003) 'European Security Strategy: A Secure Europe in a Better World', Brussels, 12 December.

Everts, S. (2004) *Engaging Iran: A Test Case for EU Foreign Policy*, London: Centre for European Reform.

Gallis, P. (2006) *NATO in Afghanistan: A test of the Transatlantic Alliance*, Washington: Congressional Research Service Report for Congress.

Gillespie, R. and Youngs, R. (eds) (2002) *The European Union and Democracy Promotion: the Case of North Africa*, London: Frank Cass.

Gordon, P. (1998) *The Transatlantic Allies and the Changing Middle East*, Adelphi Paper 322, Oxford: Oxford University Press.

Gordon, P. and Shapiro, J. (2004) *Allies at War: America, Europe and the Crisis over Iraq*, New York: McGraw-Hill.

Gowan, R. (2007) 'From Beirut to Baghdad', *E-Sharp*, September-October, 44–6.

Greilsammer, I. (1984) 'Failure of the European "Initiatives" in the Middle East', *Jerusalem Quarterly*, 33: 40–49.

Haine, J.-Y. (2004) 'Idealism and Power: The New European Security Strategy', *Current History*, 103: 107–122.

Haas, R.N. (1997) 'The United States, Europe and the Middle East Peace Process' in Blackwill, R.D. and Stürmer, M. (eds), *Allies Divided: Transatlantic Policies for the Greater Middle East*, Cambridge: Centre for Science and International Affairs.

Hollis, R. (1994) 'Israeli-European Economic Relations', *Israel Affairs*, 1(1): 118–132.

Kagan, R. (2003) *Of Paradise and Power: America and Europe in the New World Order*, New York: Alfred A. Knopf.

Karsh, E. (2003) *Rethinking the Middle East*, London: Frank Cass.

Keinle, E. (1998) 'Destabilization through partnership? Euro-Mediterranean relations after the Barcelona process', *Mediterranean Politics*, 3(2): 1–20.

Kelley, J. (2006) 'New wines in old wineskins: promoting political reforms through the new European Neighbourhood Policy', *Journal of Common Market Studies*, 44(1): 26–55.

Mair, P. and Zielonka, J. (eds) (2002) *The Enlarged European Union: Diversity and Adaptation*, London: Frank Cass.

Manners, I. (2002) 'Normative power Europe – A contradiction in terms', *Journal of Common Market Studies*, 40(2): 235–258.

Manners, I. (2008) 'The normative ethics of the European Union', *International Affairs*, 84(1): 65–80.

Neumann, I. (1998) 'European Identity, EU Expansion, and the Integration/Exclusion Nexus', *Alternatives*, 23(3): 397–416.

Onis, Z. (2006) 'Turkey's Encounter with the New Europe: Multiple Transformations, Inherent Dilemmas and the Challenges Ahead', *Journal of Southern European and the Balkans*, 8(3): 279–298.

Perthes, V. (1999) 'The advantages of complementarity: The Middle East peace process' in Gardner, H. and Stefanova, R. (eds), *The New Transatlantic Agenda: Facing the Challenges of Global Governance*, Aldershot: Ashgate.

Phillipart, E. (2003) 'The Euro-Mediterranean Partnership: A critical evaluation of an ambitious scheme', *European Foreign Affairs Review*, 8: 201–220.

Rumelili, B. (2003) 'Liminality and Perpetuation of Conflicts: Turkish-Greek Relations in the Context of Community-Building by the EU', *European Journal of International Relations*, 9(2): 213–248.

Smeland, S.P. (2004) 'Countering Iranian Nukes: a European Strategy', *The Nonproliferation Review*, 11(1): 40–72.

Smith, K.E. (2005) 'The Outsiders: The European Neighbourhood Policy', *International Affairs*, 81(4): 757–773.

Tanner, F. (2004) 'North Africa: partnership, exceptionalism and neglect' in Dannreuther, R. (ed.), *European Union Foreign and Security Policy: Towards a Neighbourhood Strategy*, London: Routledge.

Vacudova, M.A. (2005) *Europe Undivided: Democracy, Leverage and Integration after Communism*, Oxford: Oxford University Press.

Volpi, F. (2004) 'Regional Community Building and the Transformation of International Relations: The Case of the Euro-Mediterranean Partnership', *Mediterranean Politics*, 9(2): 145–164.

Yapp, M. (1991) *The Near East Since the First World War*, London: Longman.

Youngs, R. (2001) 'European Union democracy promotion policies: ten years on', *European Foreign Affairs Review*, 6(3): 355–373.

Youngs, R. (2004) 'Normative dynamics and strategic interests in the EU's external identity', *Journal of Common Market Studies*, 42(2): 415–436.

Zielonka, J. (2006) *Europe as Empire: The Nature of the Enlarged European Union*, Oxford: Oxford University Press.

8 Africa
Still a secondary security challenge to the European Union

Gorm Rye Olsen

Introduction

From the creation of the European Community in 1957, sub-Saharan Africa was arguably the most important region to the European Community among the developing areas of the world.[1] It manifested itself in the Treaty of Rome where Article 131 established the association between the European Community and the countries and territories in Africa with the aim to 'promote the economic and social development ... and to establish close relations between them and the Community as a whole' (Grilli 1994: 8–11).

During the Cold War, development assistance, mainly in the form of the successive Lomé Conventions,[2] was the only external policy instrument the European Union could use towards Africa. The end of the bipolar world and the subsequent new global political environment made clear to many European policy-makers that there was a need for a 'new' European policy that would take into account the new challenges facing Europe (Schirm 1998: 76, Howorth 2007: 52ff.). The European Community was not only met by new challenges, new possibilities also opened for Europe to play a different and more prominent role on the international scene. The new international situation opened the way for establishing the Common Foreign and Security Policy (CFSP) in the Maastricht Treaty in 1992, and subsequently the European Security and Defence Policy (ESDP) (Tardy in this volume).

This chapter will look into the changes that have taken place in the relationship between the European Union and sub-Saharan Africa in the years following the end of the Cold War, with an emphasis on the developments of the first decade of 2000. The focus is on security issues, and the initiatives launched within the framework of the CFSP and ESDP will therefore be dealt with in some detail. The chapter starts with a presentation of the analytical framework that lies behind the analysis, and also offers a discussion of the policy reflections within the EU on Africa since the end of the Cold War. The second part examines European security initiatives in Africa after the events of September 11, and questions whether they mark a genuine renewed interest towards the African continent. Finally, the third part presents an overview of the EU's development policy, humanitarian assistance policy and the policy towards migration from Africa, looking at the extent to which these policy instruments buttress the security goals and concerns of the European Union itself.

The increasing significance of Africa for Europe

Interests, values and decision-making

The changes that have taken place in the European Union's policy towards Africa will be interpreted within a framework that pays special attention to the interests and presumed values held by European decision-makers. It is assumed that interests, preferences and goals may develop over time and therefore, foreign policy behaviour may also change (Hill 2003: 95–155, 296–297). Another assumption is that it is possible to talk about the EU as an international actor with its own interests, however diffuse and amorphous they may be (Hyde-Price 2004: 102; Tardy in this volume). It is pertinent to operate with two types of EU foreign policy interests. On the one hand, there are material interests such as security, economic and political affairs, that pertain to the EU member states' priorities in these three respective fields and that are self-centred. Self-interest, or domestic interests and concerns would then be the primary triggers for foreign policy interventions.

On the other hand, there seems to be a general agreement that the EU builds its external policies on specific ideas and values which are closely associated with the question of the European Union's identity (Hill and Wallace 1996: 9; Hyde-Price 2004: 108). Christopher Hill and William Wallace argue that a number of values and principles are guiding the external policies of the EU which are defined by an emphasis on

> diplomatic rather than coercive instruments, the centrality of mediation in conflict resolution, the importance of long-term economic solutions to political problems, and the need for indigenous people to determine their fate – all of these in contradistinction to the norms of superpower politics.
>
> (1996: 9)

It is assumed that these values and principles put certain limitations on the choice of policy instruments that the EU can apply in its policy towards, in this case, Africa.

Furthermore, foreign policy interests and goals of European decision-makers cannot be seen in isolation (Hyde-Price 2004: 102). They have to be understood as the outcome of discrete political processes involving a number of different actors such as the Brussels-based institutions and the member states. As pointed out by constructivist theories, interests and decisions to a large extent are the result of interaction and socialization between actors operating both at the national as well as at the EU-level (Knill 2001; Smith 2003: 197–198; Smith 2004: 746). For this particular analysis, it means that it is necessary to be open towards the possibility that, depending on the situation, the interests of particular EU institutions and/or of a number of member states may be decisive in the decision-making process.

Finally, decision-makers and decision-making procedures change from one policy area to the other, in the Commission (first pillar of the EU structure) or in the Council of Ministers (in the definition and implementation of second pillar activities). CFSP and ESDP are intergovernmental processes involving the Council secretariat but most importantly the member states as final decision-makers. Within the Council of Ministers, decisions on external affairs are taken in unanimity and only seldom by majority voting, which complicates decision-making. The process is different in the field of development aid and humanitarian assistance. Here, the European Commission plays a leading role in a more or less close dialogue with member states, which is supposed to facilitate decision-making. The EU is involved in Africa simultaneously through first pillar and second pillar activities, and these differences impact directly on EU policy, its efficiency and visibility.

European Union policy reflections on Africa

It is in this context that Africa security developments need to be considered. Following the end of the Cold War, a significant number of civil wars, interstate wars and general instability appeared throughout sub-Saharan Africa. As a consequence, the management or at least the containment of violent conflicts on the continent have increasingly become an EU policy priority. In particular, the genocide in Rwanda in 1994 was an extremely frustrating experience for the European Union. It represented an additional push to the debate within Europe on how to prevent a recurrence of such tragedies in Africa. One step towards serious involvement in conflict prevention in Africa came in March 1996 with the appointment of an EU Special Envoy in 'order to help the countries in the region (i.e. the Great Lakes Region) to resolve the crisis affecting them' (Council of Ministers 1996).

The increasing significance of foreign and security concerns was explicitly articulated in the spring of 2000 by the EU Portuguese Presidency in its 'reflection paper' concerning the EU's future relations with Africa. The paper stressed that

> development priorities should be thought of in the context of ongoing dynamics namely those related to the reorganization of external relations (in the Commission) and the building of a European CFSP. Being

realistic about development means thinking in an integrated manner about politics, security, and trade as well as development aid itself.

(Cardoso *et al.* 2000)

The wish to see Africa as a crucial element in the Union's general external relations led to the first European–African summit, held in Cairo in early April 2000 (Olsen 2005). Thus, before the terrorist attacks on New York and Washington on September 11, 2001, security issues were fairly high on the European Union's foreign policy agenda towards Africa.

The Cairo summit and the EU attempt to formulate a coherent EU policy towards the whole of Africa were followed-up in December 2005 by the adoption of the 'EU Strategy for Africa'. It set out the first European framework to address the political goal of improving coordination, coherence and consistency of the Union's policies and instruments aimed at Africa (European Council 2005). For the time being, the final result of this process came in late 2007 with the second EU–Africa summit, held in Lisbon. The Lisbon meeting produced a concluding document describing the relationship between the two regions as a 'Strategic Partnership' (EU–African Union 2007). Peace and security were among the key issues, but immigration, trade, human rights, development and climate change also figured high on the agenda.

Behind the numerous policy declarations, it is possible to identify two debates that have taken place since the early 1990s and that have directly impacted on the EU's propensity to deal with Africa. First, the so-called 'development debate' characterized the period from 1993 to the beginning of the first decade of 2000 when the development sector in the European institutions were pulling together a strategy on how to support conflict prevention in Africa by means of development assistance (Olsen 2002: 316–322). The launch of a European debate on conflict management was followed by a number of symbolically important decisions such as the Madrid Summit in 1995, stressing that the security problems in Africa were also a concern in Europe (Olsen 2002: 317). More specifically, article 11 of the Cotonou Agreement of 2000 explicitly deals with '[p]eace-building policies, conflict prevention and resolution', and stresses that 'in situations of violent conflict, the Parties shall take all suitable action to prevent an intensification of violence' and 'shall ensure the creation of the necessary links between emergency measures, rehabilitation and development cooperation' (ACP–EU 2000).

Following the signing of the Cotonou Agreement, a number of policy statements emphasized that development policy and cooperation programmes are the most powerful instruments when the European Community wants to treat the causes of conflict. Therefore, these instruments should form part of an integrated approach to conflict prevention alongside other direct and indirect EU tools. In May 2001, the Council adopted a 'Common Position concerning conflict prevention, management and resolution in

Africa' which, in its preamble, recalls the Cotonou Agreement. As a CFSP statement, this Common Position is important as it complements the development focus of the Communication on the EU–Africa dialogue issued in June 2003 (European Centre for Development Policy Management (ECDPM) 2006: 23). The Conclusions from the Development Council in May 2002 marked the end of a period of policy reflection on conflict prevention in EU development circles. Thereafter, the EU institutions on the development side moved into an operationalization phase.

The second debate, broader and more clearly focused on security issues, established an explicit link between security and development. It began to be promoted to the public agenda by the EU foreign policy and defence circles as of 2002–03. This 'political-military' debate was formalized in 2003 when EU Foreign Ministers asked Javier Solana to produce a security concept which led to the adoption of the *European Security Strategy* (ESS) in late 2003 (ECDPM 2006: 26; Olsen 2006: 162–164). Among other issues, violent conflicts in certain sub-Saharan Africa countries were pointed out as being of special concern. The ESS clearly stressed that 'Security is a precondition for development'. As a report of the European Centre for Development Policy Management (ECDPM) put it,

> The scope of the vision of the ESS is thus broad and comprehensive and does not confine itself to traditional notions of 'hard' security. The ESS also acknowledged the influence and interplay of different areas of EU external relations. In doing so, it recognised the value of the work that had been done for years by the development side in supporting measures to promote good governance and conflict prevention.
>
> (ECDPM 2006: 24)

Subsequently, the 2005 'Africa Strategy' and its ambition to develop coordination, coherence and consistency in the European Union's foreign policy draw on both these debates. Unsurprisingly, the 'Africa Strategy' reflected the mixture of these discussions manifesting itself in the 'new' recognition within the development philosophy of the European Union, namely that peace and stability are crucial preconditions for lasting development. The realization is clearly spelled out in the document which states that 'Without peace, there can be no lasting development' (Council 2005b: 2), and that 'it is now universally recognised that there can be no sustainable development without peace and security. Peace and security are therefore the first essential prerequisites for sustainable development' (European Commission 2005: 3). It follows that the European Union steps up its efforts to promote peace and security at all stages of the conflict cycle (European Commission 2005: 21ff.). The Union has to 'set up a more comprehensive EU approach complementing these Community instruments through CFSP/ESDP approaches. A common EU policy is therefore needed.' (European Commission 2005: 22).

To sum up, the emphasis put by the EU on peace, stability and security in Africa is not only an expression of a new recognition that these circumstances are important for the promotion of development in Africa. It is also an expression of a European wish to adapt its policy to the changing global security context that made it necessary to rethink the EU's policy towards the developing world. The December 2007 Lisbon Europe–Africa summit was an element in this process. The summit gave much emphasis to the so-called 'Africa–EU political partnership'. It was no coincidence that the headline of the concluding document from the summit was 'The Africa–EU Strategic Partnership. A Joint Africa–EU Strategy'. The strategic partnership includes continuation of the existing Africa–EU Ministerial Troika system stressing that these troikas have to maintain the dialogue between the two parties through regular meetings of Senior Officials and Ministers (EU–African Union 2007: 2ff., 21).

After September 11: new and old European priorities

The fight against terrorism in Africa: a rhetorical response

There are a number of obvious and striking points of resemblance between the US post-September 11 evaluation of Africa and that of the European Union as far as the fight against international terrorism is concerned. There is no doubt that the European Union considers terrorism as a very serious threat to Europe. It is stated clearly in the European Union's security strategy where the list of 'key threats' has many similarities with those found in the US *National Security Strategy*. Terrorism is placed as one of the main threats to the EU followed by the threats from the proliferation of weapons of mass destruction, regional conflicts, state failure and organized crime. Concerning regional conflicts, the ESS points out that 'conflicts can lead to extremism, terrorism and state failure; it provides opportunities for organized crime'. On state failure, the ESS underlines that 'collapse of the state can be associated with obvious threats, such as organized crime or terrorism. State failure is an alarming phenomenon that undermines global governance and adds to regional instability' (European Council 2003: 4). Furthermore, the ESS established a close link between the new security threats and underdevelopment which is of particular importance in the case of EU policies towards sub-Saharan Africa.

Following the terrorist attacks on September 11, 2001, the pre-existing and ongoing debate on European security became strongly focused on the need to react to terrorism and on how to do so adequately (Allen and Smith 2002: 97ff.; Boer and Monar 2002: 11–28). The European Council produced a number of declarations and statements concerning international terrorism starting with the 'Conclusion and plan of action of the extraordinary European Council meeting on 21 September 2001' (European Council 2001). On the other hand and in spite of declaratory unanimity,

September 11 has had mixed effects on the attempts to develop common responses to international terrorism. A considerable number of initiatives were taken within the realm of the third pillar of the EU structure, dealing with Justice and Home Affairs. However, when it came to common initiatives within the area of defence and security policy (second pillar), there were striking and serious shortcomings. Signs of re-nationalization of these policies among the larger EU member states, not least in the United Kingdom, have been identified (Duke 2002: 153–169).

As far as Africa is concerned, the EU has restricted its post-September 11 policy to issuing a number of declarations condemning terrorism. At the first EU–Africa Ministerial Meeting held in Brussels on October 11 2001 as part of the so-called Cairo process, the discussions were strongly influenced by the attacks on the United States. The issue of the 'fight against terrorism' was added to the original agenda, and the ministers agreed on a Joint Declaration on terrorism. At the second Ministerial Meeting, held in Ouagadougou on 28 November 2002 and also within the framework of the EU–Africa dialogue, the ministers once again adopted a Joint Africa–Europe Declaration on terrorism, reiterating their commitment to fighting international terrorism and condemning all acts of terrorism (European Council 2002).[3]

The growing and rhetorical interest in Africa was also illustrated at state level. At the Franco-British summit in Le Touquet in February 2003, Jacques Chirac and Tony Blair emphasized their desire to support the efforts of the African Union to strengthen Africa's peacekeeping capabilities. 'Touquet thus meant switching their responsibility to intervene militarily in Africa to the Africans themselves', Catherine Gegout emphasizes (2005: 435). Indirectly, the British–French support of the African Union can be considered as an element in the fight against terrorism in Africa. But, most importantly, it reflected a continuation of policies and preferences which were formulated during the 1990s (Landgraf 1998; Olsen 2005), and that were little affected by the events of September 11.

The issue of fighting terrorism remained on the agenda of the EU–Africa dialogue during the years following September 11 2001, but the issue increasingly receded into the background. For example, at the EU–Africa Summit held in Dublin in April 2004, terrorism attracted only the following attention, in a document of five pages: 'Ministers reaffirmed their commitment and determination to continue to co-operate in the global fight against terrorism' (EU–African Union 2004). At the same time, traditional topics such as peace and security, governance, regional integration and trade, debt, food security and HIV/AIDS continued to be addressed at some length. In the end, if the European Union did give declaratory priority to the fight against terrorism, the actual policy priorities remained more or less unaffected by this particular security threat as the following analysis of the ESDP/CFSP initiatives launched after 2001 shows. This state of affairs was confirmed in the concluding document adopted at the second

EU–Africa summit in December 2007. The fight against international terrorism was hardly mentioned and when it was done, the threat from terrorism was put in line with 'issues relating to trans-national organised crime … mercenary activities, and human and drugs trafficking, as well as the illicit trade in natural resources, which are a major factor in triggering and spreading conflicts and undermining state structures…' (EU–African Union 2007: 6).

Africa as the new region for EU-led operations

The Common Foreign and Security Policy (CFSP) and the European Security and Defence Policy (ESDP) towards Africa have developed strongly during the past ten years. In June 2003, the EU launched its first military operation on the African continent, with Operation Artemis in the Democratic Republic of the Congo (DRC). Created in the framework of the ESDP, Operation Artemis was groundbreaking as it was simultaneously the first EU-led crisis management operation outside Europe and the first ESDP autonomous operation, i.e. implemented without resorting to NATO assets under the Berlin Plus Agreement (Gegout 2005; Ulriksen *et al.* 2004). The operation was created by UN Security Council resolution 1484 of 30 May 2003 and by the Council Joint Action of 5 June 2003 (Council of the EU 2003). It counted about 2,000 troops (Faria 2004: 43ff.; Ulriksen *et al.* 2004: 515–519). Although EU-led in principle, it benefited from a significant contribution from France that acted as the framework nation and provided the bulk of the forces. Other EU countries, as well as some future members and non-European countries, also provided personnel. The aim of Artemis was to stabilize the security situation in the crisis-ridden Ituri province in the Democratic Republic of Congo and thereby improve the humanitarian situation in and around the main town of Bunia. Many observers warned that a new outbreak of violence could threaten the ongoing national process aimed at reaching a negotiated settlement to the conflicts in the DRC (Ulriksen *et al.* 2004: 509–511; Faria 2004). In that situation, the UN Secretary-General Kofi Annan called for the establishment of a coalition of willing nations that were ready to respond to the humanitarian crisis in Ituri. At the same time, the operation acted as a 'bridging force', in the sense that it was supposed to secure an interim solution until the United Nations could deploy a strengthened brigade in the province (UNSC 2003; Tardy 2005).

Evaluated against the declared objectives, the mission was fairly successful (UN 2004: 16ff.). First of all, the security situation in Bunia was markedly improved. Second, the presence of the EU soldiers ensured that a large percentage of refugees could return to the main town. Third, economic life picked up again as the improved security situation made it possible for emergency assistance to be distributed on a much larger scale than before. Fourth, Operation Artemis did also well in that the EU troops handed over control to a regular UN force at a date agreed upon beforehand, a successful first experience for the UN and the EU with 'bridging operations' (Faria 2004: 43ff.). Finally, the operation cleared the way for the EU to increase its presence in the DRC.

In December 2004, the EU deployed police officers in the DRC, with the EUPOL mission. This was the EU's first civilian crisis management operation in Africa which, despite its civilian dimension and its limited scope, fell within the framework of ESDP. An advisory and assistance mission for security sector reform (EUSEC DRC) was also launched in June 2005 as an illustration of the European Union's engagement towards promoting stability and security in the DRC. The mission was intended to provide assistance to the local security authorities ensuring that their action was compatible with human rights, democratic principles and good governance.

Two other military missions were launched by the EU in Africa in 2006 and 2007: one in the DRC, the other in Chad and the Central African Republic. Both were autonomous operations created on the basis of a UN Security Council resolution.

During the election campaign in the spring of 2006, maintenance of order in Kinshasa was recognized by the UN as a key element for the success of the electoral process. As a consequence, following the adoption by the UN Security Council of resolution 1671 (2006), the Foreign Affairs Council decided to temporarily strengthen the EUPOL mission in Kinshasa by creating a military operation in support of the UN mission (MONUC) in the DRC (Council of the EU 2006). The EUFOR DRC was conducted within the framework of the ESDP and was assigned to support MONUC to stabilize the situation during the election process of summer 2006, protect civilians and secure the Kinshasa airport. The operation was put under the operational command of Germany, with France providing a large part of the troops. The force included an advance element of almost 1,000 soldiers in and around Kinshasa (Lange 2007), as well as almost 2,000 troops on-call 'over the horizon', concretely in neighbouring Gabon, from where they would be quickly deployable if necessary (EU Council Secretariat 2006; Howorth 2007: 238–239).

The latest EU-led military operation was created in the fall of 2007 in Chad and the Central African Republic (EUFOR Chad/CAR), as a 'bridging operation', before the UN assumes control after a one-year deployment. As the two other EU-led military operations in Africa, EUFOR Chad/CAR was created by a joint action of the Council (Council of the European Union 2007) following a resolution by the UN Security Council (2007). The mission was deployed in early 2008 for a period of one year. It is aimed at protecting civilians, particularly refugees coming from Darfur and settling down in the east of Chad and north-east of CAR; facilitating the delivery of humanitarian aid; and contributing to the protection of UN personnel and facilities. The theoretical strength of the force is

3,700 personnel, with, once again, France providing the bulk of the troops and the operational headquarters.

Finally, alongside ESDP efforts and following Operation Artemis, the EU increased its presence in Africa through European Community instruments. The General Affairs Council approved in November 2003 a draft decision to use the European Development Fund (EDF) to create a so-called 'Peace Facility for Africa' in line with the request made by the African Union (Faria 2004: 36). The 'African Peace Facility' (APF), worth €250 million, was officially established in March 2004 with the aim to support non-military aspects of African peace operations. The APF is the outcome of almost ten years of reflection by European and African decision-makers on the importance of conflict prevention for development and on the need for appropriate measures to tackle conflicts in Africa. As mentioned, years before it had fully worked out the details of its conflict prevention policy in 2001 and 2002, the EU had reached agreement with the African, Caribbean, and Pacific (ACP) countries on the need for a legal framework guiding their collaboration in this particular area (namely Article 11 in the Cotonou Agreement). There was therefore no legal obstacle to the transfer of money originally aimed at promoting socio-economic development (i.e. the EDF) to the Peace Facility (ECDPM 2006: 4ff.). Yet, at the political level, many European countries were wary of what they saw as a potential 'slippery slope' with development funds being increasingly called upon to fund security-related work.

By October 2006, the Peace Facility had supported the African Union's AMIS mission in Darfur by providing more than €242 million to its mission. It was also used to support a multilateral peace operation in the Central African Republic. In parallel, the EU has disbursed a significant amount of money to humanitarian assistance, and has funded political initiatives aimed at solving the crisis in Darfur (EU Council Secretariat 2005). The EU involvement in Darfur has been promoted by a strong European desire to have the African Union to take responsibility for security in Africa (Howorth 2007: 216). Allegedly, one aim was to avoid direct EU military involvement (Confidential interviews, Brussels, December 2005). Jolyon Howorth holds a rather critical view on the overall outcome of the EU's involvement in the management of the crisis, arguing that 'the EU has ultimately proven unable to contribute in a manner consistent with its future ambitions and historical responsibilities for Africa', and concluding that 'one is struck by the shortfall between the rhetoric and the reality' (Howorth 2007: 217).

European versus African interests

The interests motivating EU decision-makers to launch these initiatives appear to have been mixed. Howorth argues that 'accusations that it was primarily intended to get some good coverage for the EU are hard to avoid'. The Congolese crisis may also have functioned 'as a political testing ground for the EU to design forms of intervention' (Security and Defence Agenda 2007: 34, 9, 13). At the same time, as Howorth put it (2007: 239–240), the EU efforts were 'consciously framed as part of the EU's comprehensive approach to the DRC' and 'when taken together, the four EU missions in Congo do amount to a sizeable measure of assistance'.

Indeed, Operation Artemis appears to be a spectacular initiative and signalled a new and more proactive EU security policy towards sub-Saharan Africa (Ulriksen 2004: 521ff.). On the one hand, it marked the involvement of the EU as an institution in security management in Africa. On the other hand, it is both a continuation of policy reflections that were launched already during the 1990s, and the expression of national concerns.

As previously stated, France acted as the framework nation and pushed for the creation of the operation. A few weeks after the Iraq episode and the profound political crisis that it created within the EU, French president Jacques Chirac may have seen the intervention as a way to prove the capacity of the EU to act autonomously from NATO. Beyond a genuine EU will to play a role in security management in Africa, the EU may have been instrumentalized by one of its key members, France, for its own foreign policy interests, using Artemis as opportunity to present the EU as an effective and autonomous military actor (Gegout 2005: 437; Ulriksen 2004: 512; Tardy 2004). For Britain, participation in Artemis was less important. In the context of the Iraq crisis, the idea for Britain was mainly to prove its continued interest in developing a European security policy (Gegout 2005: 438). Overall, the Congo operation demonstrated that European powers could still cooperate in spite of the deep divisions caused by the war on Iraq.

In this light, Operation Artemis was not necessarily an outcome of changing preferences or change of interests within the foreign policy set-up of the EU. If the operation is interpreted as an attempt to bridge the disagreements within the European Union following the Iraq war, then it has to be understood as reflecting internal EU priorities rather than as an expression of particular European security concerns in Africa. By the same token, if it is a way for France to assert the role of the EU as an autonomous security actor, again exogenous factors prevail over endogenous, i.e. African, concerns.

In general terms, ESDP/CFSP initiatives launched towards Africa in recent years have been motivated by a whole range of different interests and concerns. It is safe to conclude that the ones analysed in this chapter were, to some extent, motivated by a concern for the consequences of conflict and instability in Africa. With the instruments supplied in the Maastricht Treaty and in the subsequent CFSP- and ESDP-related decisions, the European Union can actually launch initiatives which would have been impossible to carry out beforehand. Second, the actions taken were also motivated by concerns internal to the European Union itself. In fact, if EU action was partly motivated by concerns for Africa, most importantly they were launched for 'domestic' European reasons. The wish to raise the profile of the European Union on the international scene comes into play, as well as the will to reconcile EU member states in the wake of the 2003 Iraq war. Finally, it can be argued that the ambition to have Africans take over the responsibility for security in Africa is more an attempt to serve European interests and concerns, namely the wish not to be involved any more, rather than evidence of Europe taking care of 'African interests'.

Development and humanitarian aid in Africa: addressing needs or buttressing EU security concerns

Drawing on the previous sections, this part scrutinizes if and to what extent the development assistance policy and the humanitarian assistance policy have buttressed the security goals of the European Union in Africa. Also, the section touches upon an issue which has become an integrated part of the development-security debate in Europe, namely the politically sensitive question of how to stem the flow of illegal African migrants.

According to numerous recent policy declarations, development assistance is considered as a very important policy tool to promote stability and thus peace. By 2004, the European Union provided around 11 per cent of global aid flows (OECD 2006: 158, table 1). If the aid of the EU member states is added to this figure, 'Europe' accounted for more than 64 per cent of the global development assistance in 2004 (OECD 2006: 158, table 1).

At the UN Millennium Summit in September 2000, the EU countries promised to further increase their development aid in order to secure resources for reaching the ambitious Millennium Development Goals (MDGs). The goal of increasing European aid was later revised upwards as EU countries agreed to reach 0.51 per cent of individual gross national income in development aid by 2010 and 0.7 per cent by 2015. It was also decided that 50 per cent of the agreed increase should be allocated to the African continent (European Council 2005: 8–9). The increase in the volume of aid to sub-Saharan Africa means that the region is receiving a slightly increasing share of the total net disbursements of official development assistance from the EU, as it almost reached 37 per cent in 2005 compared with 30.4 per cent in 2001 (OECD 2006: table 29).

Parallel to the growth in aid volumes, remarkable changes took place in the geographical distribution of development aid from the EU to individual African countries. From 2001 to 2005, a number of countries experienced increases in their aid volume, whereas others had their aid reduced. For example, the aid to Ivory Coast was cut by more than 70 per cent. From 2001 to 2003, Kenya experienced significant reductions in aid allocations from the EU, but from 2004 till 2005 there was almost a doubling of the aid volume to the country. In this context, it is most interesting that a number of countries experienced significant increases in their aid alloca-tions. Measured in current prices, the DRC experienced an increase in EU aid of around 500 per cent, and Mozambique some 200 per cent, whereas the aid to Sudan jumped by no less than 1,000 per cent from 2001 to 2005 (OECD 2007: 68).

These two trends in European development assistance policy require an interpretation. The increasing political priority given to conflict manage-ment and prevention can explain the remarkable increase in aid to the DRC and Sudan. Both countries are in an extremely vulnerable situation where development aid can be one of the instruments of stabilization. And both countries are among the priorities of ESDP towards Africa. As aid increased, particularly after 2001, one could wonder whether the increase or the shift in geographical distribution were linked one way or another to the fight against terrorism. This link has proven impossible to substantiate with empirical data (Olsen 2006).

On the contrary, it seems as if the European decision-makers disburse aid to the African countries based mainly on criteria tied to the traditional aim of reducing poverty, in accordance with the UN Millennium Development Goals. At least, this type of argument could explain the significant increases in aid disbursements to the DRC, Sudan, Zambia and Mozambique. In recent years, these countries are in general among the big recipients of development aid because there is either a belief that these countries are on a positive course of development or because the needs for assistance are enormous, as underlined by the critical situation in the DRC. This 'tradi-tional' type of reasoning may also explain the reductions in aid to the Ivory Coast with its ongoing civil war and Kenya, Eritrea and Ethiopia with their continuing problems with lack of good governance. The moderate shift in the geographical pattern of distribution of EU aid to individual African countries confirms that the allocation of aid continues to be mainly based on the goal of eradicating poverty. Based on these observations, it is not possible to claim that development aid buttressed the narrow security goals of the European Union.

Analysis is slightly different insofar as the European Union's humanitar-ian assistance policy is concerned, as it appears a much more relevant instrument in supporting ESDP/CFSP initiatives aimed at enhancing security and stability. At least, one can argue that this particular policy instrument has, to a certain extent, buttressed the aim of giving priority to conflict management and conflict prevention in Africa. The combined resources of the European Community Humanitarian Aid department (ECHO) and of bilateral contributions made 'Europe' the biggest provider of humanitarian assistance during the 1990s, accounting for 53–54 per cent of global humanitarian assistance on average (ECHO 1999: 29). As a separate donor, ECHO accounted for around one-third of the amount, placing it among the top global donors of humanitarian aid (ECHO 1999: 29).

Between 2001 and 2006, on average 37 per cent of all humanitarian assistance from the EU went to Africa (ECHO 2002: 15, 20; ECHO 2006). This signifies that Africa received a considerable amount of humanitarian assistance from the European Union both before and after September 11. However, based on the actual financial decisions, it appears that after 2001 ECHO ended up disbursing significant amounts of humanitarian assistance to Afghanistan and Iraq. As a matter of fact, these two countries were the two largest recipients of disbursements of humanitarian assistance from the EU post-9/11. Afghanistan continued to be so in 2004. The amounts are remarkable compared with the disbursements to Congo and Southern Africa (ECHO 2003, 2004) which were also big crisis regions.

The significant disbursements of humanitarian assistance to Afghanistan and Iraq stress at least one important observation, that is, humanitarian assistance is increasingly considered as an integrated part of the foreign policy of the European Union. Depending on the specific case, humanitarian aid will be channelled to crises that are considered politically important, to a large extent because of intensive media coverage, and partly irrespective of the objective needs elsewhere (Macrae 2004; Macrae and Harmer 2004). During a limited number of years, the situations in Afghanistan and in Iraq have been so important to some decision-makers within the EU and to the interests of many member states that huge amounts of assistance were directed to these countries. However, this pattern of disbursement did not preclude that a significant percentage of ECHO's resources were channelled to Africa and to countries which were considered as high priority to European decision-makers within the realm of the CFSP/ESDP.

Finally, we turn to the policy initiatives aimed at curbing the illegal migration of Africans into the European Union. Migration and policies to deal with the return of rejected asylum seekers and migrants were included in article 13 of the Cotonou Treaty from 2000. The article stated that 'each of the African states [...] shall accept the return and the readmission of any of its nationals who are illegally present in the territory of a member state of the European Union'. Migration was a hot topic at the June 2002 EU summit in Seville, where the debate revealed a serious split among the member states on the question of illegal migrants. On the one hand, Britain and Spain led the charge for a tough-sounding policy that included stricter border control, visa policy and information on illegal immigrants. A key element in the British–Spanish alliance was a proposal that the EU should be able to impose sanctions in the form of withholding development aid to countries that refuse to take back their own citizens who have been denied asylum by the EU countries (*The Economist* 2002: 30–31; *Financial Times* 2002). On the other hand, France and other countries were strongly against this proposal.

Yet, despite these disagreements, the years following the Seville summit have revealed an increasing agreement among the EU members on migration.

First of all, it is remarkable that the EU members have agreed that there is a link between migration and development in Europe, and also that remittances from migrants may contribute to a positive development in their home countries. At the same time, along with the increasing consensus on the positive sides of migration, there has developed a common European understanding of the need to stem the flow of illegal migrants into the EU and instead encourage legitimate migration from Africa. Several thousand illegal migrants die every year trying to travel to Europe by sea although the numbers making this perilous journey have fallen because of joint air and sea patrols carried out by EU member states (*BBC World* 2007).

The urgent need to take action in order to stem the rising tide of illegal migration from Africa resulted in the November 2006 joint EU–Africa summit in Tripoli, Libya (Libya being one of the main transit countries for illegal migrants to Europe, along with Morocco, Senegal and Mauritania). On the one hand, EU officials offered assistance, including equipment and staff, to help Libya improve its control of illegal migrants. On the other hand, the conference focused on ways to widen the opportunities for legal migration. The European Commissioner for Justice, Freedom and Security, Franco Frattini, announced plans to provide African countries with information on job opportunities in Europe through the establishment of a European 'Job Mobility Portal' (Castelfranco 2006). Both these elements were addressed at the second EU–Africa summit held in Lisbon in December 2007. The Africa–EU Strategic Partnership stated that the 'partners will foster the linkages between migration and development, maximise the development impact of remittances, facilitate the involvement of diasporas/migrant communities in development processes'. It also said that

> Africa and the EU will jointly address the down-sides of migration. This includes jointly combating illegal migration where cooperation needs to be stepped up, including through cooperation on return and readmission of migrants [...], as well as on border control and trafficking in human beings.
>
> (EU–African Union 2007: 16)

Summing up, if the development aid policy does not seem to buttress the narrow security goals of the EU, the conclusion is more open as far as the humanitarian assistance to Africa is concerned. Depending on the specific situation, this particular policy instrument may or may not buttress the Union's security concerns. On the migration issue, a number of policy initiatives have been launched, which reflect a combination of hard security concerns and attention paid to European values. Stricter control, surveillance and return of rejected asylum seekers and illegal migrants definitely reflect attempts to take care of the EU's own material interests. On the other hand, the recognition that migration may help the development efforts of African countries can be interpreted as a reflection of norms on which the Union builds its external policies.

Conclusion

There is no doubt that sub-Saharan Africa holds an important position within the current security reflections of the European Union. The EU is preoccupied with widespread instability, violent conflicts on the continent and illegal immigration to Europe and, depending on the specific situation and the specific time, has decided to intervene within the framework of CFSP and ESDP.

Yet, this does not mean that the region has become a high-priority security concern, as indicated by the limited attention that the fight against terrorism attracts in the actual implementation of the EU's Africa policy, or by the lack of strategic thinking about the development-security nexus.

It follows that the European Union does not, as a general rule, intervene in crisis situations in Africa. As the Darfur crisis shows, the EU is willing to significantly finance armed interventions there, but having African troops carrying out the operations on the ground is also a priority.

The picture becomes somewhat blurred when individual operations are scrutinized. Then, it appears that the motives and interests behind the actual interventions are mixed. There is no doubt that internal European concerns contribute to explaining the decisions taken. Traditionally, France and Britain have had key interests in Africa and the two former colonial powers appear to have been strongly involved in the decisions on interventions analysed in this chapter. As a consequence, ESDP/CFSP interventions in Africa, in the first decade of 2000, can be interpreted as a concomitant handling of French/British national interest as well as of European Community or European Union interests.

The mixed picture of the European Union's security concerns in Africa is confirmed when the development aid policy, the humanitarian aid policy and the policy on migration are included in the analysis. Development aid policy seems to a large extent to be motivated by the aim of eradicating poverty in Africa. But at the same time, development policy did not work against the goals of promoting stability. The same picture appears when the humanitarian assistance policy is considered. However, the recent policy initiatives towards curbing illegal migration from Africa reflect serious European security concerns as well as they are the expression of European values.

Overall, Africa is still as important to the European Union as it was in 1957. European concerns have evolved, and they now definitely include the promotion of security and stability. Most probably, there is a common understanding among European decision-makers that stability and peace are crucial preconditions for eradicating poverty and for promoting development on the African continent. However, from time to time, other more narrow European security concerns seem to prevail in decision-making on Africa.

Notes

1 This chapter will consider Africa south of the Sahara and will refer to this geographic area as 'Africa'. See Roland Dannreuther's chapter in this volume for European relations with North Africa.
2 The Lomé Convention (first signed in 1975 and renegotiated three times before being replaced by the Cotonou Agreement of 2000) is a trade and aid agreement establishing a framework of cooperation between the EU and African, Caribbean, and Pacific (ACP) countries.
3 The strong denouncement at the Ouagadougou meeting may have to be considered in the context of the terrorist act that took place in Mombasa, Kenya, on the very morning of the meeting.

References

ACP–EU (2000) 'Partnership Agreement Between the Members of the African, Caribbean and Pacific Group of States of the One Part, and the European Community and its Member States, of the Other Part, signed in Cotonou, Benin on 23 June. Online, available at http://acp.int.dotnet15.hostbasket.com/en/conventions/cotonou/accord1.htm (accessed 26 May 2008).

Allen, D. and Smith, M. (2002) 'External Policy Developments', *Journal of Common Market Studies*, Annual Review of the European Union 2001/2002, 40: 97–115.

BBC World (2007) 'EU–Africa: The key issues'. Online, available at http://news.bbc.co.uk/2/hi/europe/7130402.stm (accessed on 26 May 2008).

Boer, M. and Monar, J. (2002) 'Keynote Article: 11 September and the Challenge of Global Terrorism to the EU as a Security Actor', *Journal of Common Market Studies*, Annual Review of the European Union 2001/2002, 40: 11–28.

Cardoso, F.J., Khüne, W. and Honwana, J.B. (2000) *Reflection paper. Priorities in EU Development Cooperation in Africa: Beyond 2000*, Brussels: Council of Ministers.

Castelfranco, S. (2006) 'The EU–Africa Summit Addresses European Migration', 22 November. Online, available at www.voanews.com/english/archive/2006–11/2006–11–22-voa30.cfm (accessed 26 May 2008).

Council of the European Union (2003) 'Council Joint Action 2003/423/CFSP of 5 June 2003 on the EU military operation in the DRC', *Official Journal of the EU*, L 143/50, 11 June.

—— (2005) *The EU and Africa: Towards a Strategic Partnership*, The European Council meeting, Brussels, 15–16 December.

—— (2006) 'Council Joint Action 2006/319/CFSP of 27 April 2006 on the European Union military operation in support of the United Nations Organization Mission in the Democratic Republic of the Congo (MONUC) during the election process', *Official Journal of the European Union*, L 116/98, 29 April.

—— (2007) 'Council Joint Action 2007/677/CFSP of 15 October 2007 on the European Union military operation in the Republic of Chad and in the Central African Republic', *Official Journal of the European Union*, L 279/21, 23 October.

Council of Ministers (1996) 'Joint Action 96/250/CFSP', 25 March.

Duke, S. (2002) 'CESDP and the EU Response to 11 September: Identifying the Weakest Link', *European Foreign Affairs Review*, 7: 153–169.
ECHO (1999) *Caught in the storm. Annual Review 1998*, Luxemburg.
—— (2002) *Sustaining Hope in a Changing World. ECHO 2001*, Luxemburg.
—— (2003) *Responding to New Needs. ECHO 2002*, Luxemburg.
—— (2004) *Protecting the humanitarian space. ECHO 2003*, Luxemburg.
—— (2006) *Hope After Disaster. Annual Review 2005*, Luxemburg.
The Economist (2002) 29 June.
EU–African Union (2004) Communiqué, EU–Africa Ministerial meeting in Dublin, 1 April.
—— (2007) *The Africa–EU Strategic Partnership. A Joint Africa–EU Strategy*, Adopted at the Second EU–Africa Summit, Lisbon, December 9.
EUPOL (2006) *The first European Police mission in Africa*, October (Press Document).
European Centre for Development Policy Management (ECDPM) (2006) *Mid-Term Evaluation of the African Peace Facility Framework-Contract*, Final report, Maastricht, 16 January.
European Commission (2005) *Communication from the Commission to the Council, the European Parliament and the European Economic and Social Committee. EU Strategy for Africa: Towards a Euro-African pact to accelerate Africa's development*, Brussels, 12 October.
European Council (2001) *Conclusions and Plan of Action of the Extraordinary European Council Meeting on 21 September 2001*, Brussels.
—— (2002) *Africa–Europe Dialogue (Follow-up to the Cairo Summit) – Second Ministerial Meeting*, Ouagadougou, Burkina Faso, 28 November, 15197/02, Brussels, 3 December.
—— (2003) *A Secure Europe in a Better World. European Security Strategy*, Brussels, 12 December.
—— (2005) *European Union Strategy for Africa*, Brussels.
EU Council Secretariat (2005) 'Factsheet. EU Responses to the crisis in Darfur', Brussels.
—— (2006) 'Background, DRC Elections 2006', Brussels, June.
Faria, F. (2004) *Crisis management in sub-Saharan Africa. The Role of the European Union*, Paris: European Union Institute for Security Studies.
Financial Times (2002) 13 June.
Gegout, C. (2005) 'Causes and Consequences of the EU's Military Intervention in the Democratic Republic of Congo: A Realist Explanation', *European Foreign Affairs Review*, 10(3): 427–443.
Grilli, E.R. (1994) *The European Community and the Developing Countries*, Cambridge: Cambridge University Press.
Hill, C. (2003) *The Changing Politics of Foreign Policy*, Houndmills: Palgrave Macmillan.
Hill, C. and Wallace, W. (1996) 'Introduction: actors and actions', in Hill, C. (ed.) *The Actors in Europe's Foreign Policy*, London: Routledge, 1–16.
Howorth, J. (2007) *Security and Defence Policy in the European Union*, Houndmills: Palgrave.
Hyde-Price, A. (2004) 'Interests, institutions and identities in the study of European foreign policy', in Tonra, B. and Christiansen, T. (eds) *Rethinking European Union Foreign Policy*, Manchester: Manchester University Press, 99–113.

Knill, C. (2001) *The Europeanisation of National Administrations. Patterns of Institutional Change and Persistence*, Cambridge: Cambridge University Press.

Landgraf, M. (1998) 'Peace-Building and Conflict Prevention in Africa: View from the European Commission', in Engel, U. and Mehler, A. (eds) *Gewaltsame Konflikte and ihre Präventon in Afrika*, Hamburg: Institut für Afrika-Kunde.

Lange, M. (2007) *L'opération EUFOR RD Congo: Implications pour la Politique de sécurité et de défense allemande*, Master's dissertation, Geneva: Graduate Institute of International Studies.

Macrae, J. (2004) *The New Humanitarianisms: A review of trends in Global Humanitarian Action*, HPG Report 11, April, London: ODI.

—— and Harmer, A. (eds) (2004) *Beyond the continuum. The changing role of aid policy in protracted crises*, HPG Report 18, July, London: ODI.

OECD (2006) *Journal on Development. Development Co-operation. Report 2005*, Paris: OECD.

—— (2007) *Journal on Development. Development Co-operation. Report 2006*, Paris: OECD.

Olsen, G.R. (2002) 'Promoting Democracy, Preventing Conflict: The European Union and Africa', *International Politics*, 39: 311–328.

—— (2005) 'The Africa–Europe (Cairo summit) process. An expression of 'symbolic politics', in Hänggi, H., Roloff, R. and Rüland, J. (eds) *Interregionalism and International Relations*, Abingdon: Routledge, 199–214.

—— (2006) 'The Post-September 2001 Security Agenda: Have the European Union's Policies on Africa been Affected?' in Bono, G. (ed.) *The Impact of 9/11 on European Foreign and Security Policy*, Brussels: VUB Press, 153–175.

Schirm, S.A. (1998) 'Europe's Common Foreign and Security Policy: The Politics of Necessity, Viability and Adequacy', in Rhodes, C. (ed.) *The European Union in the World Community*, Boulder: Lynne Rienner, 65–82.

Security & Defence Agenda (2007) *The EU's Africa Strategy: What are the lessons of the Congo Mission?* SDA Discussion Paper, Brussels: SDA.

Smith, K. (2003) *European Union Foreign Policy in a Changing World*, Cambridge: Policy Press.

Smith, M.E. (2004) 'Towards a theory of EU foreign policy-making: multi-level governance, domestic politics, and national adaptation to Europe's common foreign and security policy', *Journal of European Public Policy*, 11(4): 740–758.

Tardy, T. (2004) 'L'Union européenne, nouvel acteur du maintien de la paix: le cas d'Artemis en République démocratique du Congo', in Jocelyn Coulon (ed.) *Guide du maintien de la paix 2005*, Montreal: Athéna-CEPES, 35–56.

—— (2005) 'EU–UN Cooperation in Peacekeeping. A Promising Relationship in a Constrained Environment', in Martin Ortega (ed.) 'The EU and the UN: Partners in Effective Multilateralism', *Chaillot Paper 78*, Paris: EU Institute for Security Studies, 49–68.

Ulriksen, S., Gourlay, C. and Mace, C. (2004) 'Operation Artemis: The Shape of Things to Come?' *International Peacekeeping*, 11(3): 508–525.

United Nations (2004) *Operation Artemis. The Lessons of the Interim Emergency Multinational Force*, Peacekeeping Best Practices Unit, October.

UN Security Council (2003) 'UN Security Council Resolution 1484 adopted by the Security Council at its 4764th meeting on 30 May 2003' (on the situation concerning the Democratic Republic of the Congo), New York.

—— (2006) 'UN Security Council Resolution 1671 adopted by the Security Council at its 5421st meeting on 25 April 2006' (on the situation concerning the Democratic Republic of the Congo), New York.

—— (2007) 'UN Security Council Resolution 1778 adopted by the Security Council at its 5748th meeting on 25 September 2007' (on the situation in Chad, Central African Republic and the subregion), New York.

9 Chinese outlook on European security
Towards ideological convergence?

Lanxin Xiang

Introduction

For a long time, the People's Republic of China paid only marginal attention to the European integration process, and even less interest to Euro-Atlantic security issues dismissed by Beijing as Cold War concerns and Western problems. Since the beginning of the twenty-first century, however, European security policy has not only become a major focus of China's foreign policy, but has also intertwined with Beijing's broad geopolitical vision and grand strategy of 'Peaceful Rise'.

There exists a China–EU convergence in the ideological dimension that seems broader and deeper than most Europeans have so far realized. The EU and China are rapidly moving closer in their views on domestic as well as global governance. On the surface, the picture looks different, with a democratic Europe and an authoritarian China having apparently very little in common. Indeed, at the moment, a neo-Yellow Peril sentiment is brewing in Europe. 'Beware of the Chinese!' can be heard almost everywhere. China is seen as scheming to split transatlantic relations after the Iraq War, is assumed to be undermining the industrial capacity in Europe and most remarkably, is thought to be seeking dominant influence in some regions, such as Africa, that Europe has long considered to be its backyard. China is viewed as the source of global energy panic, environmental apocalypse, Europe's high unemployment rate, and the Avian Flu or whatever pandemic that might appear. After years of hesitation, some mainstream European policy elite and politicians have indeed begun to use China as a scapegoat.

Are these fears justified? While the fear caused by trade competition is nothing new in world economic history, the policy elite's fear of a Chinese plot to deepen tensions within the West is surprising since the transatlantic split is primarily an endogenous development, with no contribution from China.

What European elites miss is the historic opportunity of Europe and China coming together for a third time. Lacking a cultural sense of equality, the results of the first two encounters were unbalanced. Pioneered by the Jesuit missionaries, the first encounter during the sixteenth and seventeenth centuries was a unilateral passion on the part of Europe that was shocked by the quality of Chinese products and who eagerly absorbed China's resource portfolios, that is ideas, values and technologies. These intellectual properties directly inspired monumental events in Europe, from the French Enlightenment to the discovery of the laissez-faire economic doctrine and to the creation of an *Usong*[1] republic of the Swiss Confederation of 1848. However, the Chinese side remained indifferent to Europe's achievements, and considered Europe a barbarian land.

The second encounter, after the mid-nineteenth century, was also a one-sided affair. Ironically, the British were perceived to have opened a China that is in fact an original globalizer, who long ago created the first world market linked by the so-called Silk Road. But the violent means used by Great Britain swept away the value system the Chinese had been holding for centuries. The brutal Western shock no doubt forced China to define itself in the context of an unfamiliar world of Western dominance.

What we see today is the third encounter, with Europe and China once again redefining their relations. This time, they are better prepared for genuine understanding.

From the Chinese perspective, Sino-EU convergence is reflected by three dimensions. First, China rejects – as much as Europe does today – the traditional and now-abandoned Eurocentric view of human history, which sustains the myth that Europe's achievements derived from its cultural originality, technical innovation and free human spirit.

Second, China shares the EU view about the future international system, and wishes to work with the EU to dismantle the last bastion of the power theory of international relations, under which China had suffered greatly. The EU is the first multinational political entity that has moved beyond the logic of balance of power. This is entirely compatible with the Chinese call for the 'democratization' of international relations (*Guoji Guanxi Mingzhuhua*). The Chinese dream of the day when multipolarity and multilateralism unify the entire Eurasian continent as a result of intense institution-building activities, largely inspired by the EU's unique success.

Third, the claim that the China–EU relationship can only flourish at the expense of Europe's relationship with the United States is as absurd as the idea that China will remain under the tutelage of the West, during the process of a West-dictated globalization. Many Europeans are feeling, but not yet ready to admit, that a unified political West is disappearing. The truth is that China has simply re-entered the world after a lapse of over a century and is now ready to move beyond the balance of power system. It would be unrealistic to expect China not to use its cultural resource portfolios again, as in the seventeenth century, to influence the meaning, the context and the rules of globalization.

The EU and China: the trend of ideological convergence

Conditions for an EU–China intellectual rapprochement

Is Europe intellectually ready to understand China? First of all, the Eurocentric view of history has long been destroyed by the Europeans themselves. According to Robert Cooper (2000), a high-ranking EU official, the EU has become a post-modern entity, ahead of the rest of the world. Second, today's European political correctness about the equality of human beings contrasts with the period of 'white supremacy' of the nineteenth and the early twentieth centuries. Moreover, the Yellow Peril sentiment has never run very deep in Europe. Throughout the history of Christian Europe, China has never become Europe's much-needed other – the chosen enemy, such as global Islam – in the process of defining Europe's own identity. The Chinese have been, at the worst, harmless and convertible pagans, but never infidels. The European intellectual world is thus ready to accommodate China, even though the foreign policy community may not be. The last, but even more fundamental, condition for a rapprochement is the fact that Europe and China are rapidly converging in their views about domestic governance as well as international security. The EU has become a genuinely secular, humane society, whose governing principle is similar to Chinese political philosophy in more ways than many European elite believe. Europe seems willing to abandon a debate with China over the abstract conception of democracy (see Xiang 2007: chapter 3). In reality, the traditional Chinese governing principle has always been the promotion of familial and social harmony and justice. By this standard, European democracy works better than most other models in the world. European social democracy is highly attractive in China, as it tends to produce more harmonious societies.

Converging 'strategic cultures'?

In the global security arena, the EU and China are also beginning to converge in their perspectives on the need for using force in international affairs. The Chinese view of national security is predicated on two factors: the modern Chinese experience since the Opium War of the early 1840s and the traditional culture concerning armed conflict. The first factor is crucial, since modern China had been a victim rather than a beneficiary of the existing international system. Before the Opium War, the Chinese perception of national security had been based on a relatively benign hegemony – a Sino-centric international relations network, known as the Tributary System, in which China received tribute (formal diplomatic gestures by foreign countries to present gifts to the Chinese emperor, symbolizing acceptance of Chinese leadership) in exchange for trade and protection.

The Westphalian conception of power was unknown to the Chinese until the Opium War and was imposed by Western powers on Asia to replace the Tributary System with a new Treaty System. Operating through the open-ended competitive principles of free trade and extraterritoriality, the Treaty System never provided China with any real sense of national security. On the contrary, these two principles inevitably turned China into a major playground of the political and economic rivalry among the Great Powers. In other words, Western imperialism created a malignant balance of power that had little to do with local culture. It was a miniature version of European power politics.

In the first half of the twentieth century, the rising Japanese made an extraordinarily bold attempt at establishing a malignant hegemony in the region – the so-called Greater East Asian Co-Prosperity Sphere, to replace the Treaty System. However, this was a short-lived adventure. After a bloody civil war in the late 1940s, the Chinese Communist Party was able to seize power, with popular support mobilized successfully during the war against Japan. The dramatic end of foreign domination means that China has obtained, for the first time in modern history, the opportunity to design national security policy based upon its own national interest. But China's humiliating past since the nineteenth century has always cast a long shadow on any security policy to deal with the threat, real or potential, to its borders and neighbourhood environment. Self-reliant economic development and strong national defence have been two main objectives of the new regime.

The second factor, the influence of cultural heritage, is no less important. From the very beginning of the People's Republic, the Chinese view of security has been influenced by China's ancient tradition and attitude regarding the use of force to address security threats. Some Western scholars have labelled this factor strategic culture. According to Iain Johnston (1995: 248–251), strategic culture consists of a central paradigm, designed to answer three questions: what role warfare is to play in human affairs; the nature of threat and enemy; and the effectiveness of the use of force in dealing with the threat. Johnston believed that the dominant Chinese strategic culture is *parabellum*, a term he used to refer to Chinese cultural realism – the alleged pro-offensive approach to dealing with the threat against the enemy.

This analytical framework seems useful, especially since it is designed to correct the prevailing view in the West about inherent Chinese pacifism. But it is also misleading, because it suggests that war and peace can be considered separate subjects in Chinese tradition, ignoring the interactive dynamics of these two aspects in the use of force. The cultural realism argument ignores the Confucian tradition dictating that the Chinese forego territorial conquest and colonial adventure. Hence the traditional Chinese purpose of using force has to be fundamentally defensive, and linked to the desire of achieving a more durable peace at the frontiers through military superiority. The prevailing inclination is not aggressive or offensive.

More significantly, domestic stability always takes priority, hence true national security requires, above all, building harmony within the society that cannot be created by any conquest of foreign land. The Chinese view about internal and international politics is coherent and is essentially an ethical one. In Chinese tradition, a state is the extension of the family, as the Chinese term *Guojia* (state-family, the official term for the state) indicates. Only moral authority can guarantee long-term stability of a family as well as a state. Even in actual warfare, winning without engaging in battle is considered the most ideal result. To put it simply, there is no power politics logic in the Chinese view of using force. Any use of force must be morally justifiable.

The alleged strategic culture of China's propensity to use force is at best a pseudo-thesis, just like another pseudo-thesis: the Venus versus Mars parody, advanced by Robert Kagan (2001), about Europe's innate unwillingness to use force in world affairs. The Europeans, like the Chinese, are by no means allergic or oblivious to the use of force, they simply want to reduce the role of force in international affairs and more importantly, when force is necessary, for it to be used with the consent of the international community. The EU and China share a common interest in upholding UN authority and multilateral diplomacy for settling international disputes. However, the Sino-European preference for moral authority in using force should not be confused with universal pacifism. Neither China nor the EU holds a pacifist view rejecting the use of force under any circumstances. It is here that traditional China and post-modern Europe meet.

In sum, Europe and China seem to be on the path of understanding each other for the first time, and at an ideological level that cannot – one might add, counter-intuitively – be matched by either transatlantic ties or Sino-US relations. Today, the EU and China, established pillars of the international system, simply need to recognize the reality of multipolarity and not place their trust and security in any residual unipolar system.

The new European security environment and its impact on China's perceptions

Europe as a key geopolitical factor: Pax Bruxelliana *versus* Pax Americana

How, in recent years, have European security issues become entwined with Chinese security concerns? To answer this question, one must trace the role of Europe in the historic transformation of Chinese geopolitical perceptions since the mid-1970s. Due to the Cold War, China did not establish official ties with Europe until the early 1970s, after the rapprochement between Washington and Beijing. China established a diplomatic mission at the European Community (EC) in Brussels only in 1975.

In 1973, Johan Galtung contended that the EC was emerging as a superpower and drew attention to the importance of non-military sources of power – soft power. François Duchene (1972) also pointed out that, despite the superpower confrontation, Europe had a unique role in world peace. Throughout the Cold War, these Eurocentric predictions around a *Pax Bruxelliana* remained irrelevant to Mao's China.

Furthermore, the Nixon–Kissinger diplomacy of opening up China in the early 1970s contributed further to China's indifference towards European security issues. One reason was that the so-called Great Strategic Triangle created by Henry Kissinger – the three-way strategic game among Beijing, Moscow and Washington – in which China was a trump card against Moscow for the US containment strategy during the Cold War, prematurely promoted China into a status beyond its real hard-power capacity. In the mid-1970s, Mao announced a new foreign policy directive known as the Three-World Theory. It stipulated that China would become the leader of the Third World in a struggle against the 'First World' – the two superpowers. Europe, both Western and Eastern, belonged to the 'Second World', as strategic pawns for the superpowers. China should lead the Third World and work with this Second World in order to weaken the support for the superpowers, the Soviet Union in particular. In any case, Europe was considered as having only secondary importance while China was supposed to play the role of a first-rank power.[2]

Within the strategic triangle, China acquired a role as a leading regional power, but not quite a global power, an ambiguous status that not only satisfied Mao's personal ego, but also harked back to the ancient system of a China-centred Middle Kingdom Complex. Since the archenemy of Beijing at the time was also the Soviet Union, China needed this strategic triangle for guaranteeing its national security.

With the end of the Cold War, China's security concerns shifted fundamentally. They are almost exclusively related to the Sino-US relationship, and it is the fear of *Pax Americana* today that compels Beijing to pay attention to the difference between *Pax Bruxelliana* and *Pax Americana*. With the enormous success in its recent economic takeoff, China has undergone fundamental changes in its perspectives on foreign and security policies. Its perceptions of Europe have also begun to shift. There have been long-term trends, such as ideological, political and economic interactions that have led to the current strategic partnership between the EU and China. But important events have also triggered policy initiatives, making this partnership more sustainable, such as the terrorist attack on the United States in 2001 and the American-led Iraq War of 2003.

One important change since the end of the Cold War in Eurasian geopolitics has been the active movement to create multilateral diplomatic and security mechanisms. For the first time in history, there is no major geopolitical conflict on the Euro-Asian mainland. Instead, cooperation, integration and multilateralism are leading themes for diplomatic initiatives among the major Euro-Asian powers. Moreover, China is drawn into a continental orientation, not so much because of the fear of US strategic power in the Pacific region, as because of the changing geopolitical environment in the Eurasian land mass. China's long-term grand strategy, which was once called Peaceful Rise (*heping jueqi*) – the search for a safe environment for its economic development – has recently been focusing on the Euro-Asian continent.

From China's point of view, the most important result of Eurasian geopolitical cooperation is the constraining effect on the United States. The Bush Administration at its outset decided to target China. It seemed to Washington that China had all the right ingredients for making a new political East: the largest communist state with a rapidly growing economy. For Paul Wolfowitz (2000: 24), former Deputy Secretary of Defence in the Bush Administration, China is a contemporary version of Kaiser Wilhelm's Germany in the late nineteenth century. The September 11 attacks on the United States diverted Washington's attention away from China, having discovered a new target, but the alleged Chinese threat has by no means faded away. The irony is, as the US continues to treat Asia as one of its strategic theatres, that China is ready to break out of a regionally defined mode of foreign and security policy and beginning to think continentally and Mackinderian.[3]

From Beijing's perspective, the transatlantic rift as a result of the Iraq War seems fundamental, reaching beyond daily foreign policy issues. Based in the Cold War, shared values and institutions between the US and its allies defined the united West, but the West has now split into two. The self-declared American global crusade against international terrorism has met with European resentment that will last for a long time (Ferguson 2005).

Under these circumstances, China may gain considerable breathing space for continued economic development. However, the Chinese are not naive. The concept of the West has had a much shorter history than most people think. After all, the rise of Christian Europe has merely been 500 years, a time span considered too short to be able to set an irreversible historical trend. The Cold War strengthened the conception of a world divided into East and West, but that was an artificial, ideological division, at once a-historical. Culturally, Hungary and the former Czechoslovakia should not be considered the East, while Japan and South Korea were hardly qualified for the West.

Pundits close to the Bush Administration were by no means oblivious to the conceptual crisis of the West. Fukuyama (1992; 2002), for example, was keenly aware of the Hegelian effect of the end of the ideological divide in the world. He made a quick attempt to rescue the West through a neo-conservative interpretation of the end of history. But his thesis was not sustainable without metaphysics, and the fact that the Cold War did not have a solid metaphysical foundation forced Fukuyama (2002) to raise the question 'Does the "West" still exist as a meaningful concept?' He believed that the transatlantic rift was serious, but it was a controversy over the interpretation of international democratic legitimacy. He believed that the Europeans, paraphrasing Kagan, had no power to force their views and simply could not find the right answer to what the international democratic legitimacy was. Still, Fukuyama is off the mark, because the Cold War was a brief and abnormal episode of human history and the conceptual absurdities associated with the Cold War do not have any particular reason to survive much longer, either in their metaphysical or political forms, than the tragic episode itself.

The West may have won the Cold War, but the conceptual basis of the Cold War is fast disappearing. This provides China with a window of opportunity to achieve its own objectives. After all, China, neither on the losing nor winning side of the Cold War, has no ideological stake in this debate, and therefore is ready to benefit from the new split.

From Beijing's perspective, the transatlantic split has shown two distinctive modes of behaviour in the West, which the Chinese have not experienced since the Opium War. The United States presents itself as an individual rights-based democracy whose foreign policy is determined by national self-interest alone. The Bush Doctrine of unilateral pre-emption in the war on terrorism is the logical, but dangerous approach. The EU, however, is projecting an image of communitarian social democracy, whose worldview is rights-based (international norms and rules) rather than individual sovereign rights-based. Both for ideological and practical national security reasons, multilateralism, which is a relatively new concept in Beijing, is the logical principle that China would prefer.

China and NATO: from grievances to opportunities

China is also changing its mind about the sensitive security question of NATO's purpose. The end of the Cold War put the *raison d'être* of the political West, including the most important institutions such as NATO, into question. In the early 1990s, NATO leaders emphasized the need for NATO operations beyond the Euro-Atlantic region. The Chinese did not understand and certainly had strong grievances against the NATO argument of 'out of area or out of business'.[4] The Kosovo Operation was an occasion when China expressed its strong disagreement towards NATO. Subsequently, the Iraq War was a clear turning point in the transformation of the global geopolitical structure, and was followed by the emergence of a new Euro-Asian strategic landscape. The US-led war against Iraq triggered an anti-war *entente active* of four major powers: France, Germany, Russia and China. The impact of the Iraq War on China–NATO relations has been somewhat dramatic. As late as early 2004, Chinese policy makers still regarded NATO as a potential threat to its national security. A typical view expressed by an important Chinese analyst, warned that 'NATO will be coming to the door of China' and that the US strategy of containment against China would be nicely dovetailed by an Asian *'Petit NATO'* aimed at China, proposed by the United States and including the US, Japan and Australia (*Global Times* 2004: 3).

By the same token, NATO enlargement upset the Chinese leadership enormously. For several years, Beijing watched this development with great anxiety and believed that it was part of the US plot to use NATO to create a larger strategic encirclement around China, pushing the line of containment from Russia and Central Asia against China's borders.

China's position has evolved on these two issues. First, Beijing no longer sees NATO as a potential threat to Chinese security. On the contrary, NATO seems to have an important function for anchoring Chinese security concerns in a multilateral framework. Indeed, the paranoia of a European NATO combined with an Asian NATO to form a great strategic encirclement against China soon disappeared.[5] By 2005, major EU members of NATO continued to show no intention of helping the US in the quagmire of Iraq and NATO had become a much less sensitive topic in Beijing. In the same year, the Chinese Ambassador to the EU made diplomatic efforts to engage NATO. After the Riga NATO summit in November 2006, a Chinese commentator began to call for active collaboration with NATO, listing three key reasons: first, common interests between NATO and China, especially in the areas of combating terrorism, drug trafficking, and the proliferation of weapons of mass destruction; second, as a permanent member of the UN Security Council, China has no reason to oppose NATO peace support operations that are generally UN-mandated; third, and perhaps most important, NATO's presence in Afghanistan does not necessarily pose a threat to Chinese national security since its purpose is not aimed at China. China should overcome psychological concerns about NATO, and move beyond its historical fear of this organization. The Sino-NATO cooperation fits well with President Hu Jintao's call for building a 'Harmonious World' (Jingwei 2006).[6]

Second, China has realized that NATO enlargement was aimed at redefining the mission of an outdated Cold War military alliance. Unless an alternative target is on the horizon to replace Russia, Moscow will remain the focus of America's strategic attention.

However, the Europeans who live with Russia on the same continent had to find ways of accommodating it to avoid a new division of Europe. In the late 1990s, the first choice for an EU common strategy was Russia. This move mollified China's fear of NATO enlargement, because it seemed that the European members of NATO were still influential in its enlargement. As soon as Beijing became convinced that this project was not dictated by Washington, its attitude toward NATO expansion began to change.[7]

The EU has played a critical role in reducing China's fear of NATO. Until the first half of 2003, the new Euro-Asian strategic landscape had been marred by the lack of one crucial element: a direct strategic link between the EU and China. Their relationship had developed slowly and without strategic significance. EU countries were primarily interested in business opportunities in China. With a narrowly defined conception of national sovereignty, the Chinese government could not see why the EU should be considered an important political player in its own right. In 2004, Beijing decided that year to be the 'Year of the EU'. China had surpassed Japan in 2002 to become the second largest economic partner of the EU and the EU remains one of the biggest investors in China. The EU is now China's largest trading partner as well as a major source of technology and investment. China is also the EU's main source of imports and its second largest trading partner.

If China's perception of NATO has largely improved over the last four or five years, US and NATO policy in Afghanistan remains a source of potential tension. Beijing is alarmed by America's policy of building a stable and democratic Afghanistan in order to carry out its greater Central Asian strategy (Boucher 2006). In a nutshell, Afghanistan is to become the springboard for the US to penetrate into Central Asia and create a counter-force, a democratic bloc against the authoritarian alliance, a label referring to the Shanghai Cooperation Organization. China suspects that America is using NATO as a cover in Afghanistan to promote regime change in the region, which would pose a direct threat to the one-party regime in Beijing. It is interesting to note that the leading Chinese party newspaper *People's Daily* (2006) published a penetrating comment on this issue. According to the newspaper, 'in the long term, the United States may create a strategic misjudgement of other large countries by "setting up another cooking stove"'. It may also disrupt existing cooperative mechanisms and put Central Asian countries in a dilemma of choice. Afghanistan is the most critical pawn in the greater Central Asia strategy.

The EU approach is different. It has no long-term ambition in Central Asia and the EU members of NATO have no ulterior motives in their operations in Afghanistan. Central Asia, the historical bridge connecting Europe and the traditional Asian great powers (China and India), has re-emerged as a sphere of economic and political interest. The US, Russia and China compete for influence and access to resources in Central Asia, and the ruling elites of Central Asian countries either try to balance between the competitors or strike the most profitable alliance to ensure their rule.

In this context, the EU still plays a minor role, though interest and involvement in the region rise with security and energy issues on the forefront. The conclusion of an EU energy partnership with Kazakhstan, and Germany's effort to create a Central Asian strategy of the EU in 2006 and 2007, prove the rising interest in the region. Yet the EU has so far shown no intention of participating in a three-way competition and does not view China as a negative force in regional integration. In Central Asia, as in most other parts of the world, the EU is not in a position to engage in strategic rivalry with China and is thus willing to engage China strategically in global management. In the wake of the Iraq War, the European Commission (2003: 3, 7) issued a communication on EU–China relations in which, for the first time, China was considered a strategic partner in global governance. Few realized that this was the first time since the establishment of the UN that major foreign powers accepted China as a 'strategic partner on the international scene' (European Commission 2003: 7). The EU's different attitude toward China after the Iraq war fundamentally changed China's security environment and perceptions.

The Chinese have gained much confidence in their relations with Europe because the fear of the traditional Western alliance seems to have disappeared. Also, China and Europe share a common conception of the use of force in international affairs. During the Iraq crisis, the Chinese supported the Franco-German view precisely because they too understood that international terrorism is often a non-governmental phenomenon. It was on this basis that the Euro-Asian powers were able to reach consensus that visible intergovernmental cooperation is all the more important for achieving success in fighting an invisible and non-governmental common enemy. The war on Iraq was not relevant to the struggle against terrorism. The faulty intelligence aside, it was a traditional war of invasion, and no military success or the toppling of a dreadful regime could justify this 'war of choice', rather than 'war of necessity'.

China and Europe also begin to share a common conception of how international diplomacy should be conducted. Cold War multilateralism, practiced by Washington until recently, was embedded in the admission that in the face of the Soviet military capacity the US did not have unlimited power. As long as the United States considers itself to be the only indispensable superpower, it will show no interest in pursuing a united strategy, considering opinions and advice from friends and foes alike.

CFSP/ESDP as a step towards Eurasian strategic cooperation

China–EU interdependence

As China begins to appreciate the value of the changing global geopolitical environment for its own national security, the fact that the EU should act in unison and speak in one voice also becomes increasingly critical. Under the circumstances, China's strategic tie with the EU would serve multiple purposes. According to a senior Chinese diplomat, it will expedite the transformation of the international power configuration. The simultaneous rise of the EU and China means that both share a common desire for influencing the future international system. Moreover, the US is a stimulating factor for EU–China strategic partnership, and the Sino-EU tie will provide China with more strategic flexibility (Zhengde 2005).

The European Security and Defence Policy (ESDP) is for China a crucial step forward in the direction of Eurasian strategic cooperation. Many Chinese analysts seem to believe that the EU is destined to become one of the poles of the international order, a natural extension of its economic power. Moreover, the Chinese tend to believe that ESDP is a positive sign that EU members are seeking independence from the US. Therefore, the rise of ESDP would arguably mean the decline of NATO, depriving the US of the most powerful strategic and military instrument under the disguise of multilateralism (Hua 2002: 6).

Few people in Europe would disagree that the rise of China will become a predominant feature of the twenty-first century. However, there seems to be no agreement as to whether or not China will pose a threat to world peace or how China might be accommodated. The transatlantic divide on this issue could not be wider. Besides the Iraq War, there was also the heated dispute over the arms embargo to China. The political significance of this affair lay in the test of the Common Foreign and Security Policy (CFSP). Although the EU eventually yielded to American pressure not to lift the embargo, the very fact that the major EU powers are willing to defy Washington on China policy is very encouraging to Beijing.

EU countries do not foresee a Chinese threat and are willing to experiment with an accommodationist approach. Unlike the US, the EU seems willing to accept the scenario that China might develop a different version of political pluralism other than western-style democracy, and the logic that any sustainable political reform must be rooted in history and culture, rather than political theology. The fact that the EU is willing to consider lifting the arms embargo against China demonstrates precisely that the perceived threat is no longer there. Accordingly, Beijing has removed the EU from its national security radar screen.

However, while demonstrating great enthusiasm about ESDP, Beijing underestimated the transatlantic role in shaping EU's China policy. The Chinese learned an important lesson from the transatlantic debate about lifting the arms embargo to China. Although the result did not turn out to be what Beijing had expected, the mere fact that it created regular transatlantic dialogues on China and East Asian security issues indicates that the EU is entering the security picture of the Asia-Pacific region. China welcomes this significant development. China fully shares the EU's concern about the lack of a collective security mechanism in Asia and hopes that the EU may become a constructive helper. As Beijing's first official statement on China's EU Policy dated October 2003 emphatically pointed out (Ministry of Foreign Affairs 2003),

> The common ground between China and the EU far outweighs their disagreements. Both China and the EU stand for democracy in international relations and an enhanced role of the UN. Both are committed to combating international terrorism and promoting sustainable development through poverty elimination and environmental protection endeavours.

In the foreign policy arena, the European Union is equally important. Beijing's declared foreign policy principle is to promote peace and development (*heping yu fazhan*). This is certainly a departure from Mao's days when ideology dominated China's external relations. However, the theme of peace and development does not have a unique operating value, because every country can make this general claim. One important, but little noticed, principle that Beijing has recently added to its grand strategy of Peaceful Rise is a theory of democratization of international relations (*guoji guanxi minzhuhua*). The European Union is in fact the first successful experiment in applying democratic principles to intergovernmental relations. It is therefore not surprising that the EU is inspiring to the new generation of Chinese leaders.

China's grand strategy for the twenty-first century remains Peaceful Rise. It is impossible for China to achieve its objective without cultural and political openness to the world. China needs a long-term peaceful environment both internally and externally to integrate into the current world. Thus China's domestic agenda and foreign policy are compatible with those of the Euro-Asian partners.

Internally, the leadership in Beijing has always insisted on a political model known as socialism with Chinese characteristics. The remarkable economic success has created sufficient confidence for the leadership to deal with the question of political legitimacy. Such a realization is the first step towards political pluralism in the future. Thus, for practical reasons, a power-and-responsibility devolution process has already begun, since the economic privatization and rationalization have already forced the party to give up its monopoly in many decision-making processes.

The EU also needs the Euro-Asian continent not only to enhance its global profile, but also to speed up its common foreign and security policy. But how far the EU and China would be ready to go in order to create a new world, in which a group of secondary powers (including China, EU, Russia, and perhaps other large countries such as Brazil or India) would form a kind of *entente cordiale* in constraining US hegemony, remains an open question.

Obstacles to an EU–China strategic partnership

In this broad positive context, the current reality is also that the alleged EU–China strategic partnership has encountered a number of difficulties. Though some critical issues, such as Taiwan, are not causing major friction, other problems, such as human rights, relations with the United States, trade, UN reform, Iran, Sudan, Africa, Latin America, and others, will probably have a significant impact on the relationship.

The human rights issue is an obvious example. The German Chancellor's approach to this issue, through direct meetings with the Dalai Lama, has greatly constrained Sino-German relations. The French approach of accommodation will face increasing pressure from other EU member states. In 1989, François Mitterrand's government was one of the most outspoken critics of the Tiananmen incident. Since 1997, EU–China cooperation on

Chinese legal reforms has been considered the more practical approach to promoting political changes. This new approach to the human rights situation in China has been criticized by large segments of the public in Europe. In their view, this policy has neither improved China's human rights record, nor contributed in any way to the liberalization and democratization of the Chinese political system.

For the human rights defenders, Taiwan has been another example of EU weakness in dealing with China. China's best EU friend, France, is a case in point. After Tiananmen, France developed a non-official relationship with Taipei to whom it sold a large amount of weapons. After the Mirage jet fighters sale in December 1992, China retaliated by excluding French companies from the Chinese market and closing the French Consulate in Guangzhou. The French Government capitulated in January 1994 and signed an agreement that not only banned France from selling more arms to Taiwan but also offered recognition of China's sovereignty over the island. Since 2002, though Taiwan has remained a dynamic economic partner of France, most French politicians are willing to give priority to relations with China.

Nevertheless, former President Chirac's suggestion that the EU should lift the arms embargo on China has incurred strong opposition even in France. Many accused him of putting France on the side of an authoritarian system against a young democracy, and thereby moving away from the common EU policy on Taiwan. At the EU level, the basis of its Taiwan policy consists of three elements: recognizing one China; supporting the status quo and opposing any move away from the status quo (for example, Taiwan President Chen Shui-bian's decision to abolish the National Unification Council in February 2006); and supporting a peaceful resolution of the Taiwan issue.

The adoption by China of an Anti-Secession Law aimed at Taiwan in March 2005 convinced most EU members to postpone any decision on this issue. German Chancellor Angela Merkel opposed any lifting of the embargo and as befits a typical East German politician, seems very keen in making direct linkages between human rights issues and the arms embargo.

More importantly, sufficient incentive does not exist from the arms trade business in Europe. European weapons producers (such as the European Aeronautic Defence and Space Company (EADS)) have shown little interest in this issue because they worry more about the possibility of jeopardizing their position on the American market. To sacrifice this huge market for developing their position on a much smaller Chinese market does not make sense. Thus any EU move on this issue appears unlikely in the foreseeable future.

Recent disputes on UN reform also became obvious when, in 2005, China publicly opposed Japan's bid for permanent membership in the Security Council. Many EU countries, including France, supported both German and Japanese bids[8] (despite Italy's opposition to Germany's application).

This difference of approach between China and Europe illustrates the gap between the EU, where all erstwhile foes have reconciled, and Asia, where the wounds of World War II are still open, and where more often than not governments prefer utilizing historical issues to further their regional influence.

Some fresh disputes with respect to international issues such as the global environment, Iran, Sudan, or more generally, Africa, are also brewing. China is slow in heeding the world's public opinion on the dangers of global warming. China's record of pollution at home has also frustrated EU states. But the good news is that the Chinese government is beginning to take the environmental issue seriously and will shift its position gradually. After all, the Chinese tradition is most original in protecting nature and creating harmony between man and his environment.

On Iran, the EU-3 group (composed of France, the United Kingdom and Germany) has been very active in trying to convince Tehran, and also the United States, that multilateralism could prove to be the best way to keep Iran's nuclear ambitions under control. China's, as well as Russia's, lack of cooperation have been perceived in the EU as very unhelpful in solving this issue and perhaps also contradictory to China's avowed commitment to the cause for multilateral diplomacy and peaceful resolution of international disputes. Fortunately for China, the December 2007 US intelligence report (National Intelligence Council 2007) much pulled the rug out from under any serious consensus among the P-6[9] in promoting a much stronger sanction package. It let both Iran and China off the hook.

Last but not least, Sudan has been a source of tension. The Darfur human tragedy has been internationalized at a time when the Chinese were desperately seeking a way out of the dilemma. On the one hand, China has a large energy stake in Sudan; on the other, to persuade China to support the internationalization of a domestic chaos would require changing its long-held opposition to any military intervention in the name of human tragedy. The EU is a key supporter of the internationalization of the Darfur question; meanwhile, the surge of China's influence in Africa is causing concerns in Europe. The December 2007 Lisbon EU–African Union summit indicates that the era of colonial mother-country tutelage is finally over and that African nations are no longer interested in the economic development model founded upon the Euro-centric idea of modernization. This summit is in sharp contrast to the African summit in Beijing of November 2006. The EU is certainly worried about the Chinese ambition to secure stable access to oil-rich nations such as Nigeria or Angola. It also resents the fact that the Chinese may be providing money, as well as weapons, to non-democratic regimes such as Zimbabwe and unstable regimes such as Sudan. Put simply, the very fact that China is playing an increasingly important role in a region where Europe's influence used to be little contested constitutes a problem for the EU, and is likely to remain one in the years to come.

Conclusion

China is no longer a revolutionary power. The new continental orientation of China's grand strategy has brought about fundamental changes in its foreign policy practices. Since the mid-1990s, China has abandoned its uni-lateralist posture and begun to participate in and even initiate multilateral organizations. It is an active member of the Association of Southeast Asian Nations (ASEAN) Regional Forum (ARF), a founder of the Shanghai Coop-eration Organization (SCO), a recent member of the World Trade Organi-zation (WTO) and a constructive member of the UN Security Council. Thus China has finally stepped out of the Middle Kingdom Complex.

More interestingly, China has also discovered the unsurpassable advant-age of handling its external relations with the EU model, a seemingly messy and slow decision-making process, but one that could prevent fatal decisions. The geopolitical instinct may tell the leadership in Beijing that the Euro-Asian orientation is far superior to a Pacific orientation when searching for a safe conduit to integrate with the world. The Euro-Asian continent is absent of major strategic confrontations; a muddling-through diplomatic approach may take a long time but is safer than the water-muddying approach in the Pacific, where potentially explosive issues are abundant – such as the US–China strategic rivalry, the crisis on the Korean Peninsula, an assertive Japan and the intractable Taiwan question.

Unfortunately, many top security concerns for Beijing have insuffi-ciently involved the EU, as the latter's strategic vision is often limited by a kind of parochialism. The EU is a visible absentee in Asia. Nowhere do we see the EU playing any role in the multilateral talks over the Korean nuclear issue, nor can we see any serious performance on the part of the EU in war prevention and strategic stability in the Taiwan Strait. Without active participation in Asian security issues, the EU can hardly be qualified as a serious global player in world peace, as authors Galtung and Duchene had predicted long ago.

In sum, we are entering an important episode of human history. Indeed, this is a historic moment in which China and Europe have the opportunity to really understand one another, without cultural prejudice. China and Europe are converging remarkably on issues of global governance. This is largely the result of China looking to the Eurasian continent as the most reliable bridge to cross for an easier way into the painful process of integrating into the world. Both China and the EU are successfully build-ing their soft power. The conventional wisdom that sees China's success as based on the ability to embrace the Western conception of market economy is predicated on the idea that China will eventually rid itself of its political system. However, this belief is misguided as it considers China's traditional values and governing method as hindering economic develop-ment. Europe needs to move beyond many lingering elements of its tradi-tional Euro-centrism.

The challenge to the EU–China relationship remains formidable. On the one hand, both actors need to understand each other's real intentions. It is easy to recognize that there is no strategic rivalry defined in hard power and traditional security terms, but there are many differences concerning non-traditional security issues. The global aspect of the Sino-EU partnership is multidimensional. There is a cultural aspect: both see their relationship as a way of balancing the influence of American culture. In particular, China has been motivated by the desire of disseminating Chinese traditional values in order to help legitimate its political system. In the global fight against terrorism, both the EU and China believe that economic, cultural and political factors are closely linked and that a multipolar and multicultural environment offers the best hope of winning the battle. Moreover, both the EU and China know they have a regional role to play that may or may not create conflict with American interests. In short, they both think that balancing the US's domination will contribute to reducing international tension.

On the other hand, the EU and China must start defining their much-acclaimed yet somewhat empty strategic partnership. For any tie to be called strategic, one must include a long-term view and endurable elements. But history is full of ironies. Europe has become a secular society, a social democratic society that rejects one of its own key inventions, the Westphalian System. Therefore, aside from upholding international consensus through the UN, the most promising areas of Sino-EU strategic cooperation concern non-traditional security, especially human, energy and environmental security.

Notes

1 *Usong* is a work of political fiction (*Staatsroman*) written by the Swiss leader of the Enlightenment movement, Albrecht von Haller (1708–1777). The story tells of a Persian prince named Usong who was captured by the Chinese and after years of residence in China, returned to Persia to start reforms according to the Confucian political model, which combines a laissez-faire economy and tight law-and-order political control.
2 Mao announced the 'Three World Theory' during a meeting with President Kaunda of Zambia on 22 February 1974; see *People's Daily* (front-page), 22 February 1974.
3 For discussions on the Bush China policy, see Xiang, 2001.
4 Expression of US Senator Richard Lugar.
5 In September 2004, Professor David Calleo, a leading transatlantic expert from the United States, visited Shanghai. He expressed the view that it would be very hard to restore the transatlantic tie to what it had been. This view had a powerful impact on the Chinese. See 'Interview with David Calleo and Lanxin Xiang', *Liberation Daily*, Shanghai, 6 September 2004.
6 The concept of a Harmonious World has become an official catch-phrase in foreign and security policy, after the controversial idea of Peaceful Rise was dropped at the recent Chinese Communist Party's Seventeenth Congress.
7 This author was among the first in China to point out that NATO enlargement could also present strategic opportunities. See for example a study in Chinese

(for internal circulation) on 1 September 1999, 'The Future of Transatlantic Ties and its Impact on China and Russia', in which I argued that the most important factor that would restrain the rampant American triumphalism and unilateralism will be the European Union.

8 In the so-called G4 group, where Germany and Japan were joined by India and Brazil.

9 The P-6 group is composed of the five permanent members of the UN Security Council plus Germany.

References

Boucher, R. (2006) 'US Policy in Central Asia: Balancing Priorities (Part II)'. Statement to the House International Relations Committee, April 26. Online. Available at www.state.gov/p/sca/rls/rm/2006/65292.htm (accessed 2 May 2008).

Cooper, R. (2000) *The Postmodern State and the World Order*, London: Demos.

Duchene, F. (1972) 'Europe's Role in World Peace', in Mayne, R. (ed.) *Europe tomorrow: sixteen Europeans look ahead*, London: Fontana.

European Commission (2003) 'A maturing partnership – Shared interests and challenges in EU-China relations', Commission Policy Paper for Transmission to the Council and the European Parliament, Brussels, COM(2003) 533 final, Brussels. Online. Available at http://eur-lex.europa.eu/LexUriServ/site/en/com/2003/com2003_0533en01.pdf (accessed 2 May 2008).

Ferguson, N. (2005) *The Colossus*, London: Penguin.

Fukuyama, F. (1992) *The End of History and the Last Man*, New York: Free Press.

—— (2002) 'US vs. Them. Opposition to American policies must not become the chief passion in global politics', *Washington Post*, 11 September, p. A17.

—— (2006) *After the Neocons: America at the crossroads*, London: Profile Books.

Galtung, J. (1973) *The European Community: A superpower in the making*, London: Allen and Unwin.

Global Times (2004) 'NATO Enlargement: not far from our door, and will do more harm than good to our national interest', Beijing, April 20.

Halford Mackinder, J. (1904) *Democratic Ideals and Reality: A Study in the Politics of Reconstruction*, London: Constable and Co. Ltd.

Jingwei, Z. (2006) 'China Should Actively Develop Its Relationship with NATO', *Guangming Daily*, December 5.

Johnston, A.I. (1995) *Cultural Realism*, Princeton: Princeton University Press.

Kagan, R. (2001) *Of Paradise and Power. America and Europe in the New World Order*, New York: Knopf.

Ministry of Foreign Affairs of the People's Republic of China (2003) 'China's EU Policy Paper', 13 October. Online, available at www.fmprc.gov.cn/eng/zxxx/t27708.htm (accessed 24 May 2008).

National Intelligence Council (2007) 'Iran. Nuclear Intentions and Capabilities', *National Intelligence Estimate*, Washington, November.

People's Daily (2006) August 4.

Wolfowitz, P. (2000) 'Remembering the Future', *National Interest*, 59: 35–46.

Xiang, L. (2001) 'Washington's Misguided China Policy', *Survival*, 43(3): 7–24.

—— (2007) *Tradition and China's Foreign Relations*, Beijing: Sanlian Press.

Zhengde, H. (2005) 'Sino-EU Strategic Relationship', *Journal of International Studies*, 2(1): 104–121.

10 Does Europe matter to India?

Christophe Jaffrelot and
Waheguru Pal Singh Sidhu

Introduction

India and post-Cold War Europe[1] share at least three characteristics:
democracy (India's electorate of 600 million voters is slightly bigger than
the entire population of Europe, including Turkey), diversity (India's 22
official languages, 28 states and seven union territories make it more
varied than Europe) and internal differences (on issues ranging from
governance models, market economy, reservations [affirmative action] to
minorities, immigration, terrorism and their respective roles in the emerging world order). Yet, despite these common traits and a long common
history, Europe has only recently re-discovered India (Acharya *et al.* 2004;
Gnesotto and Grevi 2006; Islam 2008). Had this book been conceived ten
or even five years ago, it is not certain that there would have been a
chapter on India. However, despite Europe being a popular destination for
Indian tourists, India has still to re-discover Europe in any significant way.
This begs the question: does Europe matter to India?

The short answer would have to be that Europe matters far less to India
than the United States, the Russian Federation or East Asia. This is primarily on account of several economic, political, conceptual, security and institutional factors. First, in economic terms, East Asia (which includes the
burgeoning Sino-Indian trade) has overtaken Europe as India's largest
trading partner. Similarly, the United States remains India's largest single
nation trading partner and the biggest source of foreign direct investment
(FDI). Thus, in economic terms the 27-nation bloc of the European Union
(EU) has diminished in significance, particularly as only a handful of countries (France, Germany, the United Kingdom and Italy) account for the
bulk of the EU's trade, FDI, joint ventures and technology transfers.

Second, in political and strategic terms, the United States, through a
2004 bilateral agreement, offers a significant strategic military and non-
military partnership to New Delhi. The jewel in the crown of this enlarg-
ing security and political partnership is the US–India Civil Nuclear
Cooperation Initiative (CNCI), which seeks to provide for India's civil
nuclear energy needs. In contrast, Europe has been far more ambivalent

about providing access to such strategic dual-use technology, even though some countries have been more forthcoming. Moreover, as India moves from non-alignment towards multi-alignment in the emerging multi-polar world and enters into a variety of bilateral and regional arrangements, it simply does not consider Europe to be a reliable partner, although it has entered into a 'strategic partnership' (European Commission 2004) with the EU. Events of the past few years have confirmed to New Delhi that Europe is unable to stand united against either the United States, Russia or China. Thus even though several European countries are individually considered to be reliable strategic partners, collectively Europe is not considered as one of the potential 'poles' in the evolving multi-polar world (Raja Mohan 2002: 63).

Third, conceptually, independent India is justifiably regarded as a 'modern state' which emphasises sovereignty, territoriality and *raison d'état*. In contrast most states occupying the European space are considered to be 'postmodern' as they do not emphasise sovereignty or the separation of domestic and foreign affairs and increasingly regard borders as irrelevant. Thus, the European Union, which epitomises the postmodern state, 'has become a highly developed system for mutual interference in each other's domestic affairs, right down to beer and sausages' (Cooper 2002). The difference between the conceptual outlook of India and the European Union might also explain the inherent discomfiture of a modern India in engaging with a postmodern entity like the European Union. In contrast, India is more comfortable in dealing with the individual nation states that constitute the European Union, particularly the bigger states, than the collective Union. Perhaps that is why New Delhi is most at ease in its interactions with the United States, which embodies the ideal modern state.

Fourth, despite common traits, challenges and perspectives, Europe and India have divergent approaches to addressing security issues. For instance, the EU has formalised an elaborate Common Foreign and Security Policy (CFSP), a European Security and Defence Policy (ESDP), and even a European Security Strategy (European Council 2003) while India has not formally articulated a national security strategy. It needs a more deductive and interpretive approach to discern India's security and defence policies from the few statements of its decision-makers. Besides, unlike the EU, India does not believe in promoting its secular, pluralistic, and democratic ideology to other states (Bendiek and Wagner 2008).

Finally, Europe with its multiplicity of complex organisations is considered to be over-institutionalised and over-bureaucratised and, therefore, far less attractive to engage with than powerful countries, such as the United States, the Russian Federation, Britain or France, or less-institutionalised regional organisations, such as the Association of South East Asian Nations (ASEAN) or the Shanghai Cooperative Organization (SCO). Ironically, even as EU–India relations struggle to gain traction, Indo-UK and Indo-French relations continue to grow by leaps and bounds. The latter trend is evident not only in the visits by both the new British Prime Minister, Gordon Brown, and the new French President Nicholas Sarkozy to New Delhi in January 2008 but also the depth of the strategic, economic and political cooperation which is simply not reflected in India's dealings with the EU. For instance, while the Joint Communiqué issued at the end of the ninth EU–India summit in September 2008 merely 'reaffirmed their commitment to promote energy security and energy efficiency', France and India signed an 'agreement for civil nuclear cooperation' at their bilateral summit around the same time (EU–India 2008; France–India 2008). In many ways, these bilateral interactions have done more to promote Indo-European cooperation than has the EU.

To address the question of whether Europe matters to India, the chapter begins with a short historical overview of Indo-European relations including the policies and approach of independent India to Europe during the Cold War. This first part also looks at the shift in India's perspective and policies in the post-Cold War period. The second part examines the present Indian world view and the relative insignificance of Europe as a hard and soft power to India, in comparison to the United States. The third part analyses the widening social and economic gap between India and Europe and its impact on relations between the two.

India and Europe: the evolution of ties

A brief history of Indo-European relations

Indo-European relations date back to at least 326 BC when Alexander of Macedonia first reached the banks of the Indus river but developed significantly only after 1500 when India became the central focus of European explorers, traders and, eventually, colonisers. It could be argued that since then Asia in general and China and India in particular have mattered to Europe. In the 1500s Asia accounted for over 55 per cent of the global Gross Domestic Product (GDP) (Ming China: 25.0 per cent; India 24.5 per cent; and the Far East 8.4 per cent) and until the 1800s China and India accounted for well over 45 per cent of the global GDP (China 32.9 per cent and India 16.0 per cent) (Maddison 2003). It was only in the 1850s (after the Opium Wars when the British forcibly sold Indian opium to China to pay for Chinese tea which was in great demand in Europe) that the European share of global GDP reached 24.1 per cent and exceeded that of India and China. During this period Europe mattered to India to the extent that India and Indians sought to free themselves from the European colonial economic and political yoke. By the time of India's independence in 1947 its share in the 'global output had plummeted to less than 4 per cent' (Mukherjee 2007). Indeed, one key tenet of current Indian strategic thinking is to regain its position as a major global economy and, as a corollary, reclaim the share of global GDP it boasted in the 1500s.

Ironically, it was Europe that also provided the norms, ideas and education to Indians who would lead the independence struggle against the European colonial empires and establish an independent India based on European enlightenment and related liberal structures. Indeed, not only did Britain shape most of the Indian institutions during the British Raj (rule), but most of the Indian leaders who have ruled the country since independence have been trained in Europe. As a result, one of the most precious achievements of India so far, pluralistic democracy, is a by-product of the intimate relationship of India with Europe. When Prime Minister Manmohan Singh (2005) was made a Doctor *Honoris Causa* of Oxford University in 2005, he made that point clear:

> The idea of India as enshrined in our Constitution, with its emphasis on the principles of secularism, democracy, the rule of law and, above all, the equality of all human beings irrespective of caste, community, language or ethnicity, has deep roots in India's ancient civilization. However, it is undeniable that the founding fathers of our republic were also greatly influenced by the ideas associated with the age of enlightenment in Europe. Our Constitution remains a testimony to the enduring interplay between what is essentially Indian and what is very British in our intellectual heritage.

This 'soft' contribution notwithstanding, Europe (with the exception of the United Kingdom) played a limited 'hard' political, security or economic role in independent India until the 1980s. This was on account of the desire of India not to be dependent on external powers (especially the former colonial powers) for its security and economic well being. Thus while imbibing European ideals India sought to insulate itself, especially from the raging Cold War, by embarking on a policy of non-alignment. This meant that India would not formally align itself with the two Cold War blocs and would seek self-reliance to ensure its own defence. In addition, India also opted for a mixed planned economy model comprising of state-led enterprises and over-regulated limited private sector enterprises governed by the so-called 'licence Raj'[2] which effectively closed the Indian market to the world. Simultaneously the decolonisation process in Asia and Africa led to the withdrawal of Europe and European powers from the rest of the world to their own continent. This was coupled with the growing European preoccupation with the Soviet Union during the Cold War. Finally, the absence of appropriate European institutions, except for the North Atlantic Treaty Organisation (NATO), which non-aligned India abhorred, meant that Europe could not be an effective security actor on its own.

Ironically, although India professed non-alignment it became closely connected with the Soviet Union for a number of political, security and economic reasons. However, following the Soviet intervention in Afghanistan in 1979 and the arrival of the Cold War on India's doorstep, an uncomfortable

New Delhi turned to Europe to diversify its military and economic base. Interestingly, it was the extravagant military purchases made from Europe in the 1980s (aircraft carriers and aircraft from Britain, aircraft from France, submarines from Germany, missiles and torpedoes from Italy and artillery guns from Sweden) that drove India bankrupt and compelled its leaders to embark on far-reaching economic reforms in 1991. These reforms coincided with the collapse of the Soviet Union and the end of the Cold War and were particularly significant for New Delhi's ensuing strategic shift (Baru 2007).

Post-Cold War strategic shift

In the post-Cold War while the underlying objective remained to ensure India's autonomy of action in the emerging world order, New Delhi made three significant shifts in its strategic perspective to achieve this goal (Sidhu 2002). The first shift was to reluctantly but progressively dismantle the 'licence Raj', unshackle the Indian economy and link it more closely with the global economy. This paved the way for a more pragmatic and economically driven foreign policy (Schaffer 2002: 37). Today, with an annual growth rate of around 8 per cent India is already the world's third largest economy in terms of purchasing power parity (after United States and China) (International Monetary Fund 2007; World Bank 2007).

Initially, Europe played a significant role in this early phase of India's economic liberalisation, evident in the former's emergence as the single largest trade partner of India. However, by 2005, as bilateral trade between China and India continued to grow, Europe was displaced from its leading position both with India as well as in the global economy. Indeed, by 2025 the Indian economy is projected to be about 60 per cent the size of the US economy and by 2035, it will be only marginally smaller than the US economy but larger than that of Western Europe (Virmani 2005). Thus, by the middle of the twenty-first century, India (along with China and East Asia) is likely to relegate Europe's share of the global GDP to the pre-1500s level.

The second shift in India's strategic perspective was from non-alignment to multi-alignment which was premised on the perception of the emergence of a multi-polar world. 'Where leadership among the non-aligned once was the principal means of gaining international status', Teresita Schaffer and Mandavi Mehta note, 'India now seeks a seat at the high table, the United Nations Security Council and the "nuclear club", with China illustrating the standing India wants' (Schaffer and Mehta 2001). In such a scenario India has two aspirations: first to emerge as a 'pole' in its own right in this multi-polar world (Ministry of Defence 2006: 2) and, second, to align with other 'poles' which could both contribute to India's own rise and recognition as a global decision-making pole and to counter potential threats from other decision-making poles. The nuclear tests conducted in 1998 were a manifestation of the first aspiration and announced the arrival of India as an autonomous actor on the world stage. Significantly, the European Parliament (May 1998), while acknowledging that India faced serious external security problems, condemned the nuclear tests and asked India to

> sign and ratify the Comprehensive Test Ban Treaty (CTBT) and the nuclear Non-Proliferation Treaty (NPT), to support and actively contribute to the negotiations on a Fissile Material Cut-off Treaty (FMCT) and to prevent material, equipment and technology that can be used for the production of weapons of mass destruction being exported from India to other countries.

Subsequently, however, key EU states, notably the two nuclear states – France and Britain – embarked on strategic dialogues with India which tacitly acknowledged India's nuclear status and practically countermanded the EU declaration.[3] In 2005, France even sponsored the resolution supporting G4 (Germany, Japan, India and Brazil) membership in an enlarged UN Security Council, further undermining the EU declaration. These mixed signals from Europe were in contrast to the consistent Indo-US nuclear dialogue which evolved into the Indo-US nuclear deal in 2005. It would appear that in the aftermath of the nuclear tests New Delhi was taken more seriously than before. In line with the second aspiration, India also embarked on a series of strategic partnerships with the United States, the EU, Britain, France, Germany, Russia, Japan, and ASEAN. However, clearly, some of these partnerships are more strategic than others.

Not surprisingly, the third shift was the emergence of the United States as a dominant focus of India's foreign policy and, perhaps, as New Delhi's most important strategic partner. This was a dramatic reversal from the Cold War period when the United States and India had remained 'estranged democracies' (Kux 1993). There were several political, economic and societal factors that facilitated this shift. At the political level the recognition of India as a key emerging player by successive administrations, especially the George W. Bush administration, provided a tremendous impetus for enhancing strategic relations. At the economic level, despite Europe's significant role, the United States remains India's single largest trade partner and source of FDI. Finally, the huge and influential Indian diaspora in the United States further provided an impetus for improving relations. This societal driver in particular contrasted poorly with the impression of 'fortress Europe' being closed to immigrants, including Indians.

In line with these strategic shifts, India views the world in three concentric strategic circles: first the immediate neighbourhood comprising members of the South Asian Association for Regional Cooperation (Afghanistan, Bangladesh, Bhutan, the Maldives, Nepal, Pakistan and Sri

Lanka), China and Myanmar; second the extended neighbourhood, stretching from the Persian Gulf to the Straits of Malacca and from Central Asia to the Indian Ocean, which is often described as Southern Asia; and third the global stage which would include other parts of the globe where India is involved, such as Africa, Latin America and the Far East as well as institutions and organisations such as the UN, the Commonwealth and the Non-Aligned Movement. Both the United States and Russia are present in all three circles because of their physical presence in the local neighbourhood as well as their global reach. While Europe too could have been part of all three circles (given the presence of European institutions and troops in the local neighbourhood), it is curiously not considered in all three circles. In fact, Europe has been relegated to the distant global circle but is not regarded as a global player.

In the first circle, India ideally seeks primacy and veto over action of outside powers but in reality is willing to work with external powers as long as its own interests are ensured. This is evident in New Delhi's tacit endorsement of both the US and NATO presence in Afghanistan. In the second circle, India seeks to balance the role of other powers with the support of outside powers in the short term and by itself in the long term. At the global level, India seeks to become one of the 'poles' in a multi-polar world and a key player in international peace and security through membership of key global decision-making structures, such as a permanent seat on the UN Security Council and membership of an enlarged G8. In addition, as one of the top five contributors of military personnel and civilian police to UN peace operations (UN Website 2007), India was elected as a member of the UN Peacebuilding Commission and is expected to have a greater say in UN peace missions.

In addition to these areas of strategic interest, there are several issues of similar interest for New Delhi. These are described as the 'four deficits' by Indian officials and include the historical deficit (the need to reconnect economically and politically with the Gulf region, Central Asia and Southeast Asia); the security deficit (the need to deal with proliferation, proxy wars and terrorism); the economic deficit (the need to ensure access to energy and dual-use technology); and the global decision-making deficit (the need to be part of the global decision-making architecture, including the UN Security Council) (Mukherjee 2005).

Europe versus the United States: India's preferences

The charade of a strategic partnership

Against this backdrop, how does India see the role of Europe and the various European organisations in addressing the four deficits? While there are at least three European institutions of substance – NATO, the EU and the Organisation for Security and Cooperation in Europe (OSCE) – India has only developed relations with the EU. In June 2000, the first ever EU–India summit was held in Lisbon with the objective of fostering closer political ties. In doing so, India joined the small and elite club of countries (United States, Canada, Japan, Russia and China) with whom the EU holds annual summits. Since then nine EU–India summits have been held, the latest one in September 2008 in Marseille. In June 2004, as part of this process, the European Commission (2004) presented its communication regarding an 'EU–India strategic partnership', and India (India 2004) delivered its response paper in August and identified five areas of cooperation:

- multilateral cooperation in the area of conflict prevention, anti-terrorism, non-proliferation, the promotion of democracy and the defence of human rights;
- strengthening economic cooperation, especially jointly drafted regulatory policies;
- development cooperation to enable India to achieve the UN-set Millennium Development Goals;
- increasing cultural and intellectual exchange;
- enhancing the institutional framework of Indo-European relations.

However, the implementation of this programme has been mixed. The biggest achievement has been in the sphere of science and technology with the participation of India in both the ITER (International Thermonuclear Reactor Project) and the GALILEO satellite programmes. In contrast, progress in the political, economic and societal spheres has stalled.

In its response paper India extols the virtues of multilateralism and highlights the central role of the UN while simultaneously making a strong pitch for India's candidacy for permanent membership of the UNSC with the expectation that the EU would support its bid. The paper also proposes a joint India–EU group on the Middle East peace process as well as the political and economic reconstruction of Iraq and of Afghanistan but makes no mention of the Kashmir dispute. While India asserts its commitment to 'uphold human rights and fundamental freedoms', it also insists that the 'issue of human rights is solely within the national domain' and calls on the EU and itself to 'avoid a prescriptive approach' (European Commission 2004).

Similarly, the Mittal–Arcelor affair (examined in detail later) showed India the limits of doing business with and in Europe. The differences over the International Criminal Court and the convention against anti-personnel mines are also indicative of the limits in improving political relations between the two. As Rajendra Jain notes, India does not see the EU as a

credible counterweight to the United States given the structural difficulties of making multipolarity work effectively apart from the inherent constraints of an evolving CFSP in a more diverse and heterogeneous Union. India remains sceptical about the EU's political and foreign policy capabilities.

(Jain 2005)

Besides, Lorenzo Fioramonti (2007: 2) notes that

the EU is associated with the rest of the so-called First World (particularly, the United States). [...] When it comes to the political discourse in multilateral venues, the EU and the United States are seen as two faces of the same coin.

Not surprisingly then the EU–India Joint Action Plan (JAP) (European Commission 2005) announced at the New Delhi Summit in 2005 has seen very little action, especially when contrasted with the US–India Civil Nuclear Cooperation Initiative. The JAP focuses on five areas:

- strengthening dialogue and consultation mechanisms;
- political dialogue and cooperation;
- bringing together peoples and cultures;
- economic policy dialogue and cooperation; and
- developing trade and investment.

It is apparent that the JAP is a misnomer and instead of seeing action is likely to remains a mere talking-shop with emphasis on dialogue for the sake of dialogue. One possible reason for this could be that the EU is not considered to be a sovereign entity by New Delhi and, therefore unable to deliver in any of these areas, except in terms of norms and principles. Another possible factor could be the perceived inability of the EU to speak in one voice on many of these issues and the tendency of individual EU members to negotiate bilaterally with India sometimes in disregard of the stated EU policy on the subject.

Europe: a spent force compared to the United States

A significant section of the Indian elite, proud of the country's newly acquired power, does not bother to hide its disdain for a Europe seen as paralysed by its divisions and far too discreet in world affairs. According to Karine Lisbonne de Vergeron (2006: xii), for the Indian elite, 'Europe lacks a strategic vision and ranks at the bottom of the list of partners in India's multipolar understanding of the future geometry of world affairs'. Raja Mohan, one of the most influential Indian experts in international affairs, contrasts the situation of the EU and that of the United States. India's relations with Europe have been limited by the fact that New Delhi is fairly unimpressed with Europe's role in global politics. It senses that Europe and

India have traded places in terms of their attitudes towards the United States: while Europe seethes with resentment of US policies, India is giving up on habitually being the first, and most trenchant, critic of Washington. As pessimism overtakes Europe, growing Indian optimism allows New Delhi to support unpopular US policies (Raja Mohan 2006: 25).

Indeed, besides the Delhi-based strategic community the whole Indian middle class supports the Bush administration. Certainly, most of the newspapers, true to their leftist inclinations, are highly critical of the India–US rapprochement. Editorials arraign a policy selling out the independence of the country; front-page articles long for the previous non-aligned tradition; columnists attack the imperialist attitude of the United States. These are to no avail: Indian society, at least the urban middle class, remains favourably inclined towards the United States. India is the only country recording such a high opinion of the United States, after five years of war in Iraq – a war which has led to a moral divorce of America by so many European societies. In India, the level of positive opinion regarding the United States was even higher in 2005 than in 2002.

The 2005 Pew Global Attitudes survey (Pew Research Center 2005) found that 71 per cent of Indians had a favourable view of the United States, as against 54 per cent in 2002. Only 17 per cent expressed an unfavourable opinion, compared to 38 per cent in Great Britain. Of course, this opinion partly resulted from the fact that they saw this country as a land of opportunity: asked where they would recommend that a young person move in order to lead a good life, 38 per cent of Indians chose the United States – this is a figure no other country, among those surveyed, could match. Poland came a distant second with only 19 per cent.

More importantly, the United States is also appreciated in India because of its foreign policy. Fifty-four per cent of the interviewees appreciate the way George Bush was handling the world affairs. Of the 16 countries surveyed on this question, India was the only one – aside from the United States – in which a majority expressed some confidence in the American president. Revealingly, when asked whether the United States takes into account the interest of 'countries like yours', 63 per cent of Indians answer in the affirmative – more than in any other country. On Iraq, India is the only country other than the United States in which a plurality – 45 per cent – believed that the removal of Saddam Hussein from power has made the world safer – and Indians are even less likely than the Americans to say that the Iraq War has made the world more dangerous. However, just over half – 52 per cent – of the respondents favoured US-led efforts to fight terrorism, a level of support similar to many European countries.

Other opinion polls give similar results. A poll conducted by the Indian weekly *Outlook* revealed that 66 per cent believe that Bush is a friend of India, 54 per cent think that India needs the United States, 46 per cent 'love' America and the same number say that they would not mind emigrating to the United States (*Outlook*–AC Nielsen Opinion Poll 2006).

The positive view of the United States that a majority of Indians entertain can be explained from two points of view. First, so far as American society is concerned, it is seen as an efficient model for economic dynamism, social mobility and multiculturalism – as evident from the success story of the Indian minority living there. Second, so far as world affairs are concerned, the surveys mentioned above reflect the Indian appreciation of what the United States has done for India (in terms of nuclear collaboration for instance) as well as the belief that India and the United States are in the same camp today. For decades they have been adversaries because of the Cold War, but the world has changed, the fight between communism (or socialism) and capitalism is no longer the order of the day. If the key conflict may be expressed in terms of clash of civilisations, then India and the United States have a common enemy: terrorism. Though they are not reported as much as they should be in the West, bomb attacks are more and more pervasive in India. Every six months they kill dozens – if not hundreds – of people in big cities like New Delhi (62 casualties in October 2005) (BBC 2005), Bombay (188 casualties in July 2006) (BBC 2006), on the India–Pakistan 'Samjhauta Express' train in February 2007 (BBC 2007a), Jaipur (56 killed in May 2008) and Ahmedabad (49 killed in July 2008) (Sengupta 2008). For the Indian government and for the Indians as well, these terrorist actions are due to Islamist groups based in Pakistan. Therefore, India and the United States are perceived as in the same fold and as allies in the fight against terror.

Logically enough, when George Bush paid an official visit to India in March 2006, he was most warmly welcomed by the Vishwa Hindu Parishad, a Hindu nationalist outfit, on the ground that he was heading a nation which was boldly fighting 'jehadi terrorism' (United News of India 2006).

Europe: not considered a serious security actor

Given Europe's own experience with 'jehadi terrorism', with the Madrid attack in March 2004 and the London attack in July 2005, the involvement of several European states in the so-called 'war on terror' in Iraq and in Afghanistan under the NATO-led International Security Assistance Force (ISAF), it would have been logical to expect not only greater convergence but also operational interaction between India and European organisations – be they strictly European like the EU or Euro-Atlantic like NATO. However, in reality this is not the case. While the Indo-EU joint statement following the eighth India–EU summit commits both sides to continue 'their cooperation on counter-terrorism' as 'one of the priority areas for the EU–India Strategic Partnership', they have still a long way to go before practical joint anti-terrorism operations are embarked upon (India and the EU 2007: §22).

On Iraq, the Indian parliament passed a resolution criticising the US-led war as unacceptable on the grounds that this action was taken without the sanction of the UN Security Council. Subsequently, New Delhi also rejected Washington's demand for Indian troops for Iraq (Pattanayak 2005) on the same grounds. In reality, the Indian position on Iraq had little to do with the absence of a UN mandate (although this was a convenient stratagem) and more with the fact that such a war was not in India's interest. After all, New Delhi had intervened in East Pakistan (now Bangladesh) in 1971 and Sri Lanka in 1987 without a UN mandate. Given the large Indian diaspora population in Iraq and the fact that Iraq was one of the biggest oil suppliers for India often supplying the vital resource at 'prices lower than the benchmark of OPEC' (Pattanayak 2005), New Delhi was opposed not only to the war but also the UN sanctions. However, India was more than willing to respond to the UN appeal for humanitarian relief and subsequent reconstruction of the war-torn country and eventually contributed around US$40 million for this purpose.

Similarly, on Afghanistan, while both India and the EU 'reaffirmed their sustained commitment to assist the Afghan Government in the stabilisation and rebuilding of Afghanistan' there is no reference for joint action or closer bilateral cooperation (India and the EU 2007: §16). Indeed, in January 2008 visiting European Commissioner for External Relations Benita Ferrero-Waldner reminded Indians that 'with global influences come not only rights, but also responsibilities' and called on New Delhi to '[u]se your influence in the neighbourhood. You are a stable democracy here' (Press Trust of India 2008). Interestingly, while the ISAF presence has paved the way for India's engagement with the reconstruction and development of Afghanistan and its US$700 million aid has been 'widely appreciated, including by the NATO allies' (Minuto-Rizzo 2007), India has been reluctant publicly to acknowledge the role of NATO or ISAF let alone forge closer ties with them. Indeed, scholarly assessments of India's role in Afghanistan do not even mention ISAF or NATO (see D'Souza 2007).[4] While there is certainly a case for greater Indian dialogue and, perhaps, engagement with the various European security structures, there is also great hesitation on the part of New Delhi to embark on this path.

Clearly, the clarion call for the establishment of a 'global NATO' by American policy-makers and scholars is likely to go unheeded in New Delhi (Daalder and Goldgeier 2006). On the contrary, Indian scholars caution that 'the worry of NATO being labelled as a 'Global Police Force will loom large and its "Out-of-Area" Operations will remain controversial' (Rane 2005). There are several reasons why India might be reluctant to establish formal ties with European security structures like NATO or the nascent EU force. First, although a vibrant pluralistic, multi-ethnic, democracy itself, India is reluctant to spread democracy through the barrel of a gun as a matter of principle. Non-promotion of the Indian model of democracy remains a distinct trait of India's foreign policy. Second, although it has embarked on a strategy of multi-alignment, India is unlikely to enter into formal arrangements with military alliances. This would be against the very spirit of its desire to ensure autonomy of decision-making and action. Third, there is concern that such alliances undermine the UN, especially if the alliance commitment calls for action even without a UN mandate. Fourth, given the evolving strategic partnership between India and the United States, New Delhi might consider Washington to be its informal partner in NATO. Finally, with a few notable exceptions (such as strategic airlift, global positioning and state-of-the-art communications) the over one million-strong professional Indian military (the second largest in the world) with its decades-long experience in peace operations as well as counter-insurgency operations has greater capacity than the nascent EU force and, therefore, New Delhi does not see any particular advantage in such an alliance. While India would certainly benefit from the superior military technology and is willing to acquire it, New Delhi is unwilling to acquire it at the cost of entering into formal military alliances or partnerships.

These reservations notwithstanding, there is certainly a greater need for more discussion on these issues between India and Europe as the former has significant experience which might be of use to the latter. In this context, the joint workshop on 'Asian, European and African Policies, Practices and Lessons Learnt in Peace Operations in Africa' was a promising start (von Gienanth 2007). The workshop, held in New Delhi in June 2007 was the first Indian–European Dialogue on peacekeeping and was organised in the context of the German EU Presidency. It brought together leading Indian and European peacekeepers who had worked together in UN peace operations in Africa and provided a forum to exchange views on peacekeeping. This workshop was in line with one of the recommendations of the JAP, which calls for more dialogue on UN peacekeeping and peacebuilding to exchange perspectives on conceptual and operational aspects of peacekeeping operations, including post-conflict reconstruction and rehabilitation. While the prospects of fielding a joint Indo-European peace operation are still a long way off, such joint workshops are a useful first step. In a similar vein, New Delhi might also consider participating in the Partnership for Peace programme (which includes Russia and neutral Switzerland as members) to better understand NATO policies even if it is opposed to them.

The widening gap

The European economy: doomed to decline and protectionist

The Indian middle-class tends to look at Europe as mired in economic stagnation and content with the bourgeois comfort of its welfare state. For this section of Indian society, Europe is a 'has-been' because of its demographic decline and ageing population. As Lisbonne de Vergeron notices in her study (2006: xiii), 'Europe is simply unattractive to India, especially by comparison with the United States. Many Indians regard it as "socially and culturally protectionist", and as offering interest only on account of its "exotic tourist appeal" '. This perception crystallised during the Arcelor/Mittal affair which for the first time concerned the acquisition of a European firm – Arcelor – by an Indian tycoon, Lakshmi Mittal. Arcelor was born in 2002 of the merger of Arcelia from Spain, Arbed from Luxemburg and Arcelor from France. Mittal Steel, one of the largest steel companies in the world, was registered in Rotterdam in the Netherlands but was associated with India in the common man's perception because it is the birthplace of its chief executive officer, Lakshmi Mittal. On 27 January 2006, Mittal Steel made a bid of 22 billion dollars on Arcelor which was considered by Arcelor to be hostile. Guy Dollé, Arcelor's French chief executive officer, argued that 'Arcelor made perfume while Mittal Steel made *eau de cologne*'. French politicians like Dominique Strauss-Khan (former socialist minister of finance and now director general of the International Monetary Fund) described this bid as the '*OPA du Tiers monde*' (a Third World bid) and others suggested that Arcelor's shareholders might be paid in '*monnaie de singe*' (monkey's money). After three months, Mittal increased his bid by 38.7 per cent and succeeded in acquiring the firm. But by that time, the Indian media and the government had started to hit back. The Indian Minister for Commerce and Industry, Kamal Nath, warned the European Commission that opposition to the bid violates norms of the World Trade Organization and nobody in Europe paid attention to Mittal's argument that his firm and Arcelor were European companies which should better join hands to resist China's ambitions. The Indian media had a field day in vilifying the double standards of the EU, ever ready to play the capitalist game when it suits them, but refusing to play it when it does not. After all India saw no objections in allowing Lafarge to become a giant of the Indian cement industry. Why should this not be possible with the reverse scenario in the steel industry? Interestingly, the European Commission sided with the Indian government, on behalf of the principles of economic liberalism and against the economic nationalism displayed by the French and others.

At the same time France was accused of treating India as a giant garbage bin by carelessly sending the aircraft carrier *Clemenceau*, laden with undisclosed but significant amounts of asbestos, lead, mercury and other toxic chemicals, to be broken up in the scrapmetal yards of Gujarat instead of within Europe. Following several court cases in France and activities by Greenpeace, President Jacques Chirac finally recalled the ship from India and ordered an investigation.

The rising tide of racism

In contrast to the positive outlook towards the United States, the Indian perception of the arrogant attitude of the Europeans was reinforced by the racial discrimination many Indians can suffer in Europe.

Alongside multiculturalism, the British society has multiple forms of discrimination. Here it is important to distinguish between the xenophobia of extreme rightwing movements and everyday expressions of ordinary racism

(Bhatt and Mukta 2000: 437).[5] Children are the first victims of this refusal of otherness. How many second-generation immigrants in primary or secondary school have been the butt of classmates who were taken aback not only by the color of their skin but by Hindu customs such as vegetarianism, cow worship, arranged marriages, wearing the sari or the sacred rope worn by upper caste men? In Britain, the 'Shilpa Shetty affair' was revealing of this benign form of racism: a reality show of Channel Four[6] invited Shilpa Shetty, a Bollywood starlet, for a 26-day-long show in January 2007. Things turned sour when, after three weeks, the three white celebrities turned against Shilpa, criticising her diet and saying that she would prefer to be white since she bleached her facial hair. More than 40,000 complaints about racism were sent to Channel Four, mostly by Indians, and politicians had to apologise publicly. Ken Livingstone, the Mayor of London, declared that such marks of racism were unbearable, and Keith Vaz, the Leicester MP, raised the issue in the House of Commons. Gordon Brown himself had to reassert that Britain was a tolerant country and needed to remain so, during an official visit to India (BBC News 2007b).

Indians have been victims of xenophobia in a more extreme way in Germany. In August 2007, eight Indian men were the victims of a racist attack when they were beaten and chased through the streets of Leipzig by a mob of 50 shouting 'Foreigners out!' even as the townsfolk looked on. The incident not only raised the spectre of the prevalence of right-wing extremism but also of an anti-Indian bias (*Spiegel* 2007).

The case of France is different. Not only are racist attitudes commonplace there, but in contrast to the British context, the French Republic is hostile to any form of multiculturalism. The most significant measure that has been taken by the state in this respect concerned the exterior signs of religious affiliation. In 2005 it was decided that none could be worn either by the pupils or by the teachers in the premises of schools and universities. Besides the Muslim girls who wear the veil, the Sikh boys were directly affected by this new rule. Their family objected that the turban was part of their cultural attributes, to no avail. The Indian resentment vis-à-vis this regulation dominated the press coverage of the official visit Prime Minister de Villepin paid to India in September 2005.

The rising tide of racism in Europe, especially aimed at Indians, belies the professed equality, tolerance of minorities and the multicultural and multi-ethnic society that Europe seeks to propagate. In addition, these episodes also make Europe less attractive for Indians, especially when they are compared with the perceived equality, tolerance and multicultural setting that the United States offers.

Conclusion

Europe has always mattered to India in terms of norms, concepts and ideas. Therefore India will remain drawn to Europe's soft power. But will Europe continue to be a norm generator and norm upholder or will it be relegated to becoming a norm follower, espousing the ideas developed elsewhere? If it is the latter, then Europe will become even less significant to India.

In economic terms, Europe will matter. But here too unless Europe can prove to be as competitive, attractive and open, it might continue to lose out to the United States and East Asia. Economics is also likely to be the most contentious issue between India and Europe, and Europe will have to become more attractive and open for business. Europe also needs to play on its industrial strengths to re-launch its cooperation with India. Two areas here are of primary importance, infrastructure and environmental protection. Given Europe's sensitivity to environmental questions as well as its technological capabilities, this is one area where Europe can offer solutions to India's problems. In the sphere of infrastructure, energy is a priority area for India which is experiencing serious shortages of and over-dependency on oil and coal – two of the most polluting fossil fuels. India's quest for gas supplies and nuclear energy are a consequence of this resource crunch. This is another area for Europe to step up its cooperation with India.

In political and hard power terms, Europe, sadly, matters the least to India. There is certainly sympathy and expectations for Europe as a potential alternative to the United States. 'Several officials agreed that "India would benefit from a tilt of the balance of power from the United States towards the EU", for this would ensure "more stable multipolar geopolitics in the future"' (Lisbonne de Vergeron 2006: 14). However, so far this potential has remained unrealised. Were Europe to emerge as a real alternative to Washington and play a more activist role in ensuring the elevation of India to the rank of a permanent member of the UN Security Council, as well as its inclusion in an enlarged G8, it would matter to India. Besides, it might strengthen the cause of multilateralism not only in India but also at the international level by democratising the global decision-making institutions. It remains to be seen if Europe lives up to these expectations or becomes increasingly irrelevant to the rising powers in Asia and the emerging world order.

Notes

1 In the official Indian perspective 'Europe' comprises the 27 member states of the European Union (EU), the North Atlantic Treaty Organisation (NATO) members (except the United States and Canada) as well as Switzerland and the Balkan states. Significantly, India does not regard the Russian Federation as a part of Europe but locates it in 'Eurasia' along with the Central Asian republics. Thus, by extension, while the EU and NATO are regarded as European institutions, the Organization for Security and Co-operation in Europe (OSCE), due to the geographic breadth represented by its 56 participating states, and despite its name, is not really considered to be a European institution. See Ministry of External Affairs, 2007: v–viii.
2 'Licence Raj' refers to an elaborate system of controlling private sector enterprises by issuing official licences and imposing strict rules and regulations for the

conduct of their business. It resulted in red-tape, corruption, protectionism and fettered Indian entrepreneurship.
3 This approach of France and Britain was not dissimilar to that of the other permanent members of the UN Security Council (China, Russia and the United States), all of whom established strategic dialogues with India, which was against the spirit of UNSC resolution 1172 (which also condemned the Indian and Pakistani nuclear tests and called on New Delhi and Islamabad to sign the NPT and the CTBT and start negotiations on the FMCT).
4 Interestingly, in the last five years, *Strategic Analyses*, India's leading security journal, has not featured a single article on Indo-European security relations.
5 Bhatt and Mukta point out that 'the American and British New Right language of the 1980s [...] carried similar themes of "majority discrimination" and an attack on minority rights and protection'.
6 'Celebrity Big Brother', which consists of locking together so-called celebrities for four weeks and inviting the public to vote to eliminate them.

References

Acharya, A., Biato, M.F., Diallo, B., Gonzalez, F.E., Hoshino, T., O'Brien, T., Olivier, G. and Wang, Y. (eds) (2004) 'Global Views on the European Union', *Chaillot Papers* 72, Paris: EU Institute for Security Studies.

Baru, S. (2007) 'Strategic Consequences of India's Economic Performance' in Baldev Raj Nayar (ed.), *Globalization and Politics in India*, New Delhi: Oxford University Press.

BBC News (2005) 'Who is behind the Delhi bombings?', 31 October.

—— (2006) 'Mumbai Train Attacks', 30 September.

—— (2007a) 'Dozens dead in India train blasts', 19 February.

—— (2007b) 'Politicians enter Big Brother row', 27 January.

Bendiek, A. and Wagner, C. (2008) 'Prospects and Challenges of EU–India Security Cooperation', in Shazia Wuelbers (ed.), *EU India Relations: A Critique*, New Delhi: EuroIndia Centre and the Academic Foundation.

Bhatt, C. and Mukta, P. (2000) 'Hindutva in the West: mapping the antinomies of globalization', *Ethnic and Racial Studies*, 23(3): 407–441.

Cooper, R. (2002) 'The Post-Modern State' in M. Leonard (ed.), *Re-Ordering the World*, London: Foreign Policy Centre.

Daalder, I. and Goldgeier, J. (2006) 'Global NATO', *Foreign Affairs*, 85(5): 105–113.

EU–India (2008) 'EU–India Joint Press Commniqué', Marseille, 29 September.

European Commission (2004) 'An EU-India Strategic Partnership', Communication from the Commission to the Council, the European Parliament and the European Economic and Social Committee, COM(2004) 430 final, Brussels, 16 June, and annex.

—— (2005) 'EU–India Joint Action Plan', Brussels.

—— (not dated) *The European Union and India: A Strategic Partnership for the 21st Century*, brochure. Online, available at: www.ec.europa.eu/external_relations/library/publications/25_india_brochure.pdf (accessed 24 May 2008).

European Council (2003) 'A Secure Europe in a better world', *European Security Strategy*, Brussels, 12 December.

European Parliament (1998) 'Resolution on the Communication from the Commission on EU–India Enhanced Partnership', COM(96)0275-C4–0407/96, 25 May.

Fioramonti, L. (2007) 'Report on India', *The External Image of the European Union*, Garnet Working Paper, March.

France–India (2008) 'Joint Statement issued on the occasion of the France–India Summit meeting', 30 September.

von Gienanth, T. (2007) 'Asian European and African Policies, Practices and Lessons Learned in Peace Operations in Africa', Report 08/07 of joint seminar organised by Centre for International Peace Operations and the United Services Institute of India-Centre for United Nations Peacekeeping, New Delhi, June, available at: www.zif-berlin.org/Downloads/Analysen/Veroeffentlichungen/Report_Indien_final_22.08.2007.pdf (accessed 24 May 2008).

Gnesotto, N. and Grevi, G. (2006) *The New Global Puzzle: What World for the EU in 2025?*, Paris: EU Institute for Security Studies.

India (2004) 'An EU-India Strategic Partnership – India's Response', 27 August.

India and the EU (2007) *India–EU Joint Statement*, New Delhi, 30 November.

Islam, S. (2008) 'Europe Looks East-Part I', *Yale Global Online*, 30 January. Online, available at: http://yaleglobal.yale.edu/display.article?id=10272 (accessed 24 May 2008).

International Monetary Fund (2007) *World Economic Outlook Database*, October.

Jain, R.K. (2005) 'India, the European Union and Asian Regionalism', paper presented at the EUSA–AP conference on *Multilateralism and Regionalism in Europe and Asia-Pacific*, Tokyo, December.

Kux, D. (1993) *India and the United States: Estranged Democracies 1941–1991*, New Delhi: Sage.

Lisbonne de Vergeron, K. (2006) *Contemporary Indian views of Europe*, London: Chatham House and Foundation Robert Schumann.

Maddison, A. (2003) *Historical Statistics for the World Economy: 1–2003 AD*, Paris: OECD.

Ministry of Defence (2006) *Annual Report 2005–2006*, New Delhi: Government of India.

Ministry of External Affairs (2007) *Annual Report 2006–2007*, New Delhi: Government of India.

Minuto-Rizzo, A. (2007) 'NATO's Changing Role in the Post-Cold War Period', speech at the Institute for Defence and Strategic Analyses (IDSA), New Delhi, 20 April.

Mukherjee, P. (2005) Speech at Carnegie Endowment for International Peace, Washington DC, 27 June. Online, available at www.carnegieendowment.org/files/Mukherjee_Speech_06-27-051.pdf (accessed 24 May 2008).

—— (2007) Remarks at the Council on Foreign Relations, New York, 1 October. Online, available at http://www.cfr.org/publication/14339/ (accessed 24 May 2008).

Outlook–AC Nielsen Opinion Poll (2006) '66 per cent say Bush is India's Friend', 6 March. Online, available at: www.outlookindia.com/full.asp?fname=Cover%20Story&fodname=20060306&sid=1 (accessed 24 May 2008).

Pattanayak, S. (2005) 'Regime Change in Iraq and Challenges of Political Reconstruction', *Strategic Analysis*, 29(4): 629–652.

Pew Research Center (2005) 'US Image up Slightly, but Still Negative. American Character Gets Mixed Reviews', Washington DC, 23 June.

Press Trust of India (2008) 'India should use influence for neighbourhood peace: EU', 8 January.

210   C. Jaffrelot and W.P.S. Sidhu

Raja Mohan, C. (2002) 'India, Europe and the United States' in R. Jain (ed.) *India and the European Union in the 21st Century*, New Delhi: Radiant Publishers.
—— (2006) 'India and the balance of power', *Foreign Affairs*, 85(4): 17–32.
Rane, P. (2005) 'NATO Enlargement and Security Perceptions in Europe', *Strategic Analysis*, 29(3): 470–490.
Schaffer, T. (2002) 'Building a New Partnership with India', *Washington Quarterly*, 25(2): 31–44.
—— and Mehta, M. (2001) 'Rising India and US Policy Options in Asia', *South Asia Monitor*, 40(1): 1–6.
Sengupta, S. (2008) 'Facing a wave of violence, India is rattled', *New York Times*, 28 July.
D'Souza, S.M. (2007) 'India's Aid to Afghanistan: Challenges and Prospects', *Strategic Analysis*, 31(5): 833–842.
Singh, M. (2005) Address by Prime Minister at Oxford University, 8 July. Online, available at www.hinduonnet.com/thehindu/nic/0046/pmspeech.htm (accessed 24 May 2008).
Sidhu Waheguru, P.S. (2002) 'La stratégie de l'Inde: un changement de paradigme?', *Politique Étrangère*, 67(2): 315–333.
Spiegel Online International (2007) 'After attack on Indians, Germany fears for its reputation', 22 August.
United Nations Website (2007) 'Monthly Summary of Contributors of Military and Civilian Police Personnel', December. Online, available at www.un.org/Depts/dpko/dpko/contributors/ (accessed 24 May 2008).
United News of India (2006) 'VHP welcomes Bush visit', 4 March.
Virmani, A. (2005) 'World Economy: From uni-polar to tri-polar', *The Hindu Business Line*, 8 February. Online, available at: www.thehindubusinessline.com/2005/02/08/stories/2005020800030800.htm (accessed 24 May 2008).
World Bank (2007) *World Development Indicators database*, September. Online, available at: http://siteresources.worldbank.org/DATASTATISTICS/Resources/GDP_PPP.pdf (accessed 24 May 2008).

Conclusion
The unbearable weight of not being

François Heisbourg

European security is a wide and ill-defined concept: it is an aggregation of actors, threats and policies that is strongly linked with the geographical space that is Europe. European security does not in principle equate to the security of the European Union. It is a broader concept that reaches out to institutions, states and security interactions that cannot be confined to the EU.

Yet, an interesting conclusion of this volume is that the European Union is a key agent of the European Security *problématique*, a conclusion that would hardly have been drawn a decade ago. Looking at external perceptions, the very fact that some chapters tend to amalgamate Europe and the EU is revealing about the perceptions of the EU as a security actor.

This being said, Europe's evolving security role faces two paradoxes. First, the European Union is not a coherent, centrally governed international actor comparable to other continent-sized entities, be they of a strongly federal complexion – such as the United States, Brazil, India, Canada – or of a more centralized nature such as China or Russia. The scope and the weight of Europe's Common Foreign and Security Policy (CFSP) is overall not only less than the sum of its parts, it is arguably of less importance than the role played in the world by its most ambitious members, notably the United Kingdom and France. The picture is one of a 'post medieval empire' (Zielonka 2006) analogous to the Holy Roman Empire of the Middle Ages, in which the weight of some individual members was greater than the sum of the whole. Yet that same European Union, with its slow, complex and diffuse decision-making machinery has over a period of less than two decades moved from the absence of any permanent and specific foreign and security role to a situation in which it acquires an existence of its own. The EU may look like a post-modern version of the Holy Roman Empire or of a post-Renaissance Poland paralysed by the *liberum veto* of each of its members. In practice however, the trend is that of moving from non-being as a collective actor to a reality in which the EU as a whole (and not simply each of its most significant components) increasingly figures in the calculations of other actors on the international stage. It may be courted or denounced by its neighbours, partners and rivals – in the latter case more often because of its perceived inaction than for what it does – perhaps for instrumental reasons, such as the expectation of political or economic support. The EU may be flattered or cajoled rather than respected. Still, it has begun to acquire an identity of its own.

It is the existence of such a trend which tends to support Tardy's (Chapter 1) contention that the dynamics of change work in favour of the EU. The companion paradox is that of a EU whose long-lasting economic underperformance would argue against the progressive assertion of the EU collectively as a global actor. After all, in a world economy which has been growing at an average of more than 4 per cent a year during the two decades of the post-Cold War era, Europe has managed about half that rate. The EU's demographics support the image of a stagnating, greybeard-continent losing its weight in a world brimming with youthful productive energy. The negative answer to the question posed by Jaffrelot and Sidhu in Chapter 10 ('Does Europe matter to India?') flows readily from such perceptions. However, the reality underlying this perception is rather more nuanced: the EU may grow more slowly than the emerging economies, but this is typical of other mature industrial societies. Europe's post-Cold War growth rate lies in between that of the United States and Japan. Europe's demography is substantially more dynamic than that of other major players such as Russia or Japan.

The EU's enlargement has also helped to ensure that its economic weight in the world is similar to that of the United States. The EU may look old and slow, but if this were so clearly the case, how could one explain the strong attraction exercised not only on its immediate neighbourhood but also on its more distant, powerful interlocutors? China's courting of Europe as a partner fitting into its vision of a counter-hegemonic multipolar world may be far from disinterested, but the fact remains. The United States, heavily influenced by the transatlantic tensions of the Iraq crisis, may also be tempted by negative visions of Europe, with the latter being character-ized as economically challenged and militarily hopeless (Kagan 2003), but when actual policies and choices are at stake, the United States does not take Europe lightly. America's economic and political investment in Europe shows no sign of diminishing. Foreign direct investment flows between the United States and Europe far exceed those involving Asia or other regions; and there is no equivalent to the network of political relations between the United States and its European allies. The Atlantic community may be riven with disagreement, a reality which comes across in Lindley-French's descrip-tion of NATO's travails (Chapter 2), but estrangement between the United States and the EU probably flows less from Europe's perceived weakness or spinelessness (e.g. the 'caveats' in Afghanistan) than from Europe's growing ability and willingness to assert global norms at variance with US objectives (global warming and international criminal justice come to mind, not to mention 'old Europe's' principled recalcitrance on the Iraqi adventure).

Europe's attempt to set part of the global agenda is central here, rather than its weaknesses, actual or perceived, or its supposed eclipse by the rise of Asia.

However, and notwithstanding the EU's accretion of population, territory and economic dynamism through enlargement, Europe represents a diminishing share of the world's economic and demographic assets, a trait it also shares with the United States and Japan. On this score, time does not play in the EU's (or the West's) favour. But the EU can still preserve and possibly improve its relative position by working more deliberately to set favourable global norms; by creating a benign security environment; and by generating a network of support with like-minded actors on the global stage.

The prospects here differ substantially depending on which of these interlocking categories – the setting of norms, the establishment of benign security environment, the creation of a network of support – one is focusing on.

The European Union is at its most effective in setting the 'normative agenda'. Indeed, some analysts consider the EU as a 'normative power' (Manners 2002) or even a 'normative empire' representing the triumph of soft power (Laïdi 2008). This view is held not only by proponents of the EU's world vision and value system, but also by critics, such as Robert Kagan, who support a hard-power view of a Hobbesian world in which the United States displays the requisite martial qualities in contradistinction to the otherworldly Kantian Paradise created within the confines of the EU.

This norm-setting has both regional and global dimensions. The EU has been enormously effective at making its *acquis* the lodestone for most of the countries of its 'near abroad'. The wholesale adoption of an extensive range of EU norms is a prerequisite for 'joining the club'. Furthermore, the *acquis* has broadened extensively during the last twenty years or so, moving from an essentially commercial single market into the realm of monetary, economic, social, environmental, and judiciary policy. The majority of domestic legislation in all EU countries is now derived from EU laws and regulations. The successive enlargements represent unique cases of peaceful, voluntary, inclusive, empire-building in human history. Those European neighbours (e.g. Ukraine or the Transcaucasian states), who cannot join at this stage or those who currently prefer not to join (such as Norway or Switzerland) are nonetheless inexorably drawn into the normative empire's sphere of influence.

Even if one discounts – as one prudently should – the EU pretensions at generating 'effective multilateralism' across the board at the global level, the Europeans have also been quite effective at setting the terms of the global debate: international justice, the abolition of the death penalty, environmental policies. Contrary to the expectations of many, the EU's ability to engage in such standards setting has not been clearly impaired by the expanding number of member-states. A frequently-united voting bloc of 27 member-states provides substantial leverage in the UN system.

Such standard-setting is not neutral vis-à-vis the security environment and in terms of power relations. The interaction would normally be positive insofar as the adoption of EU-inspired standards will help produce a benign regional and global environment. Even if such an assumption may be correct in general terms, it does not apply in specific cases of great significance. The EU members' attempts to set norms in the OSCE context have not helped that wide-ranging organization maintain its relevance and effectiveness. Russia has been actively limiting the OSCE's ability to fulfil its missions and downgrading its political profile. Ghebali's description (Chapter 3) of this process demonstrates the negative effects of Europe's 'normative assertiveness' on the broader, fraught, strategic relationship between the EU and a Russia which does not share those norms and values. The future of EU–Russian relations is made all the more uncertain by the deeply contradictory nature of the two competing imperial contenders: an expanding, soft-power, post-modern value-driven democratic Europe on one hand, a self-centred, hard-power, pre-modern interest-focused Bismarckian Russian Federation on the other.

Similarly, the EU's 'normative assertiveness' has put the Europeans at loggerheads with the United States and China, along with other powers who share neither the EU's post-Westphalian approach to the limitation of state sovereignty nor the standards that it promotes: from landmines to the death penalty by way of Kyoto and the International Criminal Court (ICC), 'European values' and Europe's post-modern exceptionalism are not always readily endorsed in Beijing, Washington, New Delhi or Moscow.

The EU's ability to generate a more benign security environment is both aided and hindered by the 'post-medieval' nature of the Union. Enlargement and the prospect of enlargement have been extremely effective in defusing security dilemmas within the European space: the inter-ethnic tensions which did not lead to violence in the post-communist Baltic states and the Danubian basin, and the winding down of the dreadful conflicts in the Balkans, bear testimony to the power of the 'enlargement incentive'. This power may have limits: for instance, it is not yet certain that Serbia will adopt the Kantian standards of the 'normative Empire'. Nevertheless, the general rule between the Elbe and the Black Sea is that of the gradual implementation of EU norms, including in terms of the refusal of the use of force in regulating relations between states.

Conversely, enlargement projects the EU's outer limits into regions which raise new, EU-wide, security challenges: the Maghreb, Russia, and the near East are not benign or unimportant areas from the standpoint of European security. Furthermore, the EU's security environment is hardening, independently of the consequences of enlargement. Russia, for reasons and in ways which are described by Herd (Chapter 5) is moving in the direction of 'market authoritarianism', not necessarily an enemy in the Cold War sense, but far from a systematically constructive partner (see Krastev 2008). At best, it may become an interlocutor with which circumscribed strategic business (terrorism, nuclear proliferation) can be done on an *à la carte* basis. China's rise will lead to increasing opportunities for transatlantic tension flowing from the asymmetry of US and EU strategic commitments in East Asia. The broad Middle-East is a rising, not diminishing, security concern as the sources of state and non-state conflict within the region interact with the prospect of nuclear proliferation and its resulting potential of mass destruction. Africa's booming population and failing states will not give the EU any rest. Dannreuther on the Middle East (Chapter 7) and Olsen on Africa (Chapter 8) do not provide a rosy picture for what are, in geographical terms, Europe's backyard.

In order to face these challenges, current developments within the EU are only mildly encouraging. Recent initiatives are most necessary but absolutely not sufficient. The EU institutional arrangements flowing from the Lisbon Treaty (e.g. the 'mutual defence clause', the High Representative of the Union for Foreign Affairs and Security Policy, the de facto abolition of the pillar structure) will help, although it is unclear at this stage whether a stable President of the European Council and a more powerful Foreign Policy High Representative will mutually enhance the EU's ability to act globally or whether they will tend to compete against each other. The strengthening of the Schengen space, with the Prüm Convention, the establishment of the EU-wide arrest warrant, the European Commission's European Security Research Programme, the creation of an external EU border force (FRONTEX) are all steps in the right direction. However, much more will be needed to be done in doctrinal, budgetary and institutional terms. At the doctrinal level, the EU has a useful but mislabelled 'Security Strategy' (European Council 2003) which is a common vision, rather than a strategy. This common vision has not, or not yet, opened the way to the adoption of common security and defence choices by the EU's members. Such a state of affairs is not surprising given the vast disparities between the historically assertive strategies and postures of the British and the French at one end of the spectrum, and those countries which seek low-profile safety as free-riders in a NATO and EU context at the other end. In budget terms, it may be argued that the EU members are not spending enough for their defence: with a gross domestic product (GDP) the size of America's, they spend less than 40 per cent of US defence expenditure. Nevertheless, the EU as a whole spends substantially more on defence than China, Russia or Japan; and since the EU and the United States are allies, benchmarking European defence spending on the US effort is a debatable proposition. The EU's most serious defence spending problems are of a different nature. An EU which adheres to a common vision of its security cannot sustain in political terms a policy in which only two countries out of 27 bear a disproportionate share of the defence burden. With less than on-fourth of the EU's population, Britain and France together represent nearly half of EU defence spending, two-thirds of EU defence equipment spending, three-quarters of EU military research and development. Nor is the situation any better within the group of smaller countries, with the Baltic states at the strong end of the scale of effort and countries such as Luxembourg or Ireland at the weaker end. As Dunay indicates (Chapter 4), similar splits also occur within the 12 enlargement states who joined the EU in 2004 and 2007. Furthermore, these countries which have the strongest record in defence spending are usually those who also participate in expensive EU peace operations, the costs of which are not, for the most part, borne by the EU collectively. In other words, Britain, France and a handful of other states pay twice over, while most of the other EU members get a free ride. Such a situation did not matter politically when the EU as such was not involved in defence and security affairs; but as the European Security and Defence Policy (ESDP) develops, the burden-sharing debate becomes increasingly important.

From an institutional standpoint, the 'integrated' effort conducted by the European Commission in the field of security and the intergovernmental structures of ESDP and the European Defence Agency (EDA) should be more closely linked together. Whereas the Lisbon Treaty aptly creates a 'Foreign Policy Czar', what is arguably required is a 'Security and Defence Policy Czar', tapping into the whole range of the EU's assets in security and defence.

Lastly, the EU will have to make up its collective mind as to the nature of the strategic partnerships it wishes to promote in the post-Cold War era, characterized by the rise of Asia. Here, two radically different templates exist which were brought into violent collision during the Iraq crisis. On the one hand, 'the West and the Rest' vision to use the words of Huntington (1997); on the other, a prescriptive multipolar world, exemplified by the Paris–Berlin–Moscow–Beijing alignment, dubbed the 'Axis of Weasel' by some of its opponents (*New York Post* 2003) during the Iraq crisis. The strength of these polarizations is not going to diminish as China rises, followed by a very Bismarckian India, and as the United States seeks to restore its own position in the world. The prospect of an EU–China convergence painted by Xiang (Chapter 9) is intriguing in this respect, although it is hardly likely, given the contrasting values (and the very different role values play) in Chinese and European external policy. One can only wonder whether China would take the EU as seriously if the Europeans had not managed to prove their nuisance value vis-à-vis China, notably through the post-Tienanmen massacre arms embargo or in the WTO accession negotiations. Conversely, the EU has not or not yet asserted itself similarly towards India, notably on the lifting of nuclear-related restrictions after the signing of the US–India nuclear agreement. It is this lack of assertion which may help explain to some extent the EU's low standing in India's foreign policy (Sidhu and Jaffrelot, Chapter 10).

In counterpoint, Kelleher (Chapter 6) stresses that there is 'no reason to expect American political outcomes will respond to European and American present hopes for the post-Bush era' and that 'expectations may indeed be too high': the EU will have a difficult relationship to handle with post-9/11 America, even if it were to pass under the presidency of a Kennedyesque, inspiring leader willing to heal the domestic and international wounds of the 'dark ages' of Guantánamo and the Iraq intervention.

Between the unacceptable paradigm of a deliberately anti-American multipolarity and the self-fulfilling catastrophe inherent in a US-centred 'West against the Rest' vision, the EU will have to forge its own template. That will take many years, indeed decades. It will at best, always be a work-in-progress, given the enormous objective and subjective differences between the EU's numerous members. Nevertheless, we will allow ourselves to be moderately optimistic on this score: the 'Solana document' of 2003 may not be a security strategy; but it does provide a shared assessment of the international situation and a common vision of our goals, coming on the heels of the extreme divisions of the Iraq crisis. Indeed, the fundamental alternative is that of a return to the misery suffered during the Iraq crisis as a result of European division, except that what was then an exceptional episode would become the bitter staple of US-European relations, aggravated by Europe's inability to unite at a time when Asia rises and Middle-Eastern and Africa security challenges weigh ever more heavily.

Notwithstanding its current limits and constraints, the EU's ability to become an actor in defence and security will probably continue to develop for fear of worse: 'the weight of not being' is simply unbearable.

References

European Council (2003) 'A Secure Europe in a Better World', *European Security Strategy*, Brussels, 12 December.

Huntington, S. (1997) 'The West and the Rest', *Prospect*, February.

Kagan, R. (2003) *Paradise and Power: America and Europe in the New World Order*, Random House.

Krastev, I. (2008) *The Crisis of the Post-Cold War European Order*, The German Marshall Fund.

Laïdi, Z. (2008) *The Normative Empire – the Unintended Consequences of European Power*, Garnet Policy Brief no. 6, Paris, February.

Manners, I. (2002) 'Normative Power Europe – A Contradiction in Terms', *Journal of Common Market Studies*, 40(2): 235–258.

New York Post (2003) 'Axis of Weasel: Germany and France wimp out on Iraq' (headline), 24 January.

Zielonka, J. (2006) *Europe as Empire. The Nature of the Enlarged European Union*, Oxford: Oxford University Press.

Selected reading

Adamski, J., Johnson, M.T. and Schweiss, C.M. (2006) *Old Europe, New Security*, London: Ashgate.

Adler, E. and Barnett, M. (1998) *Security Communities*, Cambridge: Cambridge University Press.

Allen, D. and Smith, M. (2002) 'External Policy Developments', *Journal of Common Market Studies*, 40: 97–115.

Antonenko, O. (1999–2000) 'Russia, NATO and European Security after Kosovo', *Survival*, 41(4): 124–144.

Arbatova, N. (2000) 'Russia–NATO Relations after the Kosovo Crisis', in Y. Fedorov and B. Nygren (eds), *Russia and NATO*, Stockholm: Försvarshögskolan Strategiska Institutionen, 43–74.

Asmus, R. (2002) *Opening NATO's Door: How the Alliance Remade Itself for a New Era*, New York: Colombia University Press.

Bailes, A.J.K. (2005) 'The European Security Strategy. An Evolutionary History', *SIPRI Policy Paper No. 10*, Stockholm: Stockholm International Peace Research Institute.

Baranovsky, V. (ed.) (1997) *Russia and Europe: The Emerging Security Agenda*, Oxford: Oxford University Press.

—— (2001) 'Russia: A Part of Europe or Apart from Europe', in Archie Brown (ed.), *Contemporary Russian Politics: A Reader*, Oxford: Oxford University Press, 429–442.

Baru, S. (2007) 'Strategic Consequences of India's Economic Performance', in Baldev Raj Nayar (ed.), *Globalization and Politics in India*, New Delhi: Oxford University Press.

Barysh, K. (2005) 'EU-Russia Relations: the EU Perspective', in D. Johnson and P. Robinson (eds), *Perspective on EU–Russia Relations*, London: Routledge.

Bebler, A. (1999) *The Challenge of NATO Enlargement*, Westport: Praeger Publishers.

Bendiek, A. and Wagner, C. (2008) 'Prospects and Challenges of EU–India Security Cooperation', in Shazia Wuelbers (ed.), *EU–India Relations: A Critique*, New Delhi: EuroIndia Centre and the Academic Foundation.

Bertelsmann Stiftung (2007) 'Who Rules the World? The Results of the Second Representative Survey in Brazil, China, France, Germany, India, Japan, Russia, the United Kingdom, and the United States', Berlin, 22 October.

Bhatt, C. and Mukta, P. (2000) 'Hindutva in the West: Mapping the Antinomies of Globalization', *Ethnic and Racial Studies*, 23(3): 407–441.

Biscop, S. (2005) *The European Security Strategy: A Global Agenda for Positive Power*, Abingdon: Ashgate.

—— (2007) 'For a "More Active" EU in the Middle East. Transatlantic Relations and the Strategic Implications of Europe's Engagement with Iran, Lebanon and Israel–Palestine', *Egmont Paper 13*, Brussels: Royal Institute for International Relations.

—— (2007) 'The Ambiguous Ambition. The Development of the EU Security Architecture', *Studia Diplomatica*, LX(1): 265–278.

Biscop, S. and Andersson J.J. (eds) (2008) *The EU and the European Security Strategy: Forging a Global Europe*, London: Routledge.

Boer, M. and Monar, J. (2002) 'Keynote Article: 11 September and the Challenge of Global Terrorism to the EU as a Security Actor', *Journal of Common Market Studies*, 40: 11–28.

Bono, G. (ed.) (2006) *The Impact of 9/11 on European Foreign and Security Policy*, Brussels: Politeia and VUB Press.

Borawski, J. and Young, T.-D. (2001) *NATO after 2000: The Future of the Euro-Atlantic Alliance*, Westport: Praeger Publishers.

Bosworth, K. (2002) 'The Effect of 11 September on Russia–NATO Relations', *Perspectives on European Politics and Society*, 3(3): 361–387.

Bourlanges, J.-L. (2004) 'De l'identité de l'Europe aux frontières de l'Union', *Etudes*, 400(6): 729–741.

Bozo, F. (2001) *Two Strategies for Europe: De Gaulle, the United States, and the Atlantic Alliance*, New York: Rowman and Littlefield.

Brawley, M.R. and Martin, P. (eds) (2000) *Alliance Politics, Kosovo, and NATO's War: Allied Force or Forced Allies?*, New York: Palgrave.

Bretherton, C. and Vogler J. (1999) *The European Union as a Global Actor*, London: Routledge.

Brown, M. (ed.) (2000) *The Rise of China*, Cambridge: MIT Press.

Buzan, B. and Wæver, O. (2003) *Regions and Powers*, Cambridge: Cambridge University Press.

—— and de Wilde, J. (1998) *Security: A New Framework for Analysis*, Boulder: Lynne Rienner.

Byers, M. (2004) 'Policing the High Seas: The Proliferation Security Initiative', *The American Journal of International Law*, 98(3): 526–545.

Caan, C. and Scott, W. (2007) *Rebuilding Civil Society in Afghanistan: Fragile Progress and Formidable Obstacles*, Washington, DC: United States Institute of Peace.

Calleo, D. (2001) *Rethinking Europe's Future*, New Jersey: Princeton University Press.

Calleya, S.C. (1997) *Navigating Regional Dynamics in the post-Cold War World: Patterns of Relations in the Mediterranean Area*, Aldershot: Dartmouth Publishers.

Cannizzaro, E. (ed.) (2002) *The European Union as an Actor in International Relations*, The Hague: Kluwer Law International.

Cardoso, F.J., Kühne, W. and Honwana, J.B. (2000) *Reflection paper. Priorities in EU Development Cooperation in Africa: Beyond 2000*, Brussels: Council of Ministers.

Checkel, J.T. (ed.) (2007) *International Institutions and Socialization in Europe*, Cambridge: Cambridge University Press.

Christiansen, T., Petito, F. and Tonra, B. (2000) 'Fuzzy Politics around Fuzzy Borders: The European Union's "Near Abroad"', *Journal of Common Market Studies*, 35(4): 389–415.

Cini, M. (ed.) (2003) *European Union Politics*, Oxford: Oxford University Press.

Cooper, R. (2000) *The Postmodern State and the World Order*, London: Demos.

—— (2003) *The Breaking of Nations. Order and Chaos in the Twenty-First Century*, New York: Grove Press.

Cornish, P. and Edwards, G. (2001) 'Beyond the EU/NATO Dichotomy: The Beginnings of a European Strategic Culture', *International Affairs*, 77(3): 587–603.

—— (2005) 'The Strategic Culture of the European Union: A Progress Report', *International Affairs*, 81(4): 801–820.

Cottey, A. (1995) *East-Central Europe after the Cold War: Poland, the Czech Republic, Slovakia and Hungary in Search of Security*, New York: Macmillan.

—— (2007) *Security in the New Europe*, Hampshire: Palgrave Macmillan.

Croft, S., Redmond, J., Rees, G.W. and Webber, M. (1999) *The Enlargement of Europe*, Manchester: Manchester University Press.

—— and Terrif, T. (eds) (2000) *Critical Reflections on Security and Change*, London: Frank Cass.

Daalder, I. and Goldgeier, J. (2006) 'Global NATO', *Foreign Affairs*, 85(5): 105–113.

Daalder, I. and Lindsay, J.M. (2003) *America Unbound: The Bush Revolution in Foreign Policy*, Washington: Brookings Institution Press.

Danilov, D. (2005) 'Russia and European Security', in D. Lynch (ed.), 'What Russia Sees', *Chaillot Paper 74*, Paris: EU Institute for Security Studies, 79–98.

Dannreuther, R. (ed.) (2004) *European Union Foreign and Security Policy: Towards a Neighbourhood Strategy*, London: Routledge.

—— (2006) 'Developing the Alternative to Enlargement: The European Neighbourhood Policy', *European Foreign Affairs Review*, 11: 183–201.

—— (2007) *International Security: The Contemporary Agenda*, Cambridge: Polity.

—— and Peterson, J. (eds) (2006) *Security Strategy and the Transatlantic Alliance*, London: Routledge.

de Wijk, R. (1997) *NATO on the Brink of the New Millennium: The Battle for Consensus*, London: Brassey's.

Deighton, A. with Mauer, V. (eds) (2006) *Securing Europe: Implementing the European Security Strategy*, no. 77, Zurich: Center for Security Studies.

Diamond, L. (2005) *Squandered Victory: the American Occupation and the Bungled Effort to bring Democracy to Iraq*, New York: Holt.

Doronsorro, G. (2004) 'The EU and Turkey: Between Geopolitics and Social Engineering' in R. Dannreuther (ed.) (2004) *European Union Foreign and Security Policy: Towards a Neighbourhood Strategy*, London: Routledge.

Dror, Y. and Pardo, S. (2006) 'Approaches and Principles for an Israeli Grand Strategy towards the European Union', *European Foreign Affairs Review*, 11(1): 17–44.

Duchene, F. (1972) 'Europe's Role in World Peace', in R. Mayne (ed.), *Europe Tomorrow: Sixteen Europeans Look Ahead*, London: Fontana.

Duke, S. (1994) *The New European Security Disorder*, Oxford: St. Martin's Press.

—— (2002) 'CESDP and the EU Response to 11 September: Identifying the Weakest Link', *European Foreign Affairs Review*, 7: 153–169.

Dunay, P. (2006) 'The OSCE in Crisis', *Chaillot Paper 88*, Paris: EU Institute for Security Studies.

—— and Lachowski, Z. (2007) 'Euro-Atlantic Security and Institutions', in *SIPRI Yearbook 2007: Armaments, Disarmament and International Security*, Oxford: Oxford University Press.

——, Bailes, A.J.K. and Baranovsky, V. (2007) 'Regional Security Cooperation in the Former Soviet Area', in *SIPRI Yearbook 2007: Armaments, Disarmament and International Security*, Oxford: Oxford University Press.

Egbert, J., Lemaitre, P., and Wæver, O. (1987) *European Security: Problems of Research on Non-Military Aspects*, Copenhagen: Copenhagen Papers of the Centre for Peace and Conflict Research.

Elgström, O. and Smith, M. (eds) (2006) *The European Union's Roles in International Politics: Concepts and Analysis*, London: Routledge.

Engelbrekt, K. (2002) *Security Policy Reorientation in Peripheral Europe: A Comparative-Perspectivist Approach*, Burlington: Ashgate.

—— and Hallenberg, J. (eds) (2008) *The European Union and Strategy: An Emerging Actor*, London: Routledge.

European Council (2003) 'A Secure Europe in a Better World', European Security Strategy, Brussels, 12 December.

European Union Institute for Security Studies (2004) *European Defence: a Proposal for a White Paper*, Paris: European Union Institute for Security Studies.

Everts, S. (ed.) (2004) *A European Way of War*, London: Centre for European Reform.

—— (2004) *Engaging Iran: A Test Case for EU Foreign Policy*, London: Centre for European Reform.

Faria, F. (2004) *Crisis Management in Sub-Saharan Africa: The Role of the European Union*, Paris: European Union Institute for Security Studies.

Fawcett, L. and Hurrell, A. (eds) (1995) *Regionalism in World Politics: Regional Organization and International Order*, Oxford: Oxford University Press.

Fioramonti, L. (2007) 'Report on India', in *The External Image of the European Union*, Garnet Working Paper, March, Brussels: Garnet.

Forsberg, T. and Herd, G.P. (2005) 'The EU, Human Rights and the Russo-Chechen Conflict', *Political Science Quarterly*, 120(3): 1–24.

Friedrichs, J. (2004) *European Approaches to International Relations Theory: A House With Many Mansions*, London: Routledge.

Fukuyama, F. (2006) *After the Neocons: America at the Crossroads*, London: Profile Books.

Gallis, P. (2006) *NATO in Afghanistan: A Test of the Transatlantic Alliance*, Washington: Congressional Research Service.

Galtung, J. (1973) *The European Community: A Superpower in the Making*, London: Allen and Unwin.

Gänzle, S. and Sens, A.G. (eds) (2007) *The Changing Politics of European Security: Europe Alone?*, Hampshire: Palgrave Macmillan.

Garton Ash, T. (2004) *Free World: America, Europe, and the Surprising Future of the West*, New York: Random House.

Gat, A. (2007) 'The Return of Authoritarian Great Powers', *Foreign Affairs*, 86(4): 59–69.

Gegout, C. (2005) 'Causes and Consequences of the EU's Military Intervention in the Democratic Republic of Congo: A Realist Explanation', *European Foreign Affairs Review*, 10(3): 427–443.

George, S. and Bache, I. (2001) *Politics in the European Union*, Oxford: Oxford University Press.

Ghebali, V.-Y. (1996) *L'OSCE dans l'Europe post-communiste, 1990–1996: Vers Une Identité Paneuropéenne de Sécurité*, Brussels: Bruylant.

—— (2004) 'The OSCE Long-Term Missions: A Creative Tool under Challenge, *Helsinki Monitor*, 15(3): 202–219.

—— (2005) 'Growing Pains at the OSCE: The Rise and Fall of Russia's Pan-European Experience', *Cambridge Review of International Relations*, 18(3): 375–388.

—— and Lambert, A. (2005) *The OSCE Code of Conduct on Politico-Military Aspects of Security: Anatomy and Implementation*, Leiden/Boston: Martinus Nijhoff.

Giegerich, B. and Wallace, W. (2004) 'Not such a Soft Power: The External Deployment of European Forces', *Survival*, 46(2): 163–182.

Gill, B. and Murphy, M. (2008) *China–Europe Relations: Implications and Policy Responses for the United States*, Washington: Center for Strategic and International Studies.

Gillespie, R. and Youngs, R. (eds) (2002) *The European Union and Democracy Promotion: The Case of North Africa*, London: Frank Cass.

Ginsberg, R. (1989) *Foreign Policy Actions of the European Community: The Politics of Scale*, Boulder: Lynne Rienner.

—— (1999) 'Conceptualizing the European Union as an International Actor: Narrowing the Theoretical Capability-Expectations Gap', *Journal of Common Market Studies*, 37(3): 429–454.

—— (2001) *The European Union in International Politics: Baptism by Fire*, Lanham: Rowman and Littlefield.

Gnesotto, N. (ed.) (2002) *EU Security and Defence Policy: The first five years (1999–2004)*, Paris: EU Institute for Security Studies.

—— and Grevi, G. (eds) (2006) *The New Global Puzzle: What World for the EU in 2025?*, Paris: EU Institute for Security Studies.

Gordon, P. and Shapiro, J. (2004) *Allies at War: America, Europe and the Crisis over Iraq*, New York: McGraw-Hill.

Grant, C. with Valasek, T. (2007) *Preparing for the Multipolar World: European Foreign and Security Policy in 2020*, London: Centre for European Reform.

Grant, C. and Barysch, K. (2008) *Can Europe and China Shape a New World Order?*, London: Centre for European Reform.

Greilsammer, I. (1984) 'Failure of the European "Initiatives" in the Middle East', *Jerusalem Quarterly*, 33: 40–49.

Grilli, E.R. (1994) *The European Community and the Developing Countries*, Cambridge: Cambridge University Press.

Haaland Matlary, J. (2006) 'When Soft Power turns Hard: Is an EU Strategic Culture Possible?' *Security Dialogue*, 37(1): 105–121.

Haas, E. (2004) *The Uniting of Europe. Political, Social, and Economic Forces, 1950–1957*, Notre Dame: University of Notre Dame Press.

Haas, R.N. (1997) 'The United States, Europe and the Middle East Peace Process', in R.D. Blackwill and M. Stürmer (eds), *Allies Divided: Transatlantic Policies for the Greater Middle East*, Cambridge: Centre for Science and International Affairs.

Hallenberg, J. and Karlson, H. (eds) (2006) *Changing Transatlantic Security Relations: Do the US, the EU and Russia Form a New Strategic Triangle?*, London: Routledge.

Hänggi, H., Roloff, R. and Rüland, J. (eds) (2006) *Interregionalism and International Relations*, Abingdon: Routledge.

—— (2006) 'The Post-September 2001 Security Agenda: Have the European Union's Policies on Africa been Affected?' in G. Bono (ed.), *The Impact of 9/11 on European Foreign and Security Policy*, Brussels: VUB Press, 153–175.

Heffernan, M. (1998) *The Meaning of Europe: Geography and Geopolitics*, London: Hodder Arnold.

Heisbourg, F. (2003) *Hyperterrorisme, la Nouvelle Guerre*, Paris: Odile Jacob.

—— (2005) *La fin de l'Occident: l'Amérique, l'Europe et le Moyen-Orient*, Paris: Odile Jacob.

—— (2007) *L'épaisseur du Monde*, Paris: Stock.

Henderson, K. (ed.) (2005) *The Area of Freedom, Security and Justice in the New Europe*, Basingstoke: Palgrave.

—— (2006) *European Union's New Democracies*, London: Routledge.

Herd, G.P. (2005) 'Colourful Revolutions and the CIS: "Manufactured" versus "Managed" Democracy?', *Problems of Post-Communism*, 52(2): 3–17.

—— and Aldis, A. (eds) (2003) *Russia and the Regions: Strength through Weakness*, London: Routledge Curzon.

—— and Forsberg, T. (2006) *Divided West: European Security and the Transatlantic Relationship*, London: RIIA and Blackwells Publishing Ltd.

Heywood, P., Jones, E., Rhodes, M. and Sedelmeier, U. (eds) (2006) *Developments in European Politics*, Basingstoke: Palgrave Macmillan.

High Representative for CFSP and European Commission (2008) *Climate Change and International Security*, Paper to the European Council, S113/08, 14 March.

Hill, C. (ed.) (1996) *The Actors in Europe's Foreign Policy*, London: Routledge.

—— (2003) *The Changing Politics of Foreign Policy*, Houndmills: Palgrave Macmillan.

Hollis, R. (1994) 'Israeli–European Economic Relations', *Israel Affairs*, 1(1): 118–132.

Howorth, J. (2007) *Security and Defence Policy in the European Union*, New York: Palgrave Macmillan.

—— and Keeler, J. (eds) (2003) *Defending Europe: The EU, NATO and the Quest for European Autonomy*, New York: Palgrave Macmillan.

Hill, C. and Smith, K. (eds) (2000) *European Foreign Policy: Key Documents*, London: Routledge.

—— and Smith, M. (eds) (2005) *International Relations and the European Union*, Oxford: Oxford University Press.

Hubel, H. (ed.) (2002) *EU Enlargement and Beyond: The Baltic States and Russia*, Berlin: Spitz.

Hunter, R. (2003) 'NATO–Russia Relations after 11 September', *Journal of Southeast European and Black Sea Studies*, 3(3): 28–54.

Hyde-Price, A. (1991) *European Security Beyond the Cold War: Four Scenarios for the Year 2010*, London: Royal Institute of International Affairs.

—— (1996) *The International Politics of East Central Europe*, Manchester: Manchester University Press.

—— (2004) 'Interests, Institutions and Identities in the Study of European Foreign Policy', in B. Tonra and T. Christiansen (eds), *Rethinking European Union Foreign Policy*, Manchester: Manchester University Press, 99–113.

Ifversen, J. (2008) 'Who are the Westerners?', *International Politics*, 45(3): 236–253.

Jaffrelot, C. (2006) (ed.) *L'Inde Contemporaine: De 1950 à nos jours*, Paris: Fayard.

Johnson, D. (2005) 'EU–Russian Energy Links: A Marriage of Convenience?', *Government & Opposition*, 40(2): 256–277.

Johnston, A.I. (1995) 'Thinking about Strategic Culture', *International Security*, 19(4): 32–64.

Jones, S. (2007) *The Rise of European Security Cooperation*, Cambridge: Cambridge University Press.

Kagan, R. (2002) 'Power and Weakness', *Policy Review*, 113: 3–28.

—— (2003) *Of Paradise and Power: America and Europe in the New World Order*, New York: Alfred Knopf.

—— (2007) 'End of Dreams, Return of History', *Policy Review*, 144: 17–44.

Kaldor, M. (2004) 'A Human Security Doctrine for Europe', *The Barcelona Report of the Study Group on Europe's Security Capabilities*, Barcelona: Centre for the Study of Global Governance.

Kaplan, L. (1984) *The United States and NATO: The Formative Years*, Lexington: The University Press of Kentucky.

—— (2004) *NATO United, NATO Divided: The Evolution of an Alliance*, Westport: Praeger Publishers.

Karsh, E. (2003) *Rethinking the Middle East*, London: Frank Cass.

Katzenstein, P. (2005) *A World of Regions. Asia and Europe in the American Imperium*, Ithaca: Cornell University Press.

Kay, S. (1998) *NATO and the Future of European Security*, Lanham: Rowman & Littlefield.

Keinle, E. (1998) 'Destabilization through Partnership? Euro–Mediterranean Relations After the Barcelona Process', *Mediterranean Politics* 3(2): 1–20.

Kelleher, C. (1995) *The Future of European Security*, Washington DC: Brookings.

—— (2005) 'The Future of a Strategic Triangle', *DARE Report*, Report to Carnegie Corporation, Brown University: Watson Institute.

—— and Adomeit, H., Gaddy, C., Himmelreich, J., Kobrinskaya, I., and Milov, V. (2007) 'Debates Over Missile Defense in Europe: Sound, Fury, and Signifying? The US–German–Russian Triangle: German–Russian Relations and the Impact on the Transatlantic Agenda', Johns Hopkins University: American Institute for Contemporary German Studies.

Kelley, J. (2006) 'New Wines in Old Wineskins: Promoting Political Reforms through the New European Neighbourhood Policy', *Journal of Common Market Studies*, 44(1): 26–55.

Kelstrup, M. and Williams, M. (eds) (2000) *International Relations Theory and the Politics of European Integration*, London: Routledge.

Kemp, W.A. (2001) *Quiet Diplomacy in Action: The OSCE High Commissioner on National Minorities*, The Hague: Kluwer Law International.

Kirchner, E. and Sperling, J. (eds) (2006) *Vertices of Conflict and Cooperation: Threat Perception into the 21st Century*, London: Routledge.

Knill, C. (2001) *The Europeanisation of National Administrations: Patterns of Institutional Change and Persistence*, Cambridge: Cambridge University Press.

Knodt, M. and Princen, S. (eds) (2003) *Understanding the European Union's External Relations*, London: Routledge.

Kupchan, C. (2002) *The End of the American Era: US Foreign Policy and the Geopolitics of the Twenty-First Century*, New York: Alfred Knopf.

Kux, D. (1993) *India and the United States: Estranged Democracies 1941–1991*, New Delhi: Sage.

Laatikainen, K. and Smith, K. (eds) (2006) *The European Union at the United Nations: Intersecting Multilateralisms*, London: Palgrave Macmillan.

Lachowski, Z. (2004) *Confidence- and Security-Building Measures in the New Europe*, SIPRI Research Report No. 18, Stockholm: SIPRI.

Laïdi, Z. (2005) *La Norme sans la Force. L'énigme de la Puissance Européenne*, Paris: Science Po Les Presses.

Lake, D. and Morgan, P. (eds) (1997) *Regional Orders: Building Security in a New World*, Pennsylvania: Pennsylvania State University Press.

Lange, M. (2007) *L'opération EUFOR RD Congo: Implications pour la Politique de Sécurité et de Défense Allemande*, Geneva: Graduate Institute of International Studies, unpublished.

Leonard, M. (2005) *Why Europe Will Run the 21st Century*, London: Fourth Estate.

—— (2008) *What Does China Think?*, London: Fourth Estate.

—— and Popescu, N. (2007) *A Power Audit of EU–Russian Relations*, Brussels: European Council on Foreign Relations.

Lewis, G. and Postol, T. (2007) 'European Missile Defense: The Technological Basis of Russian Concerns', *Arms Control Today*, 37(8): 13–18.

Lindberg, T. (2004) *Beyond Paradise and Power: Europe, America and the Future of a Troubled Partnership*, New York and London: Routledge.

Lindley-French, J. (2002) 'Terms of Engagement: The Paradox of American Power and the Transatlantic Dilemma Post-11 September', *Chaillot Paper 52*, Paris: EU Institute for Security Studies.

—— (2007) *NATO: The Enduring Alliance*, London: Routledge.

—— (2008) *A Chronology of European Security and Defence 1945–2007*, Oxford: Oxford University Press.

Lindstrom, G. (ed.) (2003) *Shift or Rift: Assessing US–EU Relations after Iraq*, Transatlantic Book, Paris: EU Institute for Security Studies.

—— (2005) 'EU–US Burdensharing: Who Does What?', *Chaillot Paper 82*, Paris: EU Institute for Security Studies.

—— (2007) 'Enter the EU Battlegroups', *Chaillot Paper 97*, Paris: EU Institute for Security Studies.

Lipschutz, R. (ed.) (1995) *On Security*, New York: Columbia University Press.

Lisbonne de Vergeron, K. (2006) *Contemporary Indian Views of Europe*, London: Chatham House and Foundation Robert Schuman.

Lucarelli, S. (ed.) (2007) 'The External Image of the European Union', Garnet Working Paper no. 17/07, Brussels: Garnet.

—— and Manners, I. (eds) (2006) *Values, Images and Principles in EU Foreign Policy*, London: Routledge.

Lynch, D. (2003) 'Russia Faces Europe', *Chaillot Paper 60*, Paris: EU Institute for Security Studies.

—— (ed.) (2005) 'What Russia Sees', *Chaillot Paper 74*, Paris: EU Institute for Security Studies.

Macrae, J. (2004) *The New Humanitarianisms: A Review of Trends in Global Humanitarian Action*, HPG Report 11, April, London: ODI.

—— and Harmer, A. (eds) (2004) *Beyond the Continuum. The Changing Role of Aid Policy in Protracted Crises*, HPG Report 18, July, London: ODI.

Mahncke, D. and Monar, J. (eds) (2006) *International Terrorism: A European Response to a Global Threat?*, College of Europe Studies, Brussels: PIE Peter Lang.

Mair, P. and Zielonka, J. (eds) (2002) *The Enlarged European Union: Diversity and Adaptation*, London: Frank Cass.

Manners, I. (2002) 'Normative Power Europe: A Contradiction in Terms', *Journal of Common Market Studies*, 40(2): 235–258.

—— (2008) 'The Normative Ethics of the European Union', *International Affairs*, 84(1): 65–80.

—— and Whitman, R. (eds) (2000) *The Foreign Policies of European Union Member States*, Manchester: Manchester University Press.

Mattli, W. (1999) *The Logic of Regional Integration: Europe and Beyond*, New York: Cambridge University Press.

Mead, W.R. (2002) *Special Providence: American Foreign Policy and How it Changed the World*, New York: Routledge.

—— (2004) *Power, Terror, Peace, and War: America's Grand Strategy in a World at Risk*, New York: Knopf.

Mendelsohn, J. (2007) 'European Missile Defense: Strategic Imperative or Business as Usual', *Arms Control Today*, 37(8): 24–27.

Meyer, C. (2006) *The Quest for a European Strategic Culture: Changing Norms on Security and Defence in the European Union*, London: Palgrave Macmillan.

Missiroli, A. (2004) 'The EU and its Changing Neighbourhood: Stabilization, Integration and Partnership', in R. Dannreuther (ed.), *European Union Foreign and Security Policy: Towards a Neighbourhood Strategy*, London: Routledge, 12–26.

Moens, A., Cohen, L. and Sens, A. (2003) *NATO and European Security. Alliance Politics from the End of the Cold War to the Age of Terrorism*, Westport: Praeger.

Moravcsik, A. (1998) *The Choice for Europe: Social Purpose and State Power from Messina to Maastricht*, Ithaca: Cornell University Press.

—— (2006) *European Union and World Politics*, London: Routledge.

Morelli, V. (2006) 'The European Union's Energy Security Challenges', *CRS Report for Congress*, Washington D.C.: Library of Congress.

Mouritzen, H. (1998) *Bordering Russia: Theory and Prospects for Europe's Baltic Rim*, Aldershot: Ashgate.

Müller-Brandeck-Bocquet, G. (2006) *The Future of the European Foreign, Security and Defence Policy after Enlargement*, Baden-Baden: Nomos Verlag.

Musu, C. and Casarini, N. (eds) (2006) *The Road Towards Convergence: European Foreign Policy in an Evolving International System*, London: Palgrave Macmillan.

Neumann, I. (1998) 'European Identity, EU Expansion, and the Integration/Exclusion Nexus', *Alternatives*, 23(3): 397–416.

Niblett, R. and Wallace, W. (eds) (2001) *Rethinking European Order: West European Responses 1989–1997*, London: Palgrave.

Nowak, A. (ed.) (2006) 'Civilian Crisis Management: The EU way', *Chaillot Paper 90*, Paris: EU Institute for Security Studies.

Nye, J. (2002) *The Paradox of American Power: Why the World's Only Superpower Can't Go it Alone*, Oxford: Oxford University Press.

Olsen, G. (2002) 'Promoting Democracy, Preventing Conflict: The European Union and Africa', *International Politics*, 39: 311–328.

—— (2005) 'The Africa–Europe (Cairo summit) Process: An Expression of "Symbolic Politics"', in H. Hänggi, R. Roloff and J. Rüland (eds), *Interregionalism and International Relations: A Stepping Stone to Global Governance?*, Abingdon: Routledge.

—— and Engel, U. (eds) (2005) *The African Exception*, Aldershot & Burlington: Ashgate.

Onis, Z. (2006) 'Turkey's Encounter with the New Europe: Multiple Transformations, Inherent Dilemmas and the Challenges Ahead', *Journal of Southern European and the Balkans*, 8(3): 279–298.

Organization for Security and Co-operation in Europe (2005) 'Common Purpose. Towards a More Effective OSCE', Final Report and Recommendations of the Panel of Eminent Persons on Strengthening the Effectiveness of the OSCE, 27 June. Vienna: OSCE Secretariat.

—— (2005) *Survey of OSCE Long-Term Missions and other OSCE Field Activities*, 25 August, Vienna: OSCE Secretariat, Conflict Prevention Centre.

Ortega, M. (ed.) (2004) 'Global Views on the European Union', *Chaillot Paper 72*, Paris: EU Institute for Security Studies.

—— (2005) 'The European Union and the United Nations: Partners in Effective Multilateralism', *Chaillot Paper 78*, Paris: EU Institute for Security Studies.

Parsons, C. (2003) *A Certain Idea of Europe*, Ithaca: Cornell University Press.

Perthes, V. (1999) 'The Advantages of Complementarity: The Middle East Peace Process' in H. Gardner and R. Stefanova (eds), *The New Transatlantic Agenda: Facing the Challenges of Global Governance*, Aldershot: Ashgate.

Peterson, J. and Pollack, M. (eds) (2003) *Europe, America, Bush: Transatlantic Relations in the 20th Century*, London: Routledge.

Phillipart, E. (2003) 'The Euro-Mediterranean Partnership: A Critical Evaluation of an Ambitious Scheme', *European Foreign Affairs Review*, 8: 201–220.

Piening, C. (1997) *Global Europe: The European Union in World Affairs*, Boulder: Lynne Rienner.

Posen, B. (2004) 'ESDP and the Structure of World Power', *The International Spectator*, 39(1): 5–17.

—— (2006) 'European Union Security and Defense Policy: Response to Unipolarity?', *Security Studies*, 15(2): 149–186.

Raik, K. and Palosaari, T. (2004) 'It's the Taking Part that Counts: The New Member States Adapt to EU Foreign and Security Policy', *FIIA Report*, 10/2004, Helsinki: The Finnish Institute of International Affairs.

Raja Mohan, C. (2002) 'India, Europe and the United States' in R. Jain (ed.), *India and the European Union in the 21st Century*, New Delhi: Radiant Publishers.

—— (2006) 'India and the Balance of Power', *Foreign Affairs*, 85(4): 17–32.

Rane, P. (2005) 'NATO Enlargement and Security Perceptions in Europe', *Strategic Analysis*, 29(3): 470–490.

Reinares, F. (ed.) (2000) *European Democracies against Terrorism: Governmental Policies and Intergovernmental Cooperation*, Aldershot: Ashgate.

Reiter, D. (2001) 'Why NATO Enlargement Does Not Spread Democracy', *International Security*, 25(4): 41–67.

Rifkin, J. (2004) *The European Dream. How Europe's Vision of the Future is Quietly Eclipsing the American Dream*, New York: Tarcher Penguin.

Rumelili, B. (2003) 'Liminality and Perpetuation of Conflicts: Turkish–Greek

Relations in the Context of Community-Building by the EU', *European Journal of International Relations*, 9(2): 213–248.

Rumer, E.B. (2007) 'Russian Foreign Policy Beyond Putin', *Adelphi Paper 390*, London: International Institute for Strategic Studies.

Russet, B. (1967) *International Regions and the International System*, Chicago: Rand McNally.

Rynning, S. (2003) 'The European Union: Towards a Strategic Culture?', *Security Dialogue*, 34(4): 479–496.

Salonius-Pasternak, C. (ed.) (2007) 'From Protecting Some to Securing Many: NATO's Journey from a Military Alliance to a Security Manager', *FIIA Report*, 17/2007, Helsinki: The Finnish Institute of International Affairs.

Schaffer, T. (2002) 'Building a New Partnership with India', *Washington Quarterly*, 25(2): 31–44.

—— and Mehta, M. (2001) 'Rising India and US Policy Options in Asia', *South Asia Monitor*, 40(1): 1–6.

Schimmelfennig, F. (2003) *The EU, NATO and the Integration of Europe: Rules and Rhetoric*, New York: Cambridge University Press.

Scott, D. (2007) 'China and the EU: A Strategic Axis for the Twenty-First Century?' *International Relations*, 21: 23–45.

Sidhu, W.P.S. (2002) 'La Stratégie de l'Inde: Un Changement de Paradigme?', *Politique Étrangère*, 67(2): 315–333.

—— (2007) 'Regional Groups and Alliances' in T.G. Weiss and S. Daws (eds), *The Oxford Handbook on the United Nations*, Oxford: Oxford University Press.

Sjöstedt, G. (1977) *The External Role of the European Community*, Farnborough: Saxon House.

Sjursen, H. (2006) 'The EU as a Normative Power: How can This be?', *Journal of European Public Policy*, 13(2): 235–251.

Sloan, S. (2005) *NATO, the European Union, and the Atlantic Community: The Transatlantic Bargain Challenged*, Oxford: Rowman & Littlefield.

Smeland, S.P. (2004) 'Countering Iranian Nukes: A European Strategy', *The Nonproliferation Review*, 11(1): 40–72.

Smith, K.E. (2003) *European Union Foreign Policy in a Changing World*, Cambridge: Policy Press.

—— (2004) *The Making of EU Foreign Policy: The Case of Eastern Europe*, Basingstoke: Palgrave.

—— (2005) 'The Outsiders: The European Neighbourhood Policy', *International Affairs*, 81(4): 757–773.

Smith, M. (2006) 'The Shock of the Real? Trends in European Foreign and Security Policy since September 2001', in G. Bono (ed.), *The Impact of 9/11 on European Foreign and Security Policy*, Institute for European Studies, Brussels: Vrije Universiteit Brussel.

Smith, M.A. and Timmins, G. (eds) (2002) *Uncertain Europe: Building a New European Security Order?*, London: Routledge.

Smith, M.E. (2003) *Europe's Foreign and Security Policy. The Institutionalization of Cooperation*, Cambridge: Cambridge University Press.

—— (2004) 'Towards a Theory of EU Foreign Policy-making: Multi-level Governance, Domestic Politics, and National Adaptation to Europe's Common Foreign and Security Policy', *Journal of European Public Policy*, 11(4): 740–758.

Stone, A., Sandholtz, W. and Fliegsten, N. (eds) (2001) *The Institutionalization of Europe*, Oxford: Oxford University Press.

Tardy, T. (2004) 'L'Union européenne, nouvel acteur du maintien de la paix: le cas d'Artemis en République démocratique du Congo', in Jocelyn Coulon (ed.), *Guide du Maintien de la Paix 2005*, Montreal: Athéna-CEPES, 35–56.

—— (2005) 'EU–UN Cooperation in Peacekeeping: A Promising Relationship in a Constrained Environment', in Martin Ortega (ed.), 'The EU and the UN: Partners in Effective Multilateralism', *Chaillot Paper 78*, Paris: EU Institute for Security Studies, 49–68.

—— (2007) 'The European Union and the United Nations: Global *versus* Regional Multilateralism', *Studia Diplomatica*, LX(1): 191–209.

Tonra, B. and Christiansen, T. (eds) (2005) *Rethinking European Union Foreign Policy*, Manchester: Manchester University Press.

Trenin, D. (2006) 'Russia Leaves the West', *Foreign Affairs*, 85(4): 87–96.

Ulriksen, S., Gourlay, C. and Mace, C. (2004) 'Operation Artemis: The Shape of Things to Come?', *International Peacekeeping*, 11(3): 508–525.

Vacudova, M.A. (2005) *Europe Undivided: Democracy, Leverage and Integration after Communism*, Oxford: Oxford University Press.

Van Der Dussen, J. and Wilson, K. (eds) (1995) *The History of the Idea of Europe (What Is Europe?)*, London: Routledge.

Volpi, F. (2004) 'Regional Community Building and the Transformation of International Relations: The Case of the Euro-Mediterranean Partnership', *Mediterranean Politics*, 9(2): 145–164.

Wæver, O. (2000) 'The EU as a Security Actor: Reflections from a pessimistic Constructivist on Post-sovereign Security Orders', in M. Kelstrup and M.C. Williams (eds), *International Relations Theory and the Politics of European Integration*, London: Routledge.

Wallace, W., Wallace, H. and Pollack, M. (eds) (2005) *Policy-Making in the European Union*, Oxford: Oxford University Press.

Wallander, C. (2002) 'NATO's Price: Shape Up or Ship Out', *Foreign Affairs*, 81(6): 2–8.

Weber, K., Smith, M.E. and Baun, M. (eds) (2008) *Governing Europe's New Neighbourhood: Partners or Periphery?*, Manchester: Manchester University Press.

Whitman, R.G. (1998) *From Civilian Power to Superpower: The International Identity of the European Union*, London: Macmillan.

Winner, A. (2005) 'The Proliferation Security Initiative: The New Face of Interdiction', *Washington Quarterly*, 2(28): 129–143.

Wohlfeld, M. (1997) *The Effects of Enlargement on Bilateral Relations in Central and Eastern Europe*, Chaillot Paper 26, Paris: EU Institute for Security Studies.

Xiang, L. (2001) 'Washington's Misguided China Policy', *Survival*, 43(3): 7–24.

—— (2007) *Tradition and China's Foreign Relations*, Beijing: Sanlian Press.

Yost, D. (1998) *NATO Transformed: The Alliance's New Roles in International Security*, Washington, DC: United States Institute of Peace Press.

Youngs, R. (2001) 'European Union Democracy Promotion Policies: Ten Years on', *European Foreign Affairs Review*, 6(3): 355–373.

—— (2004) 'Normative Dynamics and Strategic Interests in the EU's External Identity', *Journal of Common Market Studies*, 42(2): 415–436.

Zellner, W. (2005) 'Russia and the OSCE: From High Hopes to Disillusionment', *Cambridge Review of International Relations*, 18(3): 389–402.

—— (2007) 'Redefining the OSCE's Future: Strategic Uncertainty and Political Contradictions Are Delaying Progress', *Conflicts, Security and Cooperation: Liber Amicorum Victor-Yves Ghebali*, Brussels: Bruylant.

Zhengde, H. (2005) 'Sino-EU Strategic Relationship', *Journal of International Studies*, 1(1): 104–121.

Zielonka, J. (2001) 'How New Enlarged Borders will Reshape the European Union', *Journal of Common Market Studies*, 39(3): 507–536.

—— (2006) *Europe as Empire: the Nature of the Enlarged European Union*, Oxford: Oxford University Press.

Index